Oral cultures past and present

THE LANGUAGE LIBRARY

EDITED BY DAVID CRYSTAL

ORAL CULTURES PAST AND PRESENT

Rappin' and Homer

Viv Edwards
Thomas J. Sienkewicz

Basil Blackwell

First published 1990
First published in USA 1991

Basil Blackwell Ltd
108 Cowley Road, Oxford, OX4 1JF, UK

Basil Blackwell, Inc.
3 Cambridge Center
Cambridge, Massachusetts 02142, USA

British Library Cataloguing in Publication Data

A CIP catalogue record for this book is available from the British Library.

Library of Congress Cataloging in Publication Data

Edwards, Viv.
    Oral cultures past and present : rappin' and Homer / Viv Edwards,
Thomas J. Sienkewicz.
      p. cm.—(The Language library)
    Includes bibliographical references.
    ISBN 0–631–16569–X
    1. Oral tradition.   2. Language and culture. I. Sienkewicz,
Thomas J. II. Title. III. Series.
GR40.E38 1991
302.2'242—dc20
                                            90-420
                                            CIP

Typeset in 10½ on 12 Ehrhardt by Best-set Typesetter Ltd
Printed in Great Britain by TJ Press, Padstow

To Anne and Chris
who heard it
from both sides of the Atlantic

Contents

Acknowledgements

This book grew out of a UK/USA collaborative research award from the British Council and Fulbright Commission which allowed us to work together during the spring of 1987, the summer of 1988 and again in the spring of 1989. We would also like to acknowledge the various organizations which have supported the research on which we draw heavily in this book. An award from the British Academy made possible research by Viv Edwards on South Asian wedding songs; Tom Sienkewicz received several grants which allowed him to study the *Sunjata*, including a National Endowment for the Humanities summer seminar at Harvard University in 1985, a NEH stipend in 1987, a fellowship from the Program for Inter-Institutional Collaboration in Area Studies at the University of Michigan in Ann Arbor and various faculty development grants from Monmouth College.

The collaboration of an American classicist and a British sociolinguist is, to say the least, an unusual undertaking which owes much more to the vagaries of history than to any conscious plan. Without two fortuitous meetings with Anne Waterman Sienkewicz—one in a student dormitory in Université Laval, Québec which developed into a long-standing friendship, the other in the Eisenhower Library at The Johns Hopkins University, Baltimore, which led to marriage—it is likely that our paths would never have crossed and that we would never have discovered a common interest in oral culture. We owe a debt of thanks not only to Anne but also the other members of our families—Chris, Dafydd, Ceri and Siân Morriss and Marie, Julia and Richard Sienkewicz—who have shown more than a little forbearance during the writing process.

We are indebted to a variety of writers whose work we have consistently enjoyed and who inspired us to get started on this book. These include Roger Abrahams, Albert Lord, Bruce Rosenberg and Geneva Smitherman. To our great regret, we discovered Rosenberg's *Can These Bones Live?* – a substantially reworked version of his earlier book on *The Art of the American Folk Preacher* – only as we went to press and so have been unable to draw upon it in the text.

For encouragement at various stages of the project, we thank Gregory Nagy, Doug Spitz, Frank Snowden, John W. Johnson and Bill Urban. We also acknowledge the valuable assistance of the staff of the University of Reading School of Education Library both during the writing process and for many years before; and to the staff of the Hewes Library at Monmouth College, especially Harris Hauge. We would also like to thank the many friends who have allowed us to experience vicariously the oral cultures to which they belong, in particular Keiko and Katoshi Aoike, Jagiro Goodwin, Chandra and Savita Katbamna, Costas Markou, Saloa Samisi, Yasmin Thébault and Carol Tomlin.

Other friends and colleagues have helped by commenting on various drafts of the book. Thanks to Rachel Dwyer, Bernice Fox, Margaret Hardwidge, Chris Morriss, Anne Sienkewicz and Ira Smolensky for the time they spent responding to our efforts, though responsibility for its limitations remains, of course, with us.

Finally, we would like to thank Roger Abrahams for allowing us to reproduce extracts on pages 000 and 000 from the 'The Toast: a neglected form of folk narrative' (in H.P. Beck (ed.), *Folklore in Action,* Philadelphia: The American Folklore Society, 1962, pp. 1–11); Donald Cosentino for musical extracts from *Defiant Maid's and Stubborn Farmers: Tradition and invention in Mende story perfomances* (Cambridge University Press, 1982) on pages 000 and 000; and Gordon Innes for the extracts from *Sunjata. Three Mandinka Versions* (School of Oriental and African Studies, 1974) on pages 000 and 000, including the musical accompaniments prepared by his colleague, Anthony King. We would also like to acknowledge the following individuals and organizations who have provided us with the illustrations included in the text: the British Museum for the Kleophrades rhapsode (Plate 9); Rebecca Busselle for the Sierra Leonean story-teller (Plate 8); Mike Levers for the Robert Daley Sound System (Plate 5); the New York Metropolitan Museum of Art for the Colossal dipylon vase (Plate 2); Laurie Sparham for the British Black story-teller (Plate 10); Bradd Shore for the Samoan orator (Plate 4); the Hulton Picture Company for Muhammad Ali (Plate 7); and Nigel Watson, Theatr Taliesin Wales, for the Bhavaiars of Gujarat (Plate 1).

Viv Edwards
Birkbeck College
London
Thomas J. Sienkewicz
Monmouth College
Illinois

List of Plates

Step into the Oral World

The Pen is Mightier than the Sword, but not the Mouth.
                                                    Charles Schultz

Rappin' and Homer? At first sight it may seem a little strange to mention in the same breath the verbal gymnastics of Black America and the epic poet of ancient Greece. During the course of this book, however, we show that there is nothing frivolous in our attempt to link the two. We are dealing in both cases with skilled exponents of highly developed oral cultures. The common bonds between Homer and the Afro-American rapper–the building blocks from which their performance is crafted, their relationship with the audience, their importance within the community–are, in the final analysis, more meaningful than the vast distances in time and space which otherwise separate them.

This book invites the reader to step, through the medium of print, into the oral world of Homer, the rapper, the orators of Madagascar and Samoa, the story-tellers of Africa and the Caribbean and many, many more. The invitation is made with full awareness that such a step can be taken only falteringly, that a literary study of oral culture is basically a contradiction in terms and that the literate observer's understanding of oral performance is inevitably a limited one. Some of these limitations need to be discussed at the start.

Writing the Spoken Word

Even our vocabulary fails us as we make the first step and speaker of 'oral literature'. Based upon a derivative of the Latin *littera*, 'a letter of the alphabet', this phrase refers to a spoken form in a written context and thus creates our first major dilemma. Yet the English language offers no satisfactory alternative (Ong 1982:10–15; and Finnegan 1977:16).

Vocabulary is not the only stumbling block for a reader. Literate preference for the written over the oral word also causes difficulty. In order to study oral events, and relay them to other literate people, the speech event must be transcribed, be 'written down'. In the process, what is an essentially dynamic oral event becomes static, invariable or even 'petrified' in written form, to use a term of Lord (1963:193). In spoken form the word is repeated and transformed every time it is used. Once written, the word can only with difficulty be changed. Consequently, written 'oral literature' is a very different phenomenon from its spoken form. It is also important for us to acknowledge from the outset that any printed version of a living oral tradition is already outdated, that what is written in this book about Afro-American preachers or the wedding songs of South Asians living in Britain may no longer be current. Changes are always taking place in oral communities and the content and form of any performance will rarely remain static over time.

Furthermore, the very process of transcription can be a distraction during the performance. Lord (1963:193) has noted that the mere presence of a collector creates circumstances abnormal for the performer, and even the use of video and recording equipment may cause both performer and audience, distracted by the equipment, to behave differently than they would in a more natural context. Inevitably, the observer has a distorted view of what is taking place. In a very real sense the literate observer, experiencing the performance in an artificial context, remains out-of-step with the full oral experience.

Another barrier, the challenge of translation, is one which exists in both the oral and the literate worlds. It is important to recognize from the start that most of the examples of oral literature cited in this book are not the actual words of the speakers but are English translations. Again and again we must rely upon a translator's interpretation. Yet the problem of translation exists not only between two different languages, but even within the same language. In a literate context, Steiner (1975:17) has shown how 'any thorough reading of a text out of the past of one's own language and literature is a manifold act of interpretation'. This process of interpretation is both temporal and cultural. The words of Jane Austen are understood differently by eighteenth- and twentieth-century readers. Canadians and Australians have different cultural referents; so, too, do White Americans and Afro-Americans.

A symptom of this distortion of the oral by the written word is the tendency of observers to judge the importance of various elements of performance from a literary perspective. Thus commentators often highlight plot over elaborate descriptive passages and other elements not essential to the main story line (Innes 1974; Johnson 1979 and 1986; Rosenberg 1970a and 1975). In so doing, they create an impression of structural simplicity rather than sophistication, and fail to recognize a plethora of culturally important detail essential for a true appreciation of performance. In a similar vein, there is often a reluctance to discuss ritual invective because of the shocking language and imagery on which it sometimes draws. Yet, as we will show later in this book, these very features, often dismissed as uncouth and distasteful, enable even the literate observer to appreciate the important social and psychological functions of such verbal behaviour and the considerable linguistic dexterity of those who engage in it.

Certainly the distinction between the pen and the mouth, highlighted in the quote by Charles Schultz at the beginning of this chapter, underscores a major difference between orality and literacy. However, it is the oral medium itself which sets up the strongest barrier between the observer and the performance. Any listener can hear the words spoken but not every listener hears these words in the same way. Not only is the terminology of oral events contextually specific, so is the event itself. Understanding a performance in an oral culture requires a special mind-set, a cultural harmony which excludes from the oral world any outsider, whether literate or not. In many ways an oral performance, which can be fully understood only by members of its audience, is as esoteric as a composition aimed at a literate elite, such as a poem of Ezra Pound.

A growing awareness of this 'observer's paradox' remoulds the literate view of oral performance. Rather than imposing an outsider's interpretation on what is taking place, literate observers, including both the authors and the readers of this book, must be ready to reorient themselves and to tap the perceptions of those intimately involved in the performance and in the oral community where it takes place. A step into the oral world thus often requires a local guide.

A Stepper's Guide

At the outset, it may be helpful to provide a brief guide to the material covered in this book. We make no claim to be comprehensive: to include material from every possible oral context would be a Herculean task beyond the scope of this book or the abilities of its authors. Instead, we have aimed at temporal and cultural variety and have included material from all six inhabited continents and from a span of time which extends from the first millennium BC to the present day.

The Mediterranean world is a particularly important source of oral material both of the past and of the present. The *Iliad* and the *Odyssey*, the two ancient Greek epics traditionally attributed to Homer, are part of an oral tradition dating back at least to 2000 BC but probably not established in written form until about the seventh century BC. The texts of these two poems are available in a variety of English translations: we use the versions of Lattimore (1961 and 1975). While the bibliography on the orality of Homer is extensive, a good place to begin is with the formulaic studies of Parry (1930; 1932) and with Lord's *The Singer of Tales* (1960). Lord is also the starting point for a study of the traditional oral epic of Yugoslavia, but his work should be supplemented by that of Rosenberg (1970a; 1975) on the links between the oral performances of ancient Greeks, Yugoslavs and Afro-Americans. Observations on the Turkish epic (Basgöz 1975) complement the material from ancient Greece and modern Yugoslavia.

In addition to epics, we refer to other forms of oral performance from the Mediterranean, including the lyric poetry of ancient Greece. The works of these poets, including Sappho, Archilochos and Pindar, are available in English translations by Lattimore (1959; 1960) and Barnstone (1972). We draw, too, on the wedding invectives of Galicia in Spain (Tolosana 1973), verbal duelling rhymes by Turkish boys (Dundes et al. 1972) and wedding songs of modern Cyprus (Markou, personal communication).

In the more northern regions of Europe, we look at the story–telling skills of Eastern European Jewish communities at the beginning of the twentieth century (Kirshenblatt–Gimblett 1977). The British Isles provide material ancient and modern: traditional narratives from Ireland (Cross and Slover 1969); children's playground lore (Opie and Opie 1977); dub poetry and oral invective from the British Black community (Dalphinis 1985) and the wedding songs of British Gujarati women (Edwards 1982b; Edwards and Katbamna 1989).

The evidence from the Americas is extensive. Rosenberg's studies (1970a; 1970b; 1975; 1987) of the oral performances of American folk preachers sparked a consciousness of the orality of such performances which is the ultimate inspiration for this book. Abrahams (1970b; 1976), Levine (1977) and Smitherman (1977) are also important sources for oral material on Afro-American speech events including 'toasts' or epics and verbal duelling. A little further afield, in the Caribbean and Guyana, there is an extensive literature on story-telling (Crowley 1966), oratory (Abrahams 1970a; 1972a) and ritual invective (Abrahams 1967; Abrahams 1972b; W. Edwards 1978).

Of the varied oral forms of Africa we shall look at *apae* or praise songs from Ghana (Yankah 1983), the *kabary* or formal speech of the Malagasy of Madagascar (Keenan 1977), riddles from Somalia (Andrzejewski 1973), epics sung by Nyanga bards of Zaire (Biebuyck and Mateene 1969; Biebuyck 1978) and stories from the Mende in Sierra Leone (Cosentino 1982) and from the Xhosa of southern Africa

(Scheub 1977). In particular, however, we shall refer to the oral epic *Sunjata*, performed in large parts of West Africa, especially Mali, Senegal and The Gambia. This epic, available in at least seven published versions, offers a panoramic view of a traditional oral culture still thriving in the modern world. These versions of *Sunjata* provide an exciting opportunity to observe the epic not as a single performance but as part of a broader tradition dating back to the lifetime of Sunjata, who ruled the ancient kingdom of Mali in the early thirteenth century AD. For ease of reference to these seven variants, we follow a shorthand based upon Okpewho (1979):

S_1	transcription of song by Bamba Suso	(Innes 1974)
S_2	transcription of song by Banna Kanuté	(Innes 1974)
S_3	transcription of song by Dembo Kanuté	(Innes 1974)
S_4	version of Mamadou Kouyaté	(Niane 1965)
S_5	transcription of song by Magan Sisòkò	(Johnson 1979)
S_6	transcription of song by Fa-Digi Sisòkò	(Johnson 1986)
S_7	version of Babu Condé	(Laye 1984)

The Asian material is equally diverse. From the Indian subcontinent we look at the *Pābūjī* epic sung in the Indian state of Rajasthan (Smith 1977; 1989) and Vedic songs and riddles (Huizinga 1949; Ong 1982). In addition there are marriage songs from China (Blake 1978; 1979), Kirghiz epics from Mongolia (Radloff 1885; Hatto 1980) and ritual poetry from Roti, an island in Eastern Indonesia (Fox 1977). Performances of Japanese serial stories in kodan theatres (Hrdličková 1969) offer important evidence about the interaction of performer and audience. There is also material from the Pacific: Maori rituals of encounter (Salmond 1977), oratory from Samoa (Holmes 1969; see plate 4) and the poetry of Kiribati, formerly the Gilbert Isles (Grimble 1957).

Written Views of the Oral World

Even with a basic familiarity with these oral cultures, the literate observer who attempts to step into the oral world can trip over other obstacles, too, self-made obstacles derived from a literate person's distorted view of the oral world. Through linguistic manipulation literates have sometimes imposed an inferior status upon those who cannot read and write. Thus 'illiteracy' has come to be synonymous with stupidity. Only those who can read and write are considered educated, just as only the lettered word has been considered worthy of the name 'literature'. Equally misguided is the literate observer's Rousseauian view of the oral word as an untarnished expression of pure nature, as

the admirable wisdom of noble savages (Hollingworth 1989). In this
way the same person of letters who, consciously or not, asserts cultural
superiority over anyone illiterate, also yearns for what is lost, for a
return to a prelettered universe unaffected by the power of the written
word.

In his definitive work on the oral songs of Yugoslav epic singers
Lord (1960) illustrates the second of these extremes. For Lord the
written word poses more an internal than an external threat to orality.
He is not as worried about the distortion brought to the oral experience
through transcription by a literate observer, as much as he fears perma-
nent transformation of the oral performer's skills by literacy. When the
oral singer learns to read and write, the performance becomes a recitation, a book, and Lord (1960:23) resolutely asserts the inferiority of
literate Yugoslav singers over their illiterate counterparts. Thus, in the
process of affirming the intrinsic value of nonliterate language, in
showing the skill of these oral singers, Lord denies to a literate person
the skills of the illiterate. Lord's position presents a dilemma. Must the
nobility of aliteracy be abandoned in the name of progress? Must
humankind give up the heritage of a rich oral culture from the past
because the modern world requires an irrevocable step into literacy?
Has literacy already tarnished beyond repair the oral traditions of the
modern world?

The Oral–Literate Continuum

The literate observer can find a safer path by thinking in terms of an
oral–literate continuum which recognizes the skills of the oral performer and, at the same time, does not view the literate person as
hopelessly cut off from oral skill. From this perspective, the written
word does not divide so much as the spoken word unites the aliterate
and the literate; that is, the presence of literacy does not remove all
trace of orality, nor must an oral culture always function independently
of literacy.

Several cultural experiences bear this out. The first is the sophisticated, highly literate, modern world of high technology in which the
spoken word of radio and television is shouting out the print media of
newspapers and books. All too often, the traditional person of letters
laments the slow death of the written word in a media-conscious
society. Ong (1978) has described this phenomenon, an orality which
functions in a literate context, as a 'secondary' form of orality in order
to distinguish it from the primary orality of a culture yet 'untouched by
writing or print'.

The sermon of the Afro-American preacher is a specific example of such secondary orality. On the one hand the preacher is steeped in the literate culture of the book, of the Bible; on the other hand the medium of the preacher's message is purely oral. As Rosenberg (1970a and 1975) has shown, there is an intrinsic similarity between the oral art of the American folk preacher and that of the Yugoslav epic singer. Despite, or because of, literacy, the preacher has a foot in each world, the oral and the literate.

The continuum between orality and literacy is evident in other modern settings. Like the preacher, the Afro-American 'toaster' or epic poet uses literate material in an oral context. Expressions such as 'the bitter cup' and 'the slumbering beast' can often be traced back to sheet music and minstrel performances where the theme of the toast was first performed. Interaction between the written and the oral is also a dominant feature in the language and lore of school children, especially in riddles. The fact that riddles have often been written down and gathered in collections does not necessarily detract from their oral nature. The primarily oral transmission of riddles is neatly captured by the Opies (1977:95–6) in the following observation:

> It is an exciting experience, for instance, to walk into a schoolroom in one of the poorest quarters of Dublin and hear a 9-year-old urchin give the cryptic description of a maid milking a cow,
>
> Ink ank under a bank
> Ten drawing four,
>
> being already aware that this was how the riddle was posed in Charles I's time:
>
> Clinke clanke under a banke,
> Ten above foure and neere the stanke,
>
> and being able to tell oneself that it was highly unlikely that the child, or any of his forebears, had ever seen these words in print, for during the centuries of the riddle's existence it only has been printed two or three times, in obscure places.

Dynamic exchanges between the oral and the written word suggest that the barrier which the scholar perceives between the literate and the oral is actually a source of enrichment for the oral artist. For instance, the death knell Lord sounded for the Yugoslav epic singer, or guslar, appears to have been premature. Guslars are still active in modern, literate Yugoslavia, although the traditional singer has had to adapt his performance to changing audiences: the typical audience of a modern guslar is composed of urban Yugoslavs and tourists rather than unlettered peasants. Rosenberg (1975) also refers to practising guslars who have adapted their art for the Yugoslav diaspora in American cities such as Detroit and Chicago. Indeed he wonders whether illiteracy was ever a precondition of orality, at least in Yugoslavia where the Turkish prohibition against the writing down of local tales may have compelled literate singers in medieval Yugoslavia to preserve their traditions in song rather than writing.

A similar tension between oral and literate traditions exists in West Africa, where a literate Islamic culture has flourished for centuries alongside unwritten traditions (Goody 1987). Islam certainly intrudes into the story of Sunjata whose genealogy is often linked with the prophet Mohammed and his close associates (Johnson 1979; 1986). It is important to remember, however, that Islamic officials neither control nor preserve the epic which continues to thrive in modern West Africa.

Like the Yugoslav epic singers, West African performers have also had to adapt to changing times. Because the royal and wealthy families who traditionally provided financial support are often no longer reliable sources of income, epic singers have had to search for new contexts for their performances. Some have performed on radio and television; others have brought their songs to the live stage in other parts of the world. *Sunjata* inevitably changes in the process, but such change is a sign of the vitality, not the mortality, of the oral tradition.

Signs of oral resilience can be found in other cultures, too. Commercially made tapes of South Asian and Greek wedding songs are now available, and themes from traditional Indian epics form the basis for modern films and strip cartoons as well as a very popular television series. Indian oral culture also thrives outside South Asia; the late 1980s, for instance, saw the cooperation of the Mandela Theatre Company and many London schools in the staging of the epic legend of the Ramayana, an event which provided the starting point for work in music, art, drama and dance for children of all ages. Also in the UK, Channel 4 television broadcast the entire Mahabharata then being performed in Glasgow.

The presence of important Indian communities in Britain has also stimulated other cultural exchanges. *Bhavai*, for instance, the folk theatre of north-west India which has a tradition dating back 700 years, acts out folk tales through a visually stunning combination of song, dance and music (see Plate 1). Each year actors, dancers and musicians born into the *Bhavai* tradition play to thousands at each performance in

Plate 1   *The Bhavaiars of Gujarat, a folk theatre group from the north-west of India which has a tradition dating back 700 years. Photograph: Nigel Watson, Theatr Taliesin Wales.*

villages throughout the state of Gujarat. On their first UK tour in 1988, a twelve-strong company, the Bhavaiars of Gujarat, not only performed traditional themes but also joined forces with the multi-ethnic community of Cardiff to create a new play, an amalgam of the songs and dances of Wales and India based on the story of Twm Siôn Cati (the Welsh Robin Hood figure).

When faced with examples such as these, we can only agree with Finnegan (1988:175) that

Orality and literacy are not two separate and independent things; nor (to put it more concretely) are oral and written modes two mutually exclusive and opposed processes for representing and communicating information. On the contrary, they take diverse forms in differing cultures and periods, are used differently in different social contexts and, insofar as they can be distinguished at all as separate modes rather than a continuum, they mutually interact and affect each other, and the relations between them are problematic rather than self-evident.

The adaptation to change seen in many different settings today also throws interesting light on a much older problem. A similar oral–literate dynamic may have played a role in the creation of the Homeric epics of ancient Greece, which, to a great extent, have moulded the literate perception of orality. Indeed, scholarly awareness of the orality of these epics has emerged only slowly, over the course of several centuries, and did not really solidify until the twentieth century with the work of Parry (1930; 1932) and Lord (1960). Even today, however, Homeric scholarship can be divided, to a certain extent, between the separatists, those who consider the poems to be the product of multiple authorship, and the unitarians, those who insist that a single literate person, perhaps working in the oral tradition, composed the poems as we have them.

Part of the Homeric debate has naturally been based upon the introduction of the Greek alphabet, which made possible the writing down of traditional oral tales. The usual assumption has been that writing was a recent invention in the time of Homer, and that written versions of the *Iliad* and the *Odyssey* appeared within decades or, at most, within a century of the introduction of writing to Greece. Yet the evidence is ambiguous and contradictory. On the one hand, Homer is said by the Greek historian Herodotos (II:53) to have lived in the mid-ninth century. On the other hand, even in the eighth century, evidence of written Greek is limited to a small number of inscriptions cut in stone or painted on pottery; and the first recorded text of Homer is that of the Peisistratids at the end of the seventh century. Thus the Homeric epics could have been composed any time in the eighth or seventh centuries BC. When they were written down for the first time is anyone's guess.

The work of Havelock (1963; 1982; 1986) has been particularly successful in demonstrating that the rise of literacy in ancient Greece was not sudden. The transition from an oral to a literate society in Greece was actually quite gradual. For several centuries, from the introduction of writing in the late ninth or eighth century until the time of Plato in the fourth century, Greek language and culture were both oral and literate, and Greek dramatists like Aischylos and Sophokles functioned in a behavioural continuum of orality and literacy in much the same way as the Afro-American preacher does today. Many signs of the same continuum are also evident in modern Greece and Cyprus (Tannen 1980b; Markou, personal communication).

This leads us inevitably to the question, 'Was Homer a rapper?' We recognize that comparison between the Greek artist and the preacher, between the rapper and Homer, should not be made lightly and may prove another stumbling block to many readers. The ancient Greeks have long held a special place as the source of Western culture and are often considered 'different' from other peoples. In particular, the Greeks are often credited with a unique ability to transcend their own environment and culture and to create universal forms of expression. Thus, Steiner (1984:135–8) argues that the syntax of the Greek language and the myths expressed in this language unite to express basic, universal forms of human expression in a way no other culture has been able to do. From this perspective, the Greeks are different because their language functions without the special code and mind-set which are basic features of other oral cultures and which allow only members of the group to understand what is being said. Homer thus speaks to humans of all times and cultures, not just his own.

This Hellenocentric viewpoint is not universally accepted, however. In the first chapter of *Dionysus Slain*, entitled 'The Greeks Aren't Like the Others', Détienne (1979) affirms the need to interpret all myth, including Greek myth, within its own ethnographic context. In reality, even the ancient Greeks share a wide range of themes, characteristics and strategies which, as we will see, are commonly found in oral communities all over the world (Sienkewicz in press). From this vantage point, orality is therefore something which has the potential to link rather than to divide. Conscious of this oral–literate continuum, we include in this book certain material, such as the sermons of Afro-American preachers, which some might not consider sufficiently oral. Yet the resilience of orality in both ancient Greece and in our modern world makes an arbitrary cut-off point inappropriate.

We inevitably deal in this book with generalizations about orality. We do not focus exclusively upon examples of primary orality, but include as sources societies, literate or not, where great importance is attached to the spoken word. While we may occasionally indulge in a shorthand and speak in terms of 'oral' and 'literate' cultures, neither term is a homogeneous, monolithic whole. Our concern is ultimately with the full range of formal human speech.

The Structure of the Book

Our goal in the following pages is to discuss several features of oral language which cross cultural and temporal boundaries. The first of these features is the dynamism of oral language: by this we mean that it is changeable and kinetic rather than static. Ong (1982:46–57) observes much the same thing when he describes orally based thought as homeostatic and situational. The dynamic nature of orality requires that we look closely, in the section called 'The Oral World's a Stage', at the performative aspects of speech events: the characteristics of the oral performer; the verbal tools of the performer; and the active role of the audience in the performance.

A second important aspect of oral language is that it is pre-eminently interactive; that is, an oral performance operates by means of a critical bond between performer and audience, a bond which Ong (1982:43–5) describes as 'agonistically toned'. All members of the oral community are drawn into this interactive performance by linguistic exchanges, such as praise and blame, boasts and self-blame, and verbal abuse. These exchanges are examined cross-culturally in the second part of this book, 'Caught in the Web of Words'.

Oral language tends to be rhapsodic, that is 'stitched together' in the original sense of the Greek word *rhapsode*. Here again our study overlaps with Ong (1982:37–41), who describes orally based thought as 'redundant or copious', 'aggregative rather than analytic', and 'additive rather than subordinate'. Therefore, the third part of this book, called 'The Tapestry of Words', deals with the connective structure of oral performances—features such as repetition and verbal elaboration which are an essential part of the oral aesthetic, and discrete forms such as proverbs, list and riddles, which carry social meaning for both oral artists and their audiences.

In the last part of the book, 'Stepping Back', we take stock of the findings of our survey and consider some of the serious misunderstandings which arise from the differences in perspective between oral and written traditions. We look in particular at the educational consequences for children who use oral strategies in classrooms where literate strategies are encouraged. We also discuss the implications of interdisciplinary study for our understanding of oral performance and for future research in this area.

Now that you are more fully prepared for the journey, you may, with book in hand, step into the oral world.

Part I

The Oral World's a Stage

'Words, words, words.'
William Shakespeare, Hamlet *Act II, Scene 2, line 195.*

In this part of the book, we focus on performance in the widest possible sense. First of all, in 'The Good Talker', we look at the various kinds of performers and the different characteristics which affect their development. Are the expectations for male artists the same as those for women? Why are accomplished performers very often good singers and musicians? To what extent is the performer's role determined by heredity? We look also at the making of the artist and the lengthy training process which is necessary for the acquisition of virtuoso status. Finally we examine the prestige accorded to performers in the oral tradition and the various roles–entertainer, historian, teacher–which they perform.

In 'Thinking on Your Feet', the focus moves from the performer to the process of composition in performance. We look at stereotyped notions of long memory and the stable text which have grown out of the different strategies and expectations associated with oral and literate traditions. Here we observe how oral composition occurs in a variety of cultural contexts as, essentially, an act of recreation in which performers, skilled in thinking on their feet, draw on traditional tools rather than rote memorization. These tools include the shared expectation of the overall pattern of the performance; the use of formulae and repeated themes; of special language, music and metre. The stability of these structural props allows the performer to think ahead, to exploit the delicate balance between stability and creativity which marks oral performance of all kinds.

Finally, in 'Can I Get a Witness?' we broaden the focus to include the audience and draw attention to the ways in which oral artist and audience function as an organic whole. We consider how the length, the pace and content of performance are often determined by the approval–or the disapproval–of the audience. An understanding of the central role of the audience in shaping performance is thus of fundamental importance in appreciating oral culture.

1

The Good Talker

---

*We are vessels of speech, we are the repositories which harbour
secrets many centuries old. . . . We are the memory of mankind; by
the spoken word we bring to life the deeds and exploits of kings for
younger generations.*

Mamadou Kouyaté, *West African griot* (S₄:1)

In oral cultures, words are at a premium. The Western literate distinction between 'performance' and 'ordinary conversation' is blurred by
the wide range of different speech events, both formal and informal,
which allow speakers to show off and enjoy their verbal skills. Sometimes these speech events are formal in nature: the singing or reciting
of oral poetry; songs of insult at weddings or battles of ritual invective
on street corners; public oratory at important family occasions and in
sermons. On other occasions, the setting is less formal: the use of
proverbs to make a point; topping the other person's story or boast with
one even more elaborate; the use of highly metaphorical and dramatic
language to animate even the most mundane conversations.

In this chapter we focus on skilled practitioners of this oral art from a
variety of cultures in many different times, including preachers in
Eastern Europe; adolescents achieving a reputation as 'good talkers' in
Black America and the Caribbean; the epic poets of ancient Greece and
twentieth-century Yugoslavia, Turkey and Africa; story-tellers in Japan;
and Maori orators in Aotearoa (New Zealand). As we consider the
importance attached to the spoken word in all these societies, our
attention is drawn especially to the high standards expected of oral
artists, to the long and arduous training which they undergo and to the
social status which they acquire through their performances.

At the start we are faced with a great confusion of terminology. Each
culture naturally has its own words for these artists, words which are
usually applied in very specific contexts of performance. Thus in the
Homeric poems the word *aoidos*, related to *aeidein* 'to sing', is used to
describe performers like Demodokos and Phemios who sing great epic

tales to live audiences, usually at banquets. Depending upon the regional languages of West Africa, the performers of the epic poem *Sunjata* are called by various forms of the word *jalo*, while different terms are used to refer to performers of hunting songs and other oral pieces (Innes 1974:3–4). Within this linguistic babel, West African artists have also come to be known as *griots*, especially by Western observers (Labouret 1951). We shall also be discussing the Yugoslav *guslar*, the traditional singer of medieval narratives of battle between Moslems and Christians, and will make at least passing reference to other performers, such as the Rajasthani *bhopo*, the Mongolian *akyn* and the Turkish *aşik*.

Unfortunately there is no one English word to refer adequately to all these diverse performers. The native English word 'bard' is too limited in its connotations. While the term 'singer' has been popularized by Lord through his work on the Yugoslavian guslars, even this term is inappropriate for many cultural contexts, notably the West Indian orator or the Japanese story-teller, where musical expertise is not a central part of the performance. For this reason, where possible, we will employ the words used for these performers in their own languages and, where a generic reference is more appropriate, we shall use the term 'good talker' which, unlike bard, singer, or griot, carries no unnecessary linguistic baggage and which emphasizes two essential features of these performers, namely, their use of the spoken, rather than the written, word and the special skills they are expected to acquire.

A Rare Commodity

Based upon the occasion and the style of their performances, good talkers can be grouped into two distinct types. In his discussion of West Indian oral culture, Abrahams (1972a) describes as 'sweet talkers' performers who use formal rhetoric to emphasize decorum and embody the moral authority of the community. They are orators who perform on family and community occasions, especially rites of passage. They are preachers who alternately taunt and woo the congregation with their words. They are the story-tellers who entertain the crowd with tales both new and old. Outside the immediate Caribbean context, these story-tellers include the griots and guslars who sing in epic poems of the heroes of the past.

The second kind of performance, labelled 'broad talk', uses joking and repartee to focus on the behaviour of people who seriously contravene community ideals. Broad talkers are likely to operate in contexts outside family, such as pool rooms, rum shops, market places and street corners rather than the home. They also can be found in the ancient Greek *symposium*, or drinking party, and at marriage ceremonies in many different cultures. While both kinds of good talker draw on the same range of linguistic resources, the sweet talker veers towards the formal and respectable and the broad talker towards the licentious. Both kinds of speaker are helping in their own way to maintain an accepted social order, though the methods they use to achieve this end are clearly very different.

Despite this respect for and centrality of the spoken word, not every member of an oral culture is an equally important 'performer'. Just the contrary is true. As we shall see, good talkers have particular expertise; they have a knowledge of a specialized language and body of information and have often undergone a lengthy process of learning and preparation. Yet this training can be of little value if the apprentice has no basic aptitude. The importance of innate talent is underlined, for instance, in the Greek tradition, where the skills of the good talkers are seen to be a god-given gift rather than a product of training or tradition. Thus, Phemios, a Greek *aoidos*, says specifically, 'I am taught by myself, but the god has inspired me in the song-ways of every kind' (*Odyssey* XXII:346–7). A similar sentiment has been expressed in twentieth-century Japan by virtuoso story-tellers who sometimes complain that the apprentices working with them are 'such blockheads that you can make nothing of them. And then it is better if such a one gives up storytelling–and the sooner the better–and goes and does useful work, maybe in a factory' (Hrdličková 1969:187).

So, too, Biebuyck and Mateene (1969:6) note a hierarchy of talent even among the Nyanga of Zaire, for whom story-telling is an everyday activity shared by everyone: 'All Nyanga know a certain number of texts; some are able to narrate, sing or recite them coherently and completely, others are confused narrators, able only to communicate the essence of their content.' We can perhaps better appreciate the rarity of performers who achieve a high level of skill by referring to a comparable situation in literate societies. Most people in the Western industrial world are functionally literate, but few succeed in writing books and even fewer win literary awards. In the same way, only a small proportion of good talkers win public acclaim for their skills.

Because descriptions of oral cultures inevitably focus on outstanding performers and performances, the uninitiated reader is led to believe that all members of the community in question are capable of comparable achievements. There are, however, many clues that virtuoso performance is the exception rather than the rule. In the *Odyssey*, for instance, the services of an *aoidos* are sought on a number of occasions.

In Ithaka, the suitors call on Odysseus' singer, Phemios, to perform for them (*Odyssey* I:325–7). Among the Phaiakians, another *aoidos*, Demodokos, is requested to sing for Odysseus and the court of King Alkinoös (*Odyssey* VIII:62–5). It is clear that the task of singing is the responsibility of a specialist rather than of the group as a whole. From this point of view, the performative talents displayed by the heroes of both Homeric epics, Achilleus in the *Iliad* (IX:185–194) and Odysseus in the *Odyssey* (XI:363–9), simply serve to set them apart from the rest of society; they have abilities not found in the average person. Indeed, Martin (1989) has illustrated the special features of Achilleus' language and has identified them with the characteristics of Homer's own performance style.

In a similar vein, Lord (1960:21–6) talks of the varying levels of performance in Yugoslav singers of heroic epics; and Johnson (1986:24) notes that in West Africa only some jeli achieve the status of master singer and then only after many years of apprenticeship. Abrahams (1970b:93) estimates that within any Afro-American neighbourhood there will be perhaps half a dozen accomplished 'toasters' or performers of epic verse. He also comments on the peculiarities and shortcomings of certain aspiring performers:

> As a storyteller, Bobby was not recognized by his perrs as outstanding. His main trouble seemed to be that he tried too hard and yet could not remember stories, especially the toasts, very well. Thus his sense of the story's direction was often impaired and this was reflected in his faltering method of delivery.

Another clue to the distinctive talents of good performers is the extensive vocabulary in many oral cultures for people who have poorly developed oral skills. This vocabulary is an indication both of the status of 'good talkers' and of the fact that by no means everyone achieves a high level of skill. For instance, poor performers in Black America are usually referred to as 'lames' (Labov 1973a). In the West Indies, great importance is attached to 'keeping company'; the 'selfish' (shy) person and the 'garden man' (loner) meet with a great deal of disapproval. 'Selfish' is often equated with 'gettin' on ignorant' and implies an inability to take a joke and reply in kind (Abrahams 1972b). In Homer unskilled artists are criticized as *aiskhistos* 'most base' (*Iliad* II:216) and even *atasthalos* 'wanton' or 'reckless' (*Odyssey* VIII:166).

So what combination of social circumstances and personal qualities produces an individual recognized by the community at large as an accomplished artist? In our opening chapter we referred to the relationship between illiteracy and the good talker and argued strongly

It has to be admitted that, despite the examples which we have offered so far, our knowledge of the different roles for men and women in oral societies remains limited and essentially culture-bound. The majority of commentators on oral culture have been male and, as such, may have found it difficult either to identify or explore female verbal art. Goldstein (1964), for instance, has commented on the fact that his wife Rochelle obtained examples of lore in Scotland that would have been inaccessible to him as a man. Similarly, while most published studies of good talkers have focused exclusively on these male contexts, it is not unlikely that female oral artists have their own performative contexts in these cultures as well. The fact remains, however, that while we may have an incomplete picture of the total context of verbal performance, there can be little doubt that the question of who performs what is often strictly determined along male–female lines in many oral cultures.

Music and the Good Talker

For many—though by no means all—performers words and music are inseparable and are combined in the form of song and instrumental accompaniment. Performances of epic poetry in the Mediterranean, West Africa and South Asia are sometimes sung rather than spoken. The wedding songs of Cyprus and North India are also set to music. In the next chapter, 'Thinking on Your Feet', we discuss the lyrical aspects of these performances. There we consider the extent to which music—or musical rhythm—is an important backcloth for many speech events not actually sung, including British Black dub poetry (or Afro-American rap) and Afro-American toasts. For the moment we focus our attention on the relationship between the good talker and music and on the integral part which music plays in a wide range of performances.

In many different cultures, the oral artist is not only a good singer but also an accomplished musician. In the ancient Greek world, for instance, the aoidos played the lyre, a stringed instrument well-suited to solo performance. Thus Demodokos and Phemios play the lyre as the court singers in the *Odyssey* (VIII:266 and XXII:332) and Achilleus consoles himself by playing this same instrument in the *Iliad* (IX:186). So, too, Trinidadian calypso singers accompany themselves on the guitar, and the Yugoslav *guslar* plays either a two-stringed plucked instrument called the *tambura* or a one-stringed instrument, called the *gusle*, from which the singer gets his name (Lord 1960:18–21). In the Indian Rajasthan different instruments are used for different epics. The *ravaṇhattho*, a type of spike-fiddle, is used in the performance of the

against the belief of some writers, including Lord (1960), that the advent of literacy leads to the inevitable demise of the oral tradition. In short, we are interested both in Lord's illiterate Yugoslav guslars and in the educated Black preacher. In addition to literacy, however, discussion of the characteristics of good talkers centres on a number of other issues which vary to a certain extent from one setting to the next: the sex of the performer; the musical skills of the oral artist; the role of heredity in the selection of individual performers; and the social standing of the artist.

In many oral societies, while both men and women can be good talkers, there are often clear expectations about which kinds of performance are considered suitable for men and which for women. Among the Nyanga of Zaire, for example, there are performances by members of both sexes and of all ages, but certain types of performance are associated more closely with either men or women (Biebuyck and Mateene 1969:7–11): *mushúmo*, or proverbs and maxims, are recited by both men and women, but more commonly by men; *iṇoṇdo* or riddles are used more by women and adolescents; and *kárịsị*, or epics like the story of Mwindo, are performed only by men. In West Africa, as well, both men and women can be singers, but only men can sing narrative while women are limited to praise poetry (Johnson 1986:25). In contrast, Guyanese *busin'*, in which each party hurls blame at the other when a perceived injustice has taken place, is an activity restricted to women (W. Edwards 1978). Similarly, ritual abuse is an exclusively female domain in South Asian weddings, where women in the bride's party sing insults at the groom's family and the women in the groom's party return these insults in kind (Edwards and Katbamna 1989). Among the Haleka of Hong Kong, however, only the bride sings laments and insults (Blake 1978).

In Greece the experience is similar. While some have suggested that the author of the *Odyssey* was actually a woman (Butler 1922), there are only a few female voices among the ancient Greek oral artists, of whom Sappho of Lesbos is perhaps the best known. In both ancient and modern Greece, the role of female artists has been restricted to specific contexts, such as the funerary lament (see Plate 2). There would seem to be a similar delineation in modern Yugoslavia and Turkey where, for instance, the good talkers who perform in the exclusively male coffee houses are inevitably male. In performances of Rajasthani epics there appears to be a clear division of role according to sex. While a male *bhopo* sings, dances and provides musical accompaniment, a female *bhopi*, usually but not always the wife of the *bhopo*, holds a lamp to illuminate some of the scenery (Smith 1977:144 and Smith 1989).

Jewish storytellers in Eastern Europe at the beginning of the twen-

Plate 2 *Colossal dipylon vase, with funeral scene. A chorus sings a lament.*
Photograph courtesy of The New York Metropolitan Museum of Art, Rogers Fund, 1914
[14.130.14].

tieth century also had expectations about the domains of male and female performers. While it was socially acceptable for both men and women to tell stories, the situations in which they operated were very different. Preachers, renowned for their story-telling skills, and wedding jesters—who were essentially professional story-tellers—were exclusively male. Other story-telling activities were also strictly determined by sex. The men would gather together while waiting for the sun to set before saying their prayers in the *besmedresh*. A Jewish immigrant in Toronto reconstructs for Kirshenblatt-Gimblett (1977:290) a typical scene in the following terms: 'As they waited for the mayrev [preacher], they gathered themselves around a table there, people gathered around. People started to tell tales. Stories were told. This one tells such a story and that one tells such a kind of story.'

However, the Eastern European story-telling tradition is by no means

limited to Jewish men. Particularly on the Sabbath, when work was taboo and men and older boys were in the synagogue, mothers or grandmothers would assume the role of story-teller in order to amuse their daughters and younger sons. Thus, although the main focus in the accounts of oral narrative in the Jewish community has tended to be on men, there is no shortage of evidence for competent female story-tellers, albeit in different settings. Nor is this division along sex lines restricted to oral narrative. A wide range of male and female domains emerge clearly, for instance, in recollections of Bialostotski's childhood, translated by Kirshenblatt-Gimblett (1977:285):

> I never heard a single anecdote or fairytale (*maysele*) from my grandfather. I also never heard a single Yiddish song from him, of course. He was totally immersed in Halakah (the legislative part of the Talmud or rabbinical literature, as opposed to Aggadah), Shulhan Aruk (the collection of laws and prescriptions governing the life of an Orthodox Jew), restrained piety, praying, prayers, Torah (Pentateuch). But my grandmother, she implanted the Yiddish folk tune in me; she told me a fairytale; she asked a riddle, and while speaking to people, freely uttered proverbs and witticisms.
>
> Was my grandmother an exception, then? Many grandmothers and mothers were like this.

Sometimes different expectations of men's and women's roles in performance give rise to open conflict within a society. In most parts of Aoteoroa, for instance, Maori orators are male elders, while on the East coast women can also take part. Consequently, when East coast communities compete in *hui*, or contests of ritual oratory, with communities from other parts of the country certain difficulties arise. A famous example of what can happen when one set of expectations is pitted against another dates back to the 1920s (Salmond 1977:212). A woman chief from the East coast was attending a funeral in the Arawa country where it was not the custom for women to make speeches. As she launched into a chant, the Arawa elders started to shout her down. The chieftainess refused to acknowledge their protests until she had reached the end of her speech, when she finally addressed them in this way:

> You Arawa men! You tell me to sit down because I am a woman, yet none of you would be in this world if it wasn't for your mothers. *This* is where your learning and your grey hairs come from!

Turning her back on them in the ultimate gesture of contempt, she then bent over and flipped her skirts. The elders said nothing further and the old woman passed into East coast history.

Pābūjī epic while the *jantar,* a stick-zither, is used for another song called the *Devnarayaṇ* (Smith 1977:144). In West Africa either a twenty-one-stringed *kora* or xylophone-like *balaphon* are used to accompany a performance. Choice of instrument in West Africa is apparently based upon background, to the extent that certain families use the kora and others use the balaphon (Innes 1974:3). On occasion, the musical instrument is even incorporated into the plot of *Sunjata.* Thus, in one version (S_2:1519–1526), the balaphon is stolen from its original owner and is eventually associated with the hero's personal jalo.

Plate 3 *A West African griot, Sidibe Jebaté, playing the kora during a performance of* Sunjata *in Bamako, Mali. Photograph: Thomas Sienkewicz.*

In most cases, the instruments are designed to allow the oral artist to perform without the help of an accompanist, although in ancient Greece some performances, such as elegy and drama, were accompanied by flute players. In West Africa, too, the singer is sometimes assisted by a musical accompanist and, at the very beginning of his performance, the griot Bamba Suso emphasizes the close interaction between himself and his accompanist Amadu Jebate:

> It is I, Bamba Suso, who am talking,
> Along with Amadu Jebate;
> It is Amadu Jebate who is playing the *kora*,
> And it is I, Bamba Suso, who am doing the talking.
>   (S_1:1–4)

The artist's respect for his instrument emerges in other contexts as well. Thus, one Yugoslav guslar, Šećo Kolić, speaking of the many years of practice needed for him to become proficient in playing the gusle, said: 'Then I learned gradually to finger the instrument, and to fit the fingering to the words, and my fingers obeyed better and better.' Another of Lord's guslars, Stjepan Majstorović, shows concern for his instrument by always carrying it around with him in a bag to protect it from harm (Lord 1960:18–19).

In Homeric epic singer and instrument are treated with equal respect. At *Odyssey* VIII:62ff. Homer describes how a herald leads the blind singer Demodokos into the banquet hall of the Phaiakians:

> . . . Pontoös set a silver-studded chair out for him
> in the middle of the feasters, propping it against a tall column,
> and the herald hung the clear lyre on a peg placed over
> his head, and showed him how to reach up with his hands and take it
> down. . . .

Later in the *Odyssey* (XXII:330ff.) another singer, Phemios, puts his instrument in a safe place before going to plead for his life before Odysseus. The songs of Greek lyric poets, too, are filled with respectful allusions to the lyre. Sappho, for example, prays to her lyre for poetic inspiration in the following poem:

> Come, holy tortoise shell,
> my lyre, and become a poem.
> (Translated by Barnstone 1972:65)

against the belief of some writers, including Lord (1960), that the advent of literacy leads to the inevitable demise of the oral tradition. In short, we are interested both in Lord's illiterate Yugoslav guslars and in the educated Black preacher. In addition to literacy, however, discussion of the characteristics of good talkers centres on a number of other issues which vary to a certain extent from one setting to the next: the sex of the performer; the musical skills of the oral artist; the role of heredity in the selection of individual performers; and the social standing of the artist.

In many oral societies, while both men and women can be good talkers, there are often clear expectations about which kinds of performance are considered suitable for men and which for women. Among the Nyanga of Zaire, for example, there are performances by members of both sexes and of all ages, but certain types of performance are associated more closely with either men or women (Biebuyck and Mateene 1969:7–11): *mushúmo*, or proverbs and maxims, are recited by both men and women, but more commonly by men; *jnondo* or riddles are used more by women and adolescents; and *kárisi*, or epics like the story of Mwindo, are performed only by men. In West Africa, as well, both men and women can be singers, but only men can sing narrative while women are limited to praise poetry (Johnson 1986:25). In contrast, Guyanese *busin'*, in which each party hurls blame at the other when a perceived injustice has taken place, is an activity restricted to women (W. Edwards 1978). Similarly, ritual abuse is an exclusively female domain in South Asian weddings, where women in the bride's party sing insults at the groom's family and the women in the groom's party return these insults in kind (Edwards and Katbamna 1989). Among the Haleka of Hong Kong, however, only the bride sings laments and insults (Blake 1978).

In Greece the experience is similar. While some have suggested that the author of the *Odyssey* was actually a woman (Butler 1922), there are only a few female voices among the ancient Greek oral artists, of whom Sappho of Lesbos is perhaps the best known. In both ancient and modern Greece, the role of female artists has been restricted to specific contexts, such as the funerary lament (see Plate 2). There would seem to be a similar delineation in modern Yugoslavia and Turkey where, for instance, the good talkers who perform in the exclusively male coffee houses are inevitably male. In performances of Rajasthani epics there appears to be a clear division of role according to sex. While a male *bhopo* sings, dances and provides musical accompaniment, a female *bhopi*, usually but not always the wife of the *bhopo*, holds a lamp to illuminate some of the scenery (Smith 1977:144 and Smith 1989).

Jewish storytellers in Eastern Europe at the beginning of the twen-

Plate 2 *Colossal dipylon vase, with funeral scene. A chorus sings a lament.*
Photograph courtesy of The New York Metropolitan Museum of Art, Rogers Fund, 1914
[14.130.14].

tieth century also had expectations about the domains of male and
female performers. While it was socially acceptable for both men and
women to tell stories, the situations in which they operated were very
different. Preachers, renowned for their story-telling skills, and wedding jesters—who were essentially professional story-tellers—were exclusively male. Other story-telling activities were also strictly determined by sex. The men would gather together while waiting for the sun
to set before saying their prayers in the *besmedresh*. A Jewish immigrant
in Toronto reconstructs for Kirshenblatt-Gimblett (1977:290) a typical
scene in the following terms: 'As they waited for the mayrev [preacher],
they gathered themselves around a table there, people gathered around.
People started to tell tales. Stories were told. This one tells such a story
and that one tells such a kind of story.'
    However, the Eastern European story-telling tradition is by no means

limited to Jewish men. Particularly on the Sabbath, when work was taboo and men and older boys were in the synagogue, mothers or grandmothers would assume the role of story-teller in order to amuse their daughters and younger sons. Thus, although the main focus in the accounts of oral narrative in the Jewish community has tended to be on men, there is no shortage of evidence for competent female story-tellers, albeit in different settings. Nor is this division along sex lines restricted to oral narrative. A wide range of male and female domains emerge clearly, for instance, in recollections of Bialostotski's childhood, translated by Kirshenblatt-Gimblett (1977:285):

> I never heard a single anecdote or fairytale (*maysele*) from my grand-father. I also never heard a single Yiddish song from him, of course. He was totally immersed in Halakah (the legislative part of the Talmud or rabbinical literature, as opposed to Aggadah), Shulhan Aruk (the collection of laws and prescriptions governing the life of an Orthodox Jew), restrained piety, praying, prayers, Torah (Pentateuch). But my grand-mother, she implanted the Yiddish folk tune in me; she told me a fairytale; she asked a riddle, and while speaking to people, freely uttered proverbs and witticisms.
>
> Was my grandmother an exception, then? Many grandmothers and mothers were like this.

Sometimes different expectations of men's and women's roles in performance give rise to open conflict within a society. In most parts of Aoteoroa, for instance, Maori orators are male elders, while on the East coast women can also take part. Consequently, when East coast communities compete in *hui*, or contests of ritual oratory, with communities from other parts of the country certain difficulties arise. A famous example of what can happen when one set of expectations is pitted against another dates back to the 1920s (Salmond 1977:212). A woman chief from the East coast was attending a funeral in the Arawa country where it was not the custom for women to make speeches. As she launched into a chant, the Arawa elders started to shout her down. The chieftainess refused to acknowledge their protests until she had reached the end of her speech, when she finally addressed them in this way:

> You Arawa men! You tell me to sit down because I am a woman, yet none of you would be in this world if it wasn't for your mothers. *This* is where your learning and your grey hairs come from!

Turning her back on them in the ultimate gesture of contempt, she then bent over and flipped her skirts. The elders said nothing further and the old woman passed into East coast history.

It has to be admitted that, despite the examples which we have offered so far, our knowledge of the different roles for men and women in oral societies remains limited and essentially culture-bound. The majority of commentators on oral culture have been male and, as such, may have found it difficult either to identify or explore female verbal art. Goldstein (1964), for instance, has commented on the fact that his wife Rochelle obtained examples of lore in Scotland that would have been inaccessible to him as a man. Similarly, while most published studies of good talkers have focused exclusively on these male contexts, it is not unlikely that female oral artists have their own performative contexts in these cultures as well. The fact remains, however, that while we may have an incomplete picture of the total context of verbal performance, there can be little doubt that the question of who performs what is often strictly determined along male–female lines in many oral cultures.

Music and the Good Talker

For many–though by no means all–performers words and music are inseparable and are combined in the form of song and instrumental accompaniment. Performances of epic poetry in the Mediterranean, West Africa and South Asia are sometimes sung rather than spoken. The wedding songs of Cyprus and North India are also set to music. In the next chapter, 'Thinking on Your Feet', we discuss the lyrical aspects of these performances. There we consider the extent to which music–or musical rhythm–is an important backcloth for many speech events not actually sung, including British Black dub poetry (or Afro-American rap) and Afro-American toasts. For the moment we focus our attention on the relationship between the good talker and music and on the integral part which music plays in a wide range of performances.

In many different cultures, the oral artist is not only a good singer but also an accomplished musician. In the ancient Greek world, for instance, the aoidos played the lyre, a stringed instrument well-suited to solo performance. Thus Demodokos and Phemios play the lyre as the court singers in the *Odyssey* (VIII:266 and XXII:332) and Achilleus consoles himself by playing this same instrument in the *Iliad* (IX:186). So, too, Trinidadian calypso singers accompany themselves on the guitar, and the Yugoslav *guslar* plays either a two-stringed plucked instrument called the *tambura* or a one-stringed instrument, called the *gusle*, from which the singer gets his name (Lord 1960:18–21). In the Indian Rajasthan different instruments are used for different epics. The *ravaṇhattho*, a type of spike-fiddle, is used in the performance of the

Pābūjī epic while the *jantar*, a stick-zither, is used for another song called the *Devnarayaṇ* (Smith 1977:144). In West Africa either a twenty-one-stringed *kora* or xylophone-like *balaphon* are used to accompany a performance. Choice of instrument in West Africa is apparently based upon background, to the extent that certain families use the kora and others use the balaphon (Innes 1974:3). On occasion, the musical instrument is even incorporated into the plot of *Sunjata*. Thus, in one version (S$_2$:1519–1526), the balaphon is stolen from its original owner and is eventually associated with the hero's personal jalo.

Plate 3 *A West African griot, Sidibe Jebaté, playing the kora during a performance of* Sunjata *in Bamako, Mali. Photograph: Thomas Sienkewicz.*

In most cases, the instruments are designed to allow the oral artist to perform without the help of an accompanist, although in ancient Greece some performances, such as elegy and drama, were accompanied by flute players. In West Africa, too, the singer is sometimes assisted by a musical accompanist and, at the very beginning of his performance, the griot Bamba Suso emphasizes the close interaction between himself and his accompanist Amadu Jebate:

> It is I, Bamba Suso, who am talking,
> Along with Amadu Jebate;
> It is Amadu Jebate who is playing the *kora*,
> And it is I, Bamba Suso, who am doing the talking.
>   (S_1:1–4)

The artist's respect for his instrument emerges in other contexts as well. Thus, one Yugoslav guslar, Šećo Kolić, speaking of the many years of practice needed for him to become proficient in playing the gusle, said: 'Then I learned gradually to finger the instrument, and to fit the fingering to the words, and my fingers obeyed better and better.' Another of Lord's guslars, Stjepan Majstorović, shows concern for his instrument by always carrying it around with him in a bag to protect it from harm (Lord 1960:18–19).

In Homeric epic singer and instrument are treated with equal respect. At *Odyssey* VIII:62ff. Homer describes how a herald leads the blind singer Demodokos into the banquet hall of the Phaiakians:

> . . . Pontoös set a silver-studded chair out for him
> in the middle of the feasters, propping it against a tall column,
> and the herald hung the clear lyre on a peg placed over
> his head, and showed him how to reach up with his hands and take it
> down. . . .

Later in the *Odyssey* (XXII:330ff.) another singer, Phemios, puts his instrument in a safe place before going to plead for his life before Odysseus. The songs of Greek lyric poets, too, are filled with respectful allusions to the lyre. Sappho, for example, prays to her lyre for poetic inspiration in the following poem:

> Come, holy tortoise shell,
> my lyre, and become a poem.
> (Translated by Barnstone 1972:65)

taught by a skilled singer, usually a member of his family. After he has reached a certain level of skill, he will begin to travel around with the singer and experience his performances. At this stage the novice may participate in portions of the performance, 'perhaps just by playing his instrument, but perhaps also by taking part in the narration, such as singing some songs or reciting some of the praises' (Innes 1974:6). Apparently, then, the West African singer is exposed to a live audience at a much earlier stage in his training than his Yugoslav counterpart.

The following description (Biebuyck and Mateene 1969:12) of the training of a Nyanga bard emphasizes both the process of selection and the intensity of instruction which is part of the experience in many cultures:

> The patterns of transmission of epics are, of course, determined by kinship and friendship. Young men who are agnatic relatives, affines, and/or blood friends of the accomplished bard learn the epic in an informal way by accompanying him as helpers whenever he goes to recite. They are usually about three in number, but not all these young men will ultimately be expert in narrating the epic. It is likely that only one of them – the more energetic, intelligent, assiduous, better-liked one – will be fully instructed by the bard in the performance of the epic in all its complexity.

Japanese story-tellers, too, undergo an extensive apprenticeship. At first, the learner's involvement is extremely limited. He will change the strips of paper inscribed with the name of the artist between one performance and the next, and turn over the story-teller's cushion on the stage. A great deal of time will be spent in detailed observation. Hrdličková (1969:185–6) describes this process in the following terms:

> Training aims to inculcate in the young novice humility and the con-sciousness of his personal insignificance and to teach him self-discipline. Then he can absorb unhindered not only the technique of his craft, but also the atmosphere. On these firm foundations he may then seek to develop his individuality and overstep the limits laid down by tradition.

Dialogue and female roles are considered to be the most difficult elements in performance and so apprentices will start by learning to recite simple narrative descriptions of battles. Only after a year or so will they go on to tales of the deeds of famous warriors where both women's roles and dialogue begin to be featured. The most difficult stories, the domestic dramas, in which dialogue is extremely important and women assume a more important role, are approached much later in the training.

A similar process of apprenticeship has been described by Abrahams (1972a) for oratory in the West Indies. Speechmaking on important family occasions, for instance, is considered a very important form of 'sweet talk'. Parents and grandparents are generally held to be responsible for teaching a child to talk sweet on these family occasions. However, if there is no one in the family with particular skills in speech making, the child will often be sent to someone in the community who has a greater level of expertise. The likelihood of tuition is increased if the child displays speaking talent.

The 'tea meetings' on the Caribbean island of Saint Vincent provide a particular incentive by offering prizes for child orators who have been trained by accomplished performers. Classes of five to ten students meet about a month before the scheduled tea meeting, and are presented with their speech or 'lesson'. In the past, children would be taught their lesson by repetition: now, however, the lesson is usually written out. The teacher offers advice on presentation and conduct and children are expected to commit the lesson to memory in the next two weeks. At this point they attend two or three more classes where the teacher criticizes and helps develop their performance. Finally, just before the tea meeting, the teacher will usually go to the student's home to hear the speech and make comments on it in front of the parents. Good students will come back year after year and learn many different speeches. In the course of training, they come to recognize the underlying structure of the speeches and learn how to elaborate and improve on the different elements rather than simply to reproduce a speech created by another person.

Abrahams (1968b) also describes the 'speech bands', or strolling players, on the islands of Nevis, Trinidad and Tobago, who used to perform a play from their repertoire at carnival or in the Christmas season. Typically these performances were led by a 'Captain', who knew the lines by memory and taught the parts to others by writing out 'lessons' or repeating the lines with them. Members of the troupe would change from year to year, but because they were organized around this central performer, there was no threat of a break in tradition. The Captain would usually have a 'number two man' who would help him in the production and who, in the course of time, would probably go off and form his own troupe.

In some situations the learning process is mediated by the family or community-approved figures; in others, the same function is served by the novice's own peer group. Blake (1978:17) notes that Chinese brides learn their abusive laments not from their mothers, but 'from older women in the village, especially a village spinster, an elder brother's wife, or a father's younger brother's wife'. There is evidence that girls even exchange these verses in school. In Afro-American communities the importance of trying out skills in a peer group situation is extremely important, especially in the context of battles of ritual invective such as 'playing the dozens' and 'sounding' (Labov 1972; Abrahams 1976), which will be discussed at greater length in chapter 6. It is only by observing and internalizing performance skills of better and often slightly older speakers that an aspiring good talker can prepare for battle. And it is only by putting these skills to the test in competition with peers that the quick-wittedness and verbal dexterity necessary for success can be acquired. Clearly, not everyone achieves a high level of skill and those who are slow or hesitant are quickly replaced by others who think they can do better.

Rewarding the Good Talker

The long training and the high degree of skill of oral artists ensure that their standing in the community is considerable. In communities which value the spoken word, the prize for the quickwitted and verbally adept is widespread respect. Anyone who can creatively manipulate the conventions to outwit an 'opponent' or produce a new and innovative performance enjoys a considerable degree of prestige. The recognition of good talkers can take a number of different forms depending on the particular social setting: sometimes performers work under the patronage of an important community figure; sometimes they enjoy both material reward and considerable social status; sometimes they are rewarded by their standing in the community.

Ancient Greece and twentieth-century West Africa are two well-known examples of societies in which oral artists operate under the patronage of a powerful person. In the *Odyssey*, the courts of both Odysseus and the Phaiakian Alkinoös have their special singers. In West Africa, where some singer families have developed special relationships with certain members of the ruling class, the association between *jalo* and patron is also very close. For instance, one singer family, the Kouyaté, is traditionally associated with the ruling Keitas, a relationship which can be traced back several hundred years: Sunjata, the hero of the most famous African epic, was a Keita and his griot was a Kuyaté (S_1:470–3).

Patronage provides the singer with material benefits (Innes 1974:4–5; Johnson 1986:26). In West Africa the griot was traditionally supported by his patron and did not have to pursue any other occupation. This relationship has been strained in colonial and post-colonial West Africa, where the ruling families no longer have the power and the means to maintain artists who have reluctantly had to adjust to new situations. Occasionally, the *jalo* mournfully alludes to the bygone days when singers did not have to work for a living. For example, one griot sings with regret that

> In Sunjata's day a griot did not have to fetch water,
> To say nothing of farming and gathering firewood.
> Father World has changed, changed.
>
> $(S_2:320-322)$

In addition to material support from patrons, the traditional singer also derives a considerable amount of prestige and social status. There are several instances in the *Sunjata* where the hero provides the griot with gifts. The most vivid occurs when the hero actually cuts off a piece of his thigh and serves it to his unsuspecting griot who is dying of hunger $(S_1:437-475)$. Such a gesture is not only life-sustaining, but is also a mark of the highest respect.

The singer's status is also recognized in other traditions. At various points in the *Odyssey*, for example, our attention is drawn to the social status of the performer whose skills are often associated with divine inspiration. Phemios, for instance, cites his relationship with the gods as a reason that Odysseus should not slay him for disloyalty in singing to his patron's enemies (*Odyssey* XXII: 344–353). And, on his departure for the Trojan war, Agamemnon held his singer in such high respect that he declared him to be adviser to his wife and regent, Klytemnestra (*Odyssey* III: 267–271).

While the concept of patronage would appear to be limited to relatively few oral cultures, the practice of remunerating the artist is extremely widespread and is not limited to specific patrons. In the *Odyssey* (VIII:474–498) the stranger Odysseus shares a choice piece of meat with the Phaiakian singer Demodokos at a banquet. Similarly, Radloff (1885:xix) tells how a Kirghiz potentate rewards an akyn with a cloak during the performance, and Biebuyck and Mateene (1969:6) mention that good Nyanga bards 'receive much food, banana beer, and small presents' for their performances.

In Yugoslavia, apparently, there was no practice of a court minstrel, although bards were often called to sing on special occasions, particularly at the courts of Turkish nobility. Among Christian nobility, however, at least in modern times, this practice seems to have been rare. Guslars were more likely to sing in coffee shops than in aristocratic courts. Lord (1960:15) describes the guslar as 'not really a professional, but his audience does buy him drinks and if he is good they will give him a little money for the entertainment he has given them'. The money, then, is as much a gesture of honour as it is of profit.

The situation in Turkey is very similar and is neatly captured in an opening formula sung by Mudami, a Turkish epic poet (Basgöz 1975:145). When experiencing a lack of response from the audience, the performer counters with:

> My dear listeners! May you be free from all worries. I hope you always carry the Sultan's firman in your pocket. May our story tonight be told for ever. I don't eat plain bread, no matter how long I remain hungry. I drink the best Yemen coffee. I smoke them only if you provide them. However, I don't mind if you don't; I'll just give them up.

The skilled artist expects – and often receives – only the best in return for a successful performance. In Eastern Europe in the 1920s and 1930s there are records of itinerant Jewish preachers hanging signs on synagogue doors announcing the theme of their sermon (Kirshenblatt-Gimblett 1977). They charged no fee but the better they preached the more money they received; if their performances were particularly good, everyone would flock around to offer them room and board. Similarly, the Japanese good talker Ichiryusai Teiho tells the story of how an old man showed his appreciation for an outstanding story-telling performance by wrapping a 500-yen banknote in a piece of paper and placing it on the stage. Another regular member of the audience would send a packet of cakes to the dressing room every day of the year (Hrdličková 1969). It is important to recognize, therefore, that this material remuneration serves as more than a livelihood for the artist. Indeed, among people like the Yugoslavians and the Nyanga, even virtuosos do not rely upon performance as their primary source of income. They are usually established in other professions within the community and perform only on special occasions. In such situations, material rewards serve to establish the artist's high standing within the community at large.

While the importance of money varies from one situation to the next, the high standing of the performer remains a constant, even in contexts such as the training of 'broad talkers', where remuneration is not an issue. The goal of this training is to establish a place in the pecking order and to gain the respect of the peer group. In a discussion of the importance of the good talker for Afro-Americans, for instance, Smitherman (1977:76–7) points out that 'Aside from athletes and entertainers, only those blacks who can perform stunning feats of oral gymnastics become culture heroes and leaders in the community. Such feats are the basic requirement of the trade among preachers, politicians, disc jockeys, hustlers, and lovers.'

The Performer in Society

A biref survey of oral cultures reveals a wide range of roles for accomplished performers including those of historian, teacher and entertainer. Of these roles the most obvious is that of entertainer. Regardless of time, place or the seriousness of the occasion, the good talker's most important task is to entertain. Homer's singers can perform at meals for the benefit of all present:

> So the famous singer sang his song, and Odysseus
> enjoyed it in his heart as he listened, as did the others
> there, Phaiakians, men of the long oar, famed for seafaring.
> (*Odyssey* VIII:367–9)

The song of the guslars was regularly heard in coffee houses, often after market day, and on special occasions such as weddings and the Islamic festival of Ramadan. Lord (1960:14) describes the role of epic poetry in Yugoslavia as 'at the present time, or until very recently, the chief entertainment of the adult male population in the villages and small towns.'. In a similar vein, in a discussion of verbal abilities in a Black neighbourhood of Washington, D.C., Hannerz (1969:85) remarks that: 'A man with good stories well told and with a quick repartee in arguments is certain to be appreciated for his entertainment value, and those men who can talk about the high and mighty, people and places, and the state of the world, may stake claims to a reputation of being "heavy upstairs".'

However, entertainment does not take place within a social vacuum. Because good talkers draw on themes, conventions and material passed from one generation to the next, there is a sense in which they are also historians. Sometimes this function is clearly articulated; on other occasions it is implicit. Noting that the typical Yugoslav guslar is only vaguely aware of his debt to the past, Lord (1960:24) suggests that his singers were 'interested in the old songs, had a passion (*merak*) for them, listened to singers and then "work, work, work" (*goni, goni, goni*).' The West African artist is more overtly conscious of this inherited tradition and his sense that what he sings is fact not fiction. For example, Mamadou Kouyaté says that

> My word is pure and free of all untruth; it is the word of my father; it is
> the word of my father's. I will give you my father's words just as I
> received them; royal griots do not know what lying is. (S$_4$:1)

Tradition is not always considered so truthful, however. Celtic bards often end their performances with this traditional tag:

That is my story! If there be a lie in it, be it so! It is not I who made or invented it. (Rees and Rees 1961:15)

The positions of the West African and Celtic singers are not really so far apart. While one speaks of truth and the other of lies, both are acknowledging their roles as transmitters, not creators. Good talkers in some cultures express the same idea by associating their song with divine inspiration and making the gods responsible for it. Thus, speaking of the male spirit of those who transmit and preserve the *Mwindo Epic*, Biebuyck and Mateene (1969:12) say that 'When asked why he learned the epic, a Nyanga bard replies that he did so as the result of a compulsory message received in the dreams from Káriṣį.' For the same reason Odysseus praises Demodokos' song for its eyewitness accuracy:

Demodokos, above all mortals beside I prize you.
Surely the Muse, Zeus' daughter or else Apollo has taught you,
for all too right following the tale you sing the Achaians'
venture, all they did and had done to them, all the sufferings
of these Achaians, as if you had been there yourself or heard it
from one who was.

(Odyssey VIII:487–492)

Especially because of this often spiritual link between the artist and the past, in many cultural traditions the good talker is considered a teacher, the guardian of social values and community ideals. Mamoudou Kouyaté, for example tells his audience:

Listen to my word, you who want to know: by my mouth will you learn the history of Mali. By my mouth you will get to know the story of the ancestor of great Mali. . . . . (S$_4$:1)

The song of the singer is the means of preserving this history, of transmitting it to the next generation. Consequently, performances are filled with explanations of West African customs. The griot Bamba Suso, for instance, is particularly fond of aetiologies such as the following, which explains certain dietary restrictions still existing among the Kante, the descendants of Sumanguru, the vanquished hero of the Sunjata epic:

They went and found a white cock,
They found self-seeded guinea corn,
They found korte powder.
That is why members of the Kanté family do not eat white chicken.

(S$_1$:831–4)

Since the white cock was used to destroy Sumanguru, it is understandable that his descendants would not wish to consume these animals
even today. By including such a passage in his song, Bamba is not only
recounting history to his audience, but he is teaching them proper
forms of behaviour within their culture.

The didactic tone is particularly strong in the *Mwindo Epic*, which
sometimes ends with the narrator's interpretation of the moral of the
epic. Thus bard Nkuba Shekarisi concludes his performance with
the following affirmations of kinship unity, the role of the chief and the
characteristics of a good life:

> He who is not advised among the people of the world is (like) a dead
> person.
> Dispersal of the people of one and the same kinship group is bad fate
> and (a cause) of vilification of the land.
> If you hear that the land of a particular chief is famous, (it means) that
> he (the chief) is in harmony with his people. Lo! The land that has no
> chief, has no people, it dies out; it is finished without hope of salvation.
> To wrong the people of the earth is (as much as) to close the path of
> salvation.
> Beauty on earth is (long) life and begetting children. Lo! He/she who
> does not beget children is already dead; he/she is finished without hope
> of salvation! (Biebuyck 1978:232)

The same observation can be made about South Asian wedding songs.
A number of social values emerge as important: men are expected to be
strong, firm and the masters in their own home; women are expected to
be respectful and obedient. Kishore Bhai, for instance, is mocked for
tolerating the whims and extravagances of his bride and is given advice
in no uncertain terms as to what he should do:

> Kishore Bhai went to Bombay, oh the sulking of a spoilt woman.
> His wife Helmeta desires expensive sarees, oh the sulking of a spoilt
> woman.
> Kishore Bhai travelled all over Bombay but could not find any suitable
> sarees, oh the sulking of a spoilt woman.
> Kishore Bhai asked his friend to show him the way out of his difficul-
> ties, oh the sulking of a spoilt woman.
> The friend advised him to order some bamboo and have a cane made,
> oh the sulking of a spoilt woman.
> The cane goes swish and the lady's desire for sarees vanishes, oh the
> sulking of a spoilt woman. (Edwards 1982b:36)

On some occasions, 'sweet talk' and formal rhetoric are used to focus
on socially acceptable behaviour. Thus the Homeric epics illustrate

various aspects of *arete*, the Greek concept of excellence. Angry Achilleus avenging the death of his friend Patroklos in the *Iliad* and crafty Odysseus struggling to find his way home in the *Odyssey* are just two examples of this ideal. Similarly the West African good talker paints the hero Sunjata with the qualities of generosity and occult power which are so important in this cultural context.

On other occasions, performers are given licence to parody the very behaviour which is felt to threaten social order. The abuse of the mother and even the grandmother in African, Caribbean and Afro-American communities, for instance, is not real; it is a ritual phenomenon which will receive closer attention in chapter 6. At various points in this book, we shall also see certain cases in which good talkers transmit views which are the very antithesis of those held dear by the mainstream culture and, at the same time, affirm the values necessary for survival within the counter-culture. Thus tales which ridicule the preacher are widespread throughout Europe and other places where the Church aligns itself with upper-class society; in a similar vein, many Afro-American stories and 'toasts,' or epic poems, extol the virtues of being 'bad', courageous, clear-headed and worldly. Heroes show nothing but disdain for the law, romantic love, pity, gratitude and other values which rest more comfortably with White middle-class society.

Vessels of Speech

Good talkers are made, not born. Although they need a natural aptitude, they nourish their talents by listening, observing and internalizing the requirements of performance, sometimes practising in private, sometimes trying out their skills in competition with others. They model themselves on other good performers, inheriting a corpus of themes, conventions and formulae which link them with an uninterrupted oral tradition. Their accomplishments as performers, however, depend not only on their ability to learn or memorize what has gone before: they must be able to manipulate the structures to their advantage, improvising, embellishing and extending. The good talker is simultaneously entertainer, historian and teacher. The gains for the outstanding performer are considerable. Sometimes they take the form of remuneration but more often the oral artist's reward is social acclaim. The good talker holds a central and vitally important role in any oral culture.

2

Thinking on Your Feet

Six Qur'ānic scholars confirmed in October 1967 that a Turkish man from Ankara, Mehmed Ali Halici, recited from memory some 6,666 verses of the Qur'ān in the space of six hours.
Source: Guinness Book of Records

When a good talker is asked whether the song remains stable over time, or whether it differs from performance to performance, the response is invariably a denial of any change. Thus in Lord (1960:27) the Yugoslav guslar Demail Zogić affirms that 'If I were to live for twenty years, I would sing the song which I sang for you here today just the same twenty years from now, word for word', a statement which reinforces the impression of literate observers that memory functions in the same way in oral and literate contexts, that an oral performer remembers in the same way that the Guiness champion memorized his verses. Yet nothing could be further from the truth. Oral performers do not necessarily learn by rote, even if they say they do. For example, Lord (1960:28) makes the following observations about Zogić's version of the song he heard from Sulejman Makić: 'Zogić did not learn it word for word and line for line, and yet the two songs are recognizable versions of the same story. They are not close enough, however, to be considered "exactly alike".'

Differences can also be found in a song sung twice by the same performer. For example, Lord (1960:28) notes that two versions of a song performed by Zogić seventeen years apart are 'remarkably close . . . though hardly word for word'. Goody and Watt (1968:32) have also observed how the Tiv genealogies change over time despite the important social role these lists play in this African society. There can thus be little doubt as to the differences between oral and literate perceptions of what memory does and how it operates. As Ong (1982:57) notes, 'In a literate culture verbatim memorization is commonly done from a text, to which the memorizer returns as often as necessary to perfect and test verbatim mastery'.

An oral performer, however, usually has no such text as a point of reference nor a board of Islamic scholars to ensure fidelity to a written text. While in a literate context memorization means word-for-word reduplication of a previous speech event, in an oral context memorization usually involves replication of the tradition, not of the specific words. Without the ability to examine several versions of the same song side-by-side, an oral singer's claim to accuracy can be based only on recollection, on a sense of continuity between past and present performances. Clearly, then, while both oral performer and literate observer recognize memory as the basic tool of the oral performer, they are dealing with rather different concepts. In order to reconcile the apparent contradiction between the singer's claim of an accurate memory with the obvious differences between performances, Lord (1960:28) suggests that the singer's claim to verbatim repetition is 'simply an emphatic way of saying "like"', an affirmation of his role in the accurate transmission of the tradition. In other words, what is only *similar* to a literate observer is the *same* in an oral context. How can this be?

Several observations provide perspective on this question. First of all, it should be emphasized that this difference between 'similar' and 'the same' is a literate, not an oral problem. The discrepancy exists only from the point of view of the literate observer. The oral performer does not perceive the contradiction between claims of accuracy and the reality of variability. As Goody (1987:88) points out, 'Without a written text it is difficult for anyone to know whether two versions of a long recitation are the "same" or not. . . . For in this situation the concept of sameness may be much looser; it may refer not to verbal identity but to some kind of unspecified structural similarity.'

Oral and literate cultures also differ in their perception of the relationship between performances. In an oral context the song is part of a living chain of performances. In a literate context the act of transcription converts performance into text. The oral witness, thus reborn into a literate world as a written record, becomes an artificial distortion of the oral experience. In the process Homer's 'winged word' is caged.

Composition in Performance

Two traditions on the Indian sub-continent illustrate the difficulties faced by those who wish to distinguish between similar and identical oral performances. First of all there are the Vedic hymns, which have existed in writing for over two thousand years, but which are still recited orally in the twentieth century. Although Peabody (1975) has shown how Vedic verses are based upon the same sort of fixed linguistic

structures found in the Homeric epics, Ong (1982:65) notes that statements made about oral memorization of these hymns have never been
fully evaluated in the context of Parry's (1932) studies on traditional
oral language. In particular, there does not yet seem to have been a
study of the effect standardized texts have had upon oral recitations of
the hymns. Could such memorization occur without reference to a text?
Furthermore, to what extent are these recitations 'similar' rather than
the same? As Ong notes:

> Mere assertions, frequently made by literates, that such lengthy texts
> were retained verbatim over generations in a totally oral society can no
> longer be taken at face value without verification. What was retained?
> The first recitation of a poem by its originator? How could the originator
> ever repeat it word for word the second time and be sure he had done
> so? A version which a powerful teacher worked up? This appears a
> possibility. But his working it up in his own version shows variability in
> the tradition, and suggests that in the mouth of another powerful teacher
> more variations might well come in wittingly or unwittingly.

At first glance, performances of the *Pābūjī* epic of Rajasthan, which has
no written tradition but which is based on a standardized narrative
about the god Lakṣmaṇa reincarnated as a warrior-prince, appear to
provide evidence for verbatim memorization of oral performance (Smith
1977). Even here, however, close comparison of several performances
reveals that while there is little variation in the story, there is significant
variation in length; that is, performances of the *Pābūjī* epic experience
the same sort of compression and expansion found in other oral contexts. While the narrative in this case is sacred and cannot be touched,
other aspects of the performance, such as the amount of descriptive
passages or of songs, are adjustable (Smith 1989).

In the end we are faced in India with an experience not unlike that in
Yugoslavia. While the oral artist does not memorize in the same way that
a Shakespearean actor does, there is a great deal of recall from performance to performance. The good talker does not speak in a vacuum but
works from a whole body of inherited knowledge which, to a certain
extent, defines not only what is said but how it is said.

So far the performance has been discussed as an act of recollection.
It is also an act of creation, or rather of recreation, which Lord calls
'composition in performance'. Lord's study of the song of Yugoslav
guslars clarifies for the literate observer the role of memory in oral
composition. Via the act of recollecting, these oral performers recreate
the tradition, not by word-for-word memorization, but by the use of
traditional formulae and themes. They are not only performers but also
accomplished creators who have perfected the art of thinking on their

feet. There are many examples of such mental agility. Several times in the *Odyssey* Odysseus fabricates a personal history and each time he speaks the circumstances and the stories are different. Sometimes the tales he recites are lies, such as those he tells to the swineherd, Eumaios (XIV:192–359), and to his wife, Penelope (XIX:165–202) while disguised as a beggar. At other times his tale is apparently true, as when he speaks before the Phaiakians (*Odyssey* IX–XII) or to his wife after their reunion at the end of the epic (XXIII:306–343). Whether these tales are true or false, the hero is able to weave the details together in the manner of an accomplished oral performer. As Homer says about Odysseus, 'He knew how to say many false things that were like true sayings' (*Odyssey* XIX:203). The jalo Fa-Digi Sisòkò also shows an ability to think on his feet, to compose during performance and to adapt his song to special situations by turning a banquet in the narrative into an occasion for an intermission, a break in the performance (S_6:1069–1072). So does the successful player of the dozens by capping the ritual insult of an opponent with something even more outrageous; or the Black preacher in moulding the sermon to the particular situation of the congregation.

In the next sections we discuss the various tools which a good talker uses in the process of composing in performance. Memory is aided by many traditional aspects of the performance, including structure, formulae, themes, language and music. The skilled performer combines all these elements in the creation of the song. In the final sections of this chapter these tools are considered, in the context of transmission and creativity, as vehicles both for the preservation of the tradition and for innovation.

The Structures of Oral Composition

The fact that the contexts of most speech events are fixed and are associated with specific structures provides a basesline for composition. This can be seen clearly, for instance, in Black church services. Most outsiders are struck not by the very predictable internal organization but by the extemporization and the apparent freedom of expression. And yet the high level of improvisation, or composition in performance, which marks these services can be shown to take place within a very well-defined structure. As Holt (1972:191) points out, the Black Church 'has a ritual nearly as rigid and unvarying as that used by the Catholic and High Lutheran services'.

Worship begins with the singing of hymns. The preacher starts in a low key, stating the topic of worship, frequently a moral virtue borrowed from puritanism. He then introduces variations on this theme, outlining the vices of humankind and warning that the guilty can never enter the kingdom of God. Next he launches on the eagerly awaited ritual of 'stylin' out', as he exhorts the congregation to redeem themselves. He builds from a slow-moving beginning to a delivery which grows in intensity, pitch and volume; the congregation's response increases proportionately. He stresses the importance of self-purification and outlines strategies for achieving this end.

Following the sermon proper, the preacher asks for 'joiners': people who have not been saved are invited to come and join the church. The end of this section of worship is marked by the singing of a favourite hymn intended to express joy that another soul has been saved. Then comes the money ritual, during which the collection is taken and the preacher often delivers a short post-sermon about the beauty of having a church to meet in and worship God. Finally the congregation is blessed and dismissed until the following Sunday. Such a rigid pattern provides an important framework in which the 'thinking on one's feet' takes place.

Similar superstructures can be outlined for many other speech events. Holmes (1969), for instance, dscribes the five main sections which make up welcoming speeches in Samoa. Each speech begins with an introduction or *tuvaoga*, which consists of proverbial phrases suggestive of the main body of the speech. The *tuvaoga* is followed by *fa'afetai i le Atua*, a thanksgiving to God for the safe arrival of the visiting party. The third section of the speech, or *'ava*, marks the presentation of a dried kava root to the chief of the visitors as a token of village hospitality and contains apologies that the root is not bigger and better. Next comes the *tapui le nu'u* in which the orator recites, in order of status, the names of all important chiefs and personages in the visitors' village. Last but not least is the *fa'aiuga* in which the speaker talks of the joys of having such distinguished guests and closes with a formula such as, 'Now my speech is finished. God bless you and protect the *malaga* (visiting party) and the village'.

While the oratory of West Indian tea meetings is very different from the speeches that accompany Samoan welcomes, these, too, follow a very definite structure. There is an expectation that the speech will begin with an address in which the speaker makes a series of comparisons with great men. The speech proper is punctuated by requests to the chairman as to whether the speaker should proceed. An appropriate joke brings the performance to a close. Such fixed features reflect the structural framework which supports the performer in composition. Within the formulaic construction of the speeches, however, performers are able to elaborate and expand according to their experience and ability.

Plate 4 *A Samoan villager serves a cup of kava to an orator chief. Photograph: Bradd Shore.*

The chart comparison overleaf of the seven published versions of *Sunjata* suggests the overall structure upon which this epic is based. Throughout the variants the structure of the epic is organized around the story of Sunjata's life, beginning with the hero's birth and ending with his victory over his antagonist Sumanguru. While most of the movements of the epic are dominated by narrative, initial and concluding sections, combining narrative with genealogies, praise songs and personal comments by the jeli, appear in all the variants. Such sections are clearly an intrinsic and standardized feature of the epic performance. Within the narrative structure there is also significant flexibility. Four versions (S_4, S_5, S_6 and S_7) begin not with the hero's conception but with accounts of the death of a buffalo woman named Du Kamisa and of the marriage of Sunjata's parents. These same versions also include an episode centring around the naming of the newborn hero. Another (S_1) includes the marriage but not the stories of Du Kamisa or Sunjata's naming; and S_3, which has an unusual interest in Sunjata's general Faa-Koli, skips over all the movements concerning Sunjata's birth and childhood and begins with the hero's exile. In S_2 Banna Kanuté organizes several themes, including those describing Sunjata's childhood and first steps and acts of jealousy against the hero, around Sumanguru's consultation of several powerful Islamic families. The only movements found in all seven versions concern the hero's exile and his victory over Sumanguru. Despite these differences, however, it is clear that each version of *Sunjata* is based upon a general

A Summary of Structural Elements in Versions of Sunjata

	Innes, 1974	Innes, 1974	Innes, 1974	Niane, 1965	Johnson, 1979	Johnson, 1986	Laye, 1984
MOVEMENT	Bamba Suso	Banna Kanuté (Dembo's younger brother)	Dembo Kanuté (Banna's older brother)	Mamadou Kouyaté	Magan Sisòkò (Fa-Digi's son)	Fa-Digi Sisòkò (Magan's father)	Babu Condé
	S_1	S_2	S_3	S_4	S_5	S_6	S_7
I Beginning	1–26	1–30	1–115	1–3	1–72	1–338	65–72
II Du Kamisa				6–9	73–940	339–997	35–64
III Marriage	27–47			4–6; 9–11	941–979	998–1043	73–94
IV Conception	48	31–197		11–12	980–1034	1044–1047	94–106
V Pregnancy	48–58	198–607		12–13	1035–1081	1048–1122	107–112
VI Birth	59–82	608–609		13–14	1082–1166	1123–1150	112–119
VII Naming				14–15	1167–1186		119–123
VIII Childhood	82–84	610–844		15–18	1187–1215 1216–1321	1151–1254	124–128
IX Walking	85–106	845–1094		18–22	1322–1579	1255–1535	129–141
X Jealousy	107–232	1095–1405		23–28	1580–1767	1536–1688	142–149
XI Exile	233–355	1406–1407	116–118	28–38	1768–2505	1689–1777 1910–2225	150–164
XII Oppression	356–362	1408–1564	119–336	38–42	2506–2808	1778–1909 2246–2769	165–166 173–178
XIII Embassy	363–436		337–521	42–47	2809–3147	2226–2534	178–184
XIV Return	437–663		522–624	47–51	3148–3298	2535–2631	185–189
XV Impasse	664–692	1565–1689	625–828	51–56	3299–3355	2632–2667	189–193
XVI Seduction	693–830		829–916	56–58	3356–3419	2668–2745	166–173 193–194
XVII Provision	831–842	1690–1895	917–973	58–64	3420–3462	2746–2828	193–203
XVIII Victory	843–871	1896–1985	974–1014	64–70	3463–3517	2829–2904	203–209
XIX Empire	872–1243	1986–2063	1015	70–83	3518–3627	2905–3081	210–220
XX Ending	1244–1305	2064–2067	1016–1020	83–84	3628–3631	3082–3083	221–223

structure which is recognizable to both performer and audience but which, to a certain extent, can be expanded or contracted by an individual jalo. Like the oratory of West Indian tea meetings or the sermons of Afro-American preachers, *Sunjata* reveals an underlying structure which is the baseline for both the composition and evaluation of the performance.

Shared assumptions about the superstructure of a performance provide the main orientation for the performer. However, the good talker makes parallel assumptions concerning the infrastructure of the speech event. Perhaps the most widely discussed of the infrastructural supports is the use of formulae. While Parry and Lord have identified formulae as the basic building blocks of oral epic composition, they are, in fact, a basic feature of oral composition of all kinds. Parry's (1930:80) definition of a formula as 'a group of words which is regularly employed under the same metrical conditions to express a given essential idea' emphasizes the fixed nature of traditional language, which provides singers with set phrases and expressions upon which to construct their song. For example, Parry notes in the Homeric epics the frequency in the last half of a hexameter line of a noun-epithet formula in the Greek nominative case and beginning with a simple consonant. The phrase *polutlas dios Odysseus* ('much-enduring holy Odysseus') appears in this position 38 times; *thea glaukopis Athene* ('bright-eyed goddess Athena') 50 times; and *Poseidaon enosichthon* ('Poseidon the earthshaker') 23 times. A parallel use of noun–epithet combinations, such as *knjigu sarovitu* 'well-writ letter', *visoku planinu* 'high mountain', and *gradu bijelome* 'white city', is noted by Lord (1960:42) in the second half of the Yugoslavian singer's line. The fixed line position of these phrases facilitates not only the composition of the line, but of the entire epic.

Some of the elaborate descriptive epithets found in the *Mwindo Epic* of the Nyanga are collected by Biebuyck (1978:76):

Mwindo is Little-one-just-born-he-walked (Kabutwakenda), Little-Castaway (Katawa), Man-of-many-feats, Little-one-who-does-not-eat-terrestrial-foods, or Cultivator-of-marvelous-things. Characters such as Mukiti, Nkuba, and Iyangura... are occasionally designated by recurring epithets: Master-of-the-unfathomable, Flashes, Opener-Cleaver, Mother-of-the-cradling-string, Birth-Giver, Master-of-strength.

Other types of formulaic phrases in the epic noted by Biebuyck (1978:76–9) include names ('Father-of-Mwindo' *Shemwindo*), titles ('Master-of-the-river' *Minerusi*), expressions of time ('when days had passed' *ematu akie ameta*) and expressions of location ('in the place where the child was dwelling in the womb of its mother' *akwarikanga amwana mubura wina*). From these lists it is clear that each artist, whether in Greece, Yugoslavia or Zaire, has a repertoire of such traditional language on which to build. While singing these phrases, the performer can be thinking ahead to what will be sung next.

Afro-American toasts (Abrahams 1962; Jackson 1974; Labov et al. 1981) have a great deal in common with epic compositions. They are, for example, not learned by rote; rather, the toaster, just like the Yugoslav or Nyanga teller of tales, learns the conventions, the formulae and the themes associated with this poetic tradition. The structure of the line and the couplet provide the backbone for composition in performance. The four-stressed rhymed line, sometimes divided into two, often gives rise to clichés which are used repeatedly for both rhyme and stress purposes. Thus, a gun is a 44 or 45 or 38 depending on which rhyme is needed. There is a similar use of a standard repertoire of metaphorical and proverbial clichés such as 'like a rat eats cheese', 'king of the sea', 'more dead than alive', 'like a ten-ton truck'. However, it is important to remember that not all images are clichés. A successful toast teller is someone who can not only use the conventions of the toast to best effect but who is also artful and innovative.

A particularly important use of the formula is to mark the boundaries of the performance, to provide some cues to the audience that the performance is beginning or ending. At the start of a performance the artist is likely to employ various means of gaining the attention of the audience. Labov (1972), for instance, reports that an Afro-American player of the dozens may initiate a verbal duel by saying that

> I don't play the dozens, the dozens ain't my game
> But the way I fucked your mama is a goddam
> shame.

The other person can take up the challenge but has the option of backing down by using a set formula, 'I don't play that game' or 'I laugh, joke and smoke but I don't play'. Alternatively, others present may act as catalysts for competition by making remarks like

> Are you going to let him say that about your mama?

or

> He's talking about YOUR mother so bad
> He's making ME mad.

Many other speech events also open in a fixed way. One such introductory device in story-telling is the deliberate use of a word which attracts the attention of the audience. Foley (1977:151), for instance, notes the functional similarity between the Serbo-Croatian exclamation *ej!* and the interjection *hwæt* ('lo') in the poem of *Beowulf*. Both words signal a beginning to the audience. To these we might add the use of Bahamian *Bunday* (Crowley 1966), a word used to capture the attention of the audience and to gauge their response at the beginning, during and at the end of story-telling performances.

Sometimes introductory words include temporal formulae, such as 'Once upon a time', which remind the audience of the relationship between performance time and narrative time. Thus in the invocation of the *Odyssey* (I:10) there is a reference to the Muse singing the song *amothen*, 'from somewhere', So, too, Foley (1977:151–2) notes that the bard of *Beowulf* speaks of *geardagum*, of the 'year-days' when these events took place, and the Serbo-Croatian may remind the audience that *Davno nekad u zemanu bilo* ('It happened once in time long past').

In some cases performer and audience even share introductory formulae. Dalphinis (1985:182), for instance, describes the way in which the Hausa narrator seeks permission from the audience to start with *Gata non gata nan ku* ('Here's a story for you') to which the audience replies *Ta zo mu ji ta* ('Let us hear it!'). Dillard (1963:36) cites French Creole examples of such formulaic exchanges at the beginning of some Haitian story-telling sessions:

> In the old days the Creole story-teller would always announce his intention of beginning a tale by the exclamation '*Tim-tim!* whereupon the audience would shout in reply, '*Bois sec*', and the story-teller would cry again, '*Cassez-li*', to which the chorus would add ... '*dans tchu (bond) macaque*'. Thus the story-teller intimated that he had no intention of merely 'joking', but intended to tell the whole truth and nothing else – 'a real good story' – *tois fois bonne conte*.

It is also possible to mark an opening with a fixed routine rather than with set words or formulae. In *Sunjata*, for instance, the temporal shift from real time to story time is often accomplished via genealogical passages. A significant feature of these genealogies is that they can run either backwards or forwards in relation to the time of the epic. Thus a genealogy can trace Sunjata's ancestors back to the distant past or it can go forward in time to present. Through this temporal focus the audience are able to adjust their personal time to that of the narrative.

Another sort of fixed routine, found in a wide variety of cultural contexts, is the use of first person plural forms which grammatically draw singer and audience together into a communal experience. Sometimes the artist uses a sort of 'regal plural', as in the invocation of the *Odyssey*, where the singer prays to the Muse to sing the tale *hemin* 'to us' (I:10). More often first person plural forms are combined with direct address of the audience. One Serbo-Croatian singer, for example, begins by encouraging the audience in this way (Foley 1977:152):

> *De sedimo da se veseljimo*
> 'Let us make merry where we sit!'

and in the first two lines of *Beowulf*,

> *Hwæt, we Gar-Dena   in geardagum,*
> *peodcyninga prym gefrunon*

> 'Lo, we have heard the glory of the Spear-Danes, in year-days,
> O the chieftain-kings, how the noble ones performed valor.' (translated
> by Foley 1977:151)

The bard's language shows that both singer and audience have heard about the tales of the ancient kings.

Maori rituals of encounter accomplish much the same thing by using commands in a series of challenges, calls and chants. The main part of the ritual, the *whaikoorero* or oratory, is marked by *whakaaraara*, a warning shout like

> Be alert! Be watchful! Be alert on this terrace!
> Be alert on that terrace! Be watchful! Be wakeful!
>   (Salmond 1977:207)

Endings, too, are usually clearly marked. Various concluding formulae can be observed in a variety of contexts: 'De wire bend, De story end' in the Caribbean (Dillard 1962); 'I've been through a little mousehole; my tale is finished' in the Languedoc (Massignon 1968); and the African formula

> 'This is my story which I have related. If it be sweet, or if it be not sweet,
> take some elsewhere and let some come back to me.' (Haley 1972)

Such patterns mark the beginning and ending of the performance and draw the audience into the speech event.

Another form of formulaic language is to be seen in canonical parallelism, a phenomenon observable from Finland to Canaan, and Mongolia to Cuna, in societies distant in both time and space. In canonical parallelism ritual language draws on pairs or dyadic sets of words. For instance, in the oratory of Roti (Fox 1977), an island off Timor in Eastern Indonesia, '*benga*' (word) forms a set with '*dasi*' (voice); '*-fada*' (to tell) and '*-tuda*' (to fall) form another set.

1. *Benga la-fafada*   Word is continuously told
2. *Ma dasi laka-tutuda*   And voice continually let fall

These pairs of words are incorporated in *bini*, or ritual poems, which can vary in length from two lines to several hundred lines. Any individual hoping to be recognized as a promising chanter would need to know between 1,000 and 1,500 of these sets.

Also related to formulae are the thematic patterns which structure the song. These themes, according to Lord (1960:69), are not a 'fixed set of words, but a grouping of ideas'. Scenes depicting such events as departure, arrival, arming, fighting, and eating, suggest a certain set of ideas and vocabulary to the singer as he thinks out his song. These scenes can be expanded or contracted at will. Thus Homer can describe a warrior putting on his armour in a single line (*Iliad* III:339) or expand the same theme into nine lines (*Iliad* III:330–8) by listing each piece of armour in turn. So, too, Lord (1960:83–4) explains how the guslar Sulejman Makić within a single performance can vary his use of the theme of writing a letter or a decree:

> In the compass of 322 lines of a short version of a single song six letters have been written. Each letter has been given in full; in one case it was dictated and then written; in two instances the general contents of the letters were given in indirect form and then the letter was written; in three cases the singer merely states that someone wrote a letter, and he gives the letter in full.

In the Afro-American toasting tradition, recurrent themes include the hero's descent into hell and his defeat of the devil; the fight with a bartender; and the courtroom scene. Large units from one toast can freely be transferred to another. Take the situation, described by Abrahams (1970b), where the hero is responding to his sentence from the judge. In one toast it appears as:

> 55 ain't no big time
> I got a brother in Sing Sing doing ninety nine

In another we find:

> Judge, 99 years ain't no goddam time
> My father's in Alcatraz doing two-ninety-nine

To a certain extent, then, development of a particular theme occurs at the discretion of the artist as the performance evolves.

The use of such fixed expressions as the building blocks of the song is evident in a line-by-line analysis of repetition in the Homeric epics. In the first twenty-five lines of the *Odyssey* Parry (1930:117–25) notes thirty-four phrases which are repeated word for word elsewhere in Homer. One quarter of these expressions are repeated eight or more times. Such formulaic repetition also appears in the *Pābūjī* epic, in which Smith (1977:147) notes about thirty appearances of the same couplet in a single performance. In the Yugoslav songs, Lord notes a large group of phrases which are used regularly and are often found together, which 'emerge like trained reflexes' (1960:58). Thus, comparison of two versions of a favourite piece sung in the same year by Demail Zogić (Lord 1960:58–60) reveals many formula clusters and word-for-word repetition of lines.

On the other hand, the singer is not strictly bound by such repetition and is free to mould it to his own uses. Lord's comparison of songs sung by Halil Bajgorić fifteen years apart (1960:60–3) shows much less use of such repeated phrasing. It would seem that there is a correlation between frequency of performance and formulaic repetition; in other words, the more often a singer performs the same song, the more stable the vocabulary and the phrasing.

Special Language

Many kinds of oral performance are marked by a special language, often archaic in nature, which establishes the esoteric knowledge of the speaker. The archaic language of the Homeric epics, for instance, includes words like the adjective *atrugetos* ('unfruitful'), which was unintelligible even in the time of Homer (Page 1959:226). Other expressions, like Achilleus' memorable epithet *podas okus* 'swift-footed', are based on archaic grammatical features. According to Page (1959:229–30), such archaisms, used in a formulaic context, are survivals from the earliest Mycenaean origins of the epics.

Other archaisms in the Homeric epics are the so-called aeolisms, including endings such as *-essi*, words compounded with *eri-*, and forms such as *pt-* instead of *p-*. These linguistic forms were once thought to be evidence that the epics, written in Ionic Greek, were actually transliterations from an older dialect, usually identified with Aeolic Greek (Murray 1924:232–4). The decipherment of Linear B, however, has shown that these words are, for the most part, not Aeolic at all, but are derivatives of Mycenaean poetry handed down in the oral tradition (Webster 1964:159–62). Preservation of Mycenaean forms in the Homeric epic reflects the conservative nature of the singer's language, which is used simultaneously to preserve and create the song during the performance (Parry 1932:23–45).

In this context, even the Ionic Greek of the Homeric epics is significant. While the epics may have originated in Ionia, use of this dialect for performances of the Homeric epics in the rest of Greece reflects the unifying feature of the epic, which served as a bond for pan-Hellenic culture. In fact, the integration of this dialect into oral tradition was so strong that lyric poets from other parts of Greece sometimes used Homeric vocabulary, instead of their own dialect forms, in their poems. Sappho's poem about the marriage of Andromache and Hektor (Barnstone 1972:80), for example, is filled with words which belong not to Sappho's Lesbian dialect but to Homeric epic (Campbell 1967:273–4).

Special language is also found in the *bylinas*, oral performances of epics in north-eastern Russia, about which Nilsson (1968:205) makes the following observation: 'The bylinas contain not a few enigmatical elements which cannot be explained from Russian, and in the "Kalevala" epics are found diverging forms, and Swedish loan-words which are not used elsewhere; some words are even misunderstood by the singers. Three-fifths of their lexicon is not in use in everday speech.' Even today some elements of the language of the Maori rituals of encounter are so old as to be incomprehensible to present-day speakers, and it is unlikely that any single individual on Roti in Eastern Indonesia can understand in its entirety their rich tradition of ritual poetry, which the Rotinese consider to be both a special code derived from the language of their ancestors and a tangible link with the past.

Incomprehensible vocabulary is also a feature of the *Sunjata* epic, about which Innes (1974:12–13) notes the following:

> There are some words and phrases which are ambiguous and considerably more which are totally obscure, but as far as can be determined, this does not trouble the listeners or the griots. In fact, it seems likely that when a person is listening to a narration he is carried along by it without realizing that there is an occasional phrase which he does not understand. It is only when a Mandinka informant is taken through a transcription word by word by someone such as myself that he comes to realize that he is not at all sure of the meaning of every word. That this should be so is of course not at all surprising. Mandinka speakers have been accustomed since childhood to hear certain phrases used in the context of the Sunjata epic and they probably never inquired very closely into what exactly they meant. It is sufficient that these are the phrases which are used in this particular context. They no doubt have a feeling of appropriateness, of rightness, perhaps of conveying a certain aura.

These mysterious words are thus some of the blocks used by the singer to build each performance of the epic. They are 'appropriate' and 'right' in part because they have always been there, even if not always fully understood.

On the other hand, while the use of archaic or arcane words is conspicuously absent among the Nyanga poets of Zaire, even here special features of the language can be noted. First of all, in several of the published songs there are frequent transitions from the Nyanga language to the related and neighbouring Hunde, a language also understood by the Pygmies who play an important role in the plot of the epic. The special nature of this blending, emphasized by the transcriber of the epics, Biebuyck (1978:6), who understood only Nyanga and had to seek translations of the Hunde passages during his fieldwork, indicates the function of the epic as a unifier of several peoples who live in the same geographic area and share a similar heritage. Biebuyck (1978:40) also observes that the language of the epic differs from the ordinary language of the Nyanga in a significant way: '... the richness, diversity, amplitude, and poetry of the language are far beyond the capacity of the common speaker or narrator. The choice of words and expressions is incredibly rich and nuanced. The metaphorical usage of standard verbs and other expressions is sometimes carried to an extreme.' From these observations, it is clear that when a Nyanga bard performs the *Mwindo Epic* he uses a language which sets the performance and its audience apart from the everyday and from the rest of the world.

The style of an Afro-American preacher also contains specialized language features, often called 'tonal semantics', such as the elongated articulation, heavy breathing, lengthy pauses and interjections of expressions like 'ha', 'aha' and 'uh-huh' which signal the dramatic high point of the sermon. Take, for instance, this excerpt from the sermon 'The Midnight Prayer Meeting' (Smitherman 1977:138):

So there was Paul and Silas, had been thrown into jail for preaching and converting the peoples unto the Word of the Lord. And it was gittin on into the midnight hour, they went to singin, prayin, and callin on God. Church, I wonder what they did say when they cried out unto the Lord. Some folk say they said: I-I-I-I-I-I love the uh-uh ha-the Lord, the Lord. He heard, he hear-d my-y-y-y-y cry. But, naw, I don't think that was it. Somebody else said they said. AAAAA-maz-Amazing Grace, uh-huh, uh, ha, how sweet, how sweet, yassuh, the sound. But naw, I don't think that was it, either.

By now, the preacher's congregation is ecstatically tense, poised on edge, nearing their emotional plateau, and waiting to see what kind of 'on time' call the preacher is going to issue forth in expounding what *he* thinks Paul and Silas must have said. The preacher continues and shifts to talk-singing right in the middle of his sentence:

> I believe, church, I believe, yassuh, help me Lord, I believe, uh-huh, I believe that ol Paul and Silas, looked up toward Heaven, and said, ha, sa-----id, Father, Faaaaa---ther, I-I-I-I-I stretch my hand, aha, to ---- to-------toooooooo ---Thee, cause, Lo------rd, no other, no other, help I-I-I-I-I-I kn----ow.

The association of tonal semantics with the high point of the sermon marks it out as 'special' and 'appropriate' for the audience. Like the canonical parallelism of Roti, or the archaic language of Maori rituals, this characteristic use of tonal quality is one of the props which supports the preacher as he thinks on his feet.

Music and Metre

In the previous chapter we discussed the musical skills of the oral artist. Here we will consider how music serves as an important compositional frame for the song. Manding performers, for example, have a set of traditional instrumental pieces used to accompany the epic. Innes (1974:20−4) transcribes eight of these accompaniments.

1 Kura (Tolonjongo)

2 Sunjato Faso

3 Sunjata Mang Bori Long

4 Janjungo

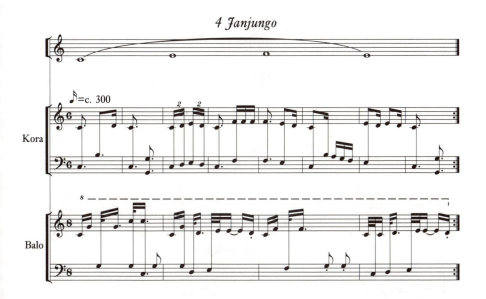

5 Mang Kaira (Manga Yura)

6 Nyaama Nyaama Nyaama

7 Kankinya

8 Manding

Sometimes these songs are even mentioned by the singer. Jalo Banna Kanuté mentions in his performance that *Janjungo* was sung before Sunjata himself (S$_2$:131–3) and that *Kura* was first sung when the hero was conceived (S$_2$:243–4). These accompaniments are thus consciously traditional and archaic and provide a set musical structure for the performance of the Manding epic.

There is some indication in Manding performances of a tie between musical and narrative themes. The griot Banna, for example, switches from *Kura*, his basic accompaniment, to *Manga Yura* at the point in the narrative (S$_2$:1472) when the character named Manga Yura enters the story (Innes 1974:138). Such adaptation of music to content has also been observed in the epics of the Kirghiz in Mongolia (Hatto 1980:304).

In the *Pābūjī* epic a basically linear form must be adapted to the strophic structure of the music. Smith (1977:145–6) notes the expansion of each pair of lines by the addition of linguistic 'fillers', such as particles, vocatives and pronouns, needed to fit the various tunes used during a performance. Thus, the following couplet

tārā nakhatariyā jhila galati mājhala raina;
      dīnā
sīdhā khara   [place-name] rai jūnai māragā.
      cālyā

which means

The stars and constellations were shining and fading at midnight;
he/she/they rode straight off on the ancient road to such and such a
place.

is expanded three different ways in the course of a single performance.
Each of these versions is used in a different musical context, which
determines the form, of the expansion. In one version the couplet
becomes

tārā he re *hakhatariyā*
    khamā *jhila galatori jī o mājhala rain;*
    chataradhāri o rājā the *sīdhā khara cālyā*
sīdhā he re ghorā jī
    e khara cālyā jī *pusakara jī rai jūnai mā-*
    o-jī-e-māragā thāri rai-gi sā vo ī amara vātā.

In another place the couplet becomes

e *tarā nakhatariyā* jī re *jhila galatori* e *mājhala*
    raina! mārū *sīdhā*
    hā̃ jī rāja bhalai *khara dīnā jī*
jī o bhāi sīdhā
    hā̃ jī rāja bhalai khara dīnā jī
jī o bhāi sīdhā
    hā̃ jī rāja vo khara dīnā jī
kolū rai jūnai hamé *mā-i-*
    -e-māragā chatradhāri jī o.

The change in tune thus determines the structure of the song.

A recent development which shows a similar dependence on musical
rhythm is the Black speech event known in North America as 'rap'
and in the UK as 'dub' or 'toasting'. The rap or Black British 'toast',
however, is quite distinct from the Afro-American toast described
elsewhere in this book which is performed independently of a musical
backing. The voice of the performer, often a disc jockey operating a
sound system or mobile discotheque, is heard over the rhythm back-

Plate 5   *Robert Daley's Young Warrior Sound System. It is often the disc jockey who performs the 'rap' or 'toast' over the rhythm background of a popular song. Photograph: Mike Levers, Open University.*

ground of a popular song. The performer improvises a monologue which is spoken, not sung, to music which has a strong, repetitive beat. Some record companies, capitalizing on the development of dub, produce two versions of the same song: an 'A' side with both words and music and a 'B' side with the music only for those who wish to provide their own words. Take the following toast by David South and Trevor Cameron, two ten-year-old London Jamaican boys (S. Hoyle, personal communication). Their performance is a parody of a Harry Belafonte song, called 'There's a hole in my bucket', and is spoken in time with the beat and phrasing of a record called *Kambola*.

DAVID: Cos there's a hole in your glasses, dear Trevor,
            Cos there's hole in your glasses, dear Trevor,
TREVOR: Well, mend it David, mend it
DAVID: Alright. What should I mend it with, Trevor?
            What should I mend it with, Trevor?

TREVOR: With a stick, David, with a stick. What you mean!
DAVID: No, man. I should mend it with plasticine. Yeah!
TREVOR: It make you run wild like with lips of oil.
         It make you run wild on the front line.
DAVID: Mend it with plasticine, you can't see through.
TREVOR: You mend it with plasticine, I can't see through.
DAVID: Go on stick a little hole in the plasticine
         Fe stick a little hole in the plasticine.

The pattern of responses suggested by 'There's a hole in my bucket' clearly forms a framework for the toast, but so, too, does the rhythm of the backing music which is as important a compositional prop for these two young performers as it is for the singers of the *Pābūjī* epic or for the West African *jalo.*

Closely related to music is the rhythmical nature of the oral language which is usually metrically structured, even when unaccompanied by music. Indeed, the importance of metre to performance was recognized by Aristotle who defined both epic and tragedy as 'metrical representations of heroic action' (*Poetics* 1449b). Oral performances in ancient Greece used special metres according to context and theme. Epic poems were recited in dactylic hexameter; iambic metre was used especially for abusive or invective contexts. The Greek lyric poets expanded the repertoire of metres, but the traditional, oral use of particular metres were retained for a long time. Indeed, at *Poetics* 1059b–1060a Aristotle, arguing for the strict division of metres according to performative contexts in Greece, observes that for epic

> experience has shown that the heroic hexameter is the right metre. Were anyone to write a narrative poem in any other metre or in several metres, the effect would be wrong. The hexameter is the most sedate and stately of all metres and therefore admits of rare words and metaphors more than others, and narrative poetry is itself elaborate above all others. ... So no one has composed a long poem in any metre other than the heroic hexameter. As we said above, Nature shows that this is the right metre to choose. (translated by Fyfe 1982:95)

Instead of the hexameter line found in Homer, Yugoslav epics are based upon a ten-syllable line with a syntactic pause (Lord 1960:32). While set rhythmical units structure both the Greek and Yugoslav epics, metre has been more difficult to establish in African contexts, where it is often impossible to identify regular rhythmical units in performances. In an ethnomusicological study, however, Jones (1964) has suggested a very close bond between music and words in Manding epics, where the musical rhythm provides a structure for the composition of the song. Bird (1972:210) notes how the lines of *Lagasa* ('Frivol-

ity'), a song by Seydou Camara, a Manding hunter's bard, are formed
in three or four accented syllables to fit the beat of the metrical meas-
ure. Such a musical structure has been labelled by Bird (1972 and
1976) and others as a 'language external constraint' as opposed to the
'language internal constraint' of grammar, rhyme, or metre. Biebuyck
(1978:40–1) has described the effect of such a system upon the
language of the *Mwindo Epic* of Nyanga bards who must '. . . [keep] in
unison with the basic percussion system, speaking faster or more slowly
as required, making sophisticated use of elisions, adding short, well-
placed words to their songs to satisfy the rhythm, changing the tense or
aspect of a verb, adding suffixes to differentiate the meaning, redupli-
cating the stem, or repeating the expression.'

Afro-American toasts also involve improvisation within a framework
of linguistic and rhythmic conventions. Thus, while the story line is
constant (though subject, on occasion, to considerable expansion) and
the rhythms change relatively little, there is enormous variation from
one performance to the next. A particular line may be of one length
with a certain number of stresses when performed on one day and of
another length with a different number of stresses when recited by the
same person on the next day. Usually, the changes are superficial: word
order may be changed or different accents used. On some occasions,
however, a stock word or phrase may be added, thus changing the
pattern of stresses.

Stability and Creativity in Transmission

One result of the traditional structures of oral language is a linguistic
conservatism which goes beyond the archaic words and phrases discussed above and preserves a whole way of life and thought. Thus
Page (1959:218) has demonstrated how the Homeric epics 'describe in
accurate detail places and objects which never existed in the world after
the Mycenaean era'. The body shield of Achilleus and the boar's tusk
helmet in *Iliad* X, known from archaeological evidence to have been
common in fifteenth century BC Greece, were extinct by the twelfth
century and therefore could not have been known to the singers of the
archaic and classical Greek periods. In the same way the catalogues of
warriors in *Iliad* II preserve references to geographic locations unknown
after the Mycenaean period in Greece.

Stability is carried even further in the *Pābūjī* epic, which, as we have
seen, tells a sacred, unchangeable story in a formulaic and improvised
context. While the fixed nature of the *Pābūjī* performance may be
connected with its religious subject and its liturgical use at night wakes,

a similar process of fixation in an oral context may have occurred with the Homeric texts, which may have acquired less and less variability through frequency of performance and through a process of panhellenization making the Ionic epic the communal property of all Greeks (Nagy 1979:7–9).

Preservation of a cultural past also occurs in the oral heritage of Afro-Americans. The animal stories known as Ananse, for example, have been shown not only to be African in origin, but also African in vocabulary and philosophy (Dance 1978). This same conservatism can be detected in Afro-American toasts, many of which are very old and celebrate mythical figures such as the archetypal bully, Stagolee, or an historical event like the sinking of the Titanic. Toasts also retain literary and archaic expressions such as 'the bitter cup', 'the slumbering beast', 'Stranger, stranger, who may thou be?' which would have been used by the original composers. The extent of this conservatism is often not always apparent to the outsider who may not understand references to past events. For instance, the fact that drugs were introduced to Harlem by the Chinese explains why a Chinaman is used in the following toast as the symbol for the drug supplier:

> Turnin' dollar tricks to make up a fix
> And the Chinaman is doin' all the pimpin'.
> (Labov et al. 1981:338)

Thus, because the Chinaman is getting the money, he is metaphorically doing the pimping.

Riddles offer further evidence for the stability of oral language. In the English-speaking world printed riddle books, popular with children and adults alike, data back some four centuries and allow us to establish the ancient pedigree of many of the riddles still in circulation today. The Opies (1977), for instance, comment on the fact that some of the riddles sent by children to comics and magazines in the hope of financial reward are by no means recent creations. They compare the example of the riddle posed in the 1950s by an eleven-year-old girl in Oxford:

> What can go under the water, and over the water, without getting wet?–An egg in a duck's back.

with

> W^t is that as goes under water & ou^r water, & touches not the water.–an egge in a ducks belly.

recorded by a member of the Holme family of Chester some three hundred years earlier.

In the case of nursery lore, we learn a particular rhyme as children and it is not usually until we have grown up and have children or grandchildren that we pass this verse on–a transmission period of anything between twenty and fifty years. The situation is very different for playground lore. Verses are passed from one child to the next. Most children play with agemates so that if a particular rhyme can be shown to have been in circulation for fifty or a hundred years it is very likely to have passed along a chain of two to three hundred hearers and tellers. As the Opies (1977:28) comment: 'The wonder is that it [the original

Plate 6 *'When Susie was a baby' . . . a hand clapping rhyme which is part of a tradition passed down not by parents but by slightly older children. In this case, Alex learns from Siân who has been in school some six months longer. Photograph: Viv Edwards.*

verse] remains alive after so much handling, let alone that there is so much resemblance to the original wording.'

Despite the many stable elements of the oral performance, no two performances are exactly alike. As discussed above, the good talker does not memorize a song word for word but instead weaves together traditional language and elements in order to recreate the tradition during the performance. Because oral transmission is essentially creative transmission, the end result bears the mark of contributions from many generations. Although there are certain fixed elements which guide the artist and provide a framework for composition, the way in which these elements are realized and combined is very much an individual matter. Each generation makes its mark on the tradition which is the collective property of the group; the same is true of each performer.

Indian wedding songs, for instance, are rooted in a tradition of competitive invective which dates back centuries and retains many conservative elements in both language and mores. However, there is no difficulty in situating the example below very firmly in the twentieth century.

In the cloudy skies the rockets fly
And look at the world below
Siris Bhai of today is driving around in a car
While uneducated Dakshaben is still learning her letters.
Siris Bhai of today wears a watch
While uneducated Dakshaben goes around asking the time.
Siris Bhai of today reads the newspaper
Whilst uneducated Dakshaben goes around asking the news.

(Edwards 1982b:37)

Stability is thus balanced by creativity. The same pattern can be seen at work in performances by individuals. One area where the individual performer can make a personal mark is in the use, for instance, of thespian techniques such as gestures and facial expressions. Another striking feature of oral narrative is the wide range of vocal effects. Performers identify strongly with a protagonist in the story and often become that character. They use a wider variety of speaking tempos; they rasp, shout and use falsetto to achieve the desired persona, imitating the voice, gestures and posture of each character in the story.

Such thespian techniques can be noted in many cultural contexts. In Plato's *Ion* (535c), a rhapsode or reciter of Homer tells Sokrates that 'whenever I speak of sad and touching scenes, my eyes are full of tears; when it is something terrible or awful, my hair stands up straight with fear and my heart leaps!' (translated by Rouse 1956). As Dorson (1962) points out, Abraham Lincoln, renowned for his mimicry of characters and acting out of parts, demonstrated similar qualities. He is reputed to have reproduced a range of dialects and speech defects and to have gyrated his arms and legs in accompaniment to the text. Likewise, the performer of the following lines from *Sunjata* must have accompanied recitation with gesture:

> But great Jibirila had an arrow,
> And if he took that arrow like this
>   and put it into his hand like this,
> He did not even put it in the bow and
>   pull the bow and fire it.
>   (S_3:709–711)

An Afro-American story-teller named Suggs also exhibits a wide range of thespian techniques:

> Whichever kind of tale he related, he projected himself completely into the situation; he talked with animation and gusto, sometimes changing from third to first person in the course of the relation, as he identified himself with the chief actor ... A sweeping range of inflection enabled Suggs to simulate the shrieking woman at a revival meeting with a high-pitched electric shout, and in a breath he was back to the rumbling tones of the preacher. Telling a personal experience with a ghost train, he conveyed the mood in short, staccato sentences with his volume turned low. (Dorson 1962:83)

Similar observations can also be made of sermons in the Black Church (Mitchell 1970). The story of Peter building the church on solid rock rather than on shifting sand may well be brought to life by the preacher lifting his foot in the air and placing it back down firmly to symbolize the solid ground. Or he may evoke the image of Jesus climbing Mount Calvary by throwing his handkerchief over his shoulder for the cross and stooping up and down the aisle. So, too, Herington (1985:13) has suggested that the thespian talents of Homeric rhapsodes were not a late development but are an intrinsic part of the performative quality of the poem: '... Homeric poetry ... seems to have been designed from the first to be *acted*. It demands impersonation; it demands skillful variations in tone, tempo, and dynamic; and there are some points, also, where it seems imperiously to exact from the speaker some form of physical gesture.'

It is not only individuals who make their mark on the performance. Sometimes the process of composition can draw on whole groups of people. Grimble (1957:204) describes the way in which a poet in Kiribati will retire to a lonely sport to allow the divine spark of inspiration to stir within him. When he is ready he sets off in search of five friends whom he brings back to work together and further refine his first attempts: 'It is the business of his friends to interrupt, criticize, interject suggestions, applaud or howl down, according to their taste ... They will remain without food or drink under the pitiless sun until night fall, searching for the right word, the balance, and music to convert it into a finished work of art.'

The effects of group creativity can also be noted in the remarkable way in which childhood lore is transmitted at breakneck speed from one part of the country to another and even from one country to the next. As the Opies (1977:25–7) recount, the 'Ballad of Davy Crockett', a song especially aimed at children, was first broadcast on radio at the beginning of 1956 and rapidly reached the number one record spot. The rather tame official version which started

> Born on a mountain top in Tennessee
> Greenest state in the Land of the Free

was rapidly replaced by more scurrilous juvenile transformations. A composition starting with the line 'The Yellow Rose of Texas' was reported from Perth, Scotland, in April 1956 and Alton, Battersea, Great Bookham and Reading in the south of England in July 1956. Along the way, various local adaptations were made. Swansea school children, for instance, had built in a reference to a local eating place:

> Born on a table top in Joe's Café,
> Dirtiest place in the U.S.A.
> Polished off his father when he was only three,
> Polished off his mother with D.D.T.
>   Davy, Davy Crockett,
>   King of the Wild Frontier

Subsequently, the Joe's Café reference was reported from various southern England locations. Unbeknown to the Opies' network of teacher correspondents, however, news had been received on 3 January, before the song was even broadcast in the United Kingdom, that a similar version had been sweeping the schools in Sydney, Australia:

> Reared on a paddle, pop in Joe's café,
> The dirtiest dump in the U.S.A.
> Poisoned his mother with D.D.T.
> And shot his father with a .303.
>> Davy, Davy Crockett,
>> The man who is no good.

Comparison of the British and Australian variants of this American song confirms the dynamic of stability and creativity upon which oral performance is based.

Thinking on Your Feet ...

We began this chapter with a reference to Mehmed Ali Halici whose perfect recitation of 6,666 verses of the Qur'ān gained him an entry in the *Guinness Book of Records*. We have argued, however, that the stereotype of good talkers as repositories for the kind of rote learning embodied in this example bears little resemblance to reality. Although oral artists depend heavily on their memories, oral and literate inter-pretations of this process are quite different. In literate cultures, the text provides a stable point of reference which ensures word-for-word accuracy. In oral cultures, the primary concern is with recreating the tradition and artists produce performances which are similar rather than identical.

The accomplishments of oral artists thus go well beyond mere recita-tion. Each performance is an act of re-creation. Performers draw on a wide range of compositional supports: the expected structure of the speech event; the special language, the music, the metre, the formulae and routines traditionally associated with it. Within this framework, they are free to think ahead and to combine the different building blocks to best effect. On both individual level and at the level of the group, we cannot fail to be struck by the delicate balance in oral performances between stability and creativity, between conservatism and flux. The accomplished oral artist has a mental and verbal ability second to none.

3

Can I Get a Witness?

Each piece of oral literature is realized in its actual performance and—the relevant point here—before a particular audience. It is directly influenced, and thus moulded, by the audience as well as the composer.

Finnegan, *Orality and Literacy*

In literate societies, the performer is largely in command. A written, memorized script prescribes the performance from which the artist varies little, regardless of the reactions of the audience. Changes from one performance to the next are determined in advance more by the preferences of the individual artist or director, or their perceptions of the audience's taste; rarely do such changes occur during an actual performance and in direct response to a specific audience. In oral cultures, in contrast, performer and audience are part of a single performative dynamic. They share a set of assumptions about what is good and acceptable. If performers stray from these norms, the audience will hold them in check. Not only does the oral artist mould performance to accommodate audience reaction, but the division between audience and performer is much less clear-cut. Performance is viewed much more as interaction between artist and audience.

In this chapter we explain the special insights into oral culture which may be gained by giving greater prominence to the role of the audience in performance. We show that performer and audience are part of one organic whole: to fail to give due recognition to the role played by the audience in performance is seriously to misrepresent orality and oral culture. However, the decision to take the audience seriously raises many questions which have tended to receive relatively little attention. In which ways do performers acknowledge the importance of their audience? What kind of social control do the audience exert over the performer? And what effect can this have on the structure and content of performance?

Sensitivity to the Audience

The central role of the audience in oral culture has long been overlooked. The growing awareness of its importance in shaping the nature,
pace and length of performance is in fact a very recent phenomenon.
Scholars from a literary tradition have tended to interpret oral culture
through literate eyes, reducing dynamic performances to static written
texts, and basing their critical commentary on the resulting literary
artifact rather than on the real thing. Students of oral culture are thus
confronted with the 'observer's paradox'. We want to understand the
mechanics and aesthetics of performance, but our very presence in the
audience is likely to affect the way that events unfold. Sometimes this
influence is obvious; sometimes it is subtle; but, on all occasions, it is
potentially significant.

A wide range of examples points to the effect of the observer on
performance. At the least, the artist may feel it necessary to make
reference to the outsider during the performance. In one recorded
version of *Sunjata*, for example, the jalo concludes his presentation by
speaking directly to Gordon Innes (S_2:2064–7), the scholar who had
arranged for the performance. Similarly, the Turkish aşik Sabit Mudami improvised a song welcoming Ilban Basgöz, his transcriber, as a
member of the audience (Basgöz 1975:155). In both cases, the artist is
acknowledging the unusual circumstances of the performance by allud-
ing to the researcher. It would seem that Mudami is also attempting to
put his audience at ease in the presence of an outsider.

Two situations described in *The Singer of Tales* further illustrate the
fragile relationship between artist and audience. In each case, the
context of the performance is unnatural and the guslar performs not
in a coffee house, but more privately, at the specific request of Lord.
On one occasion, Lord (1960:113) asked Petar Vidić to perform the
same song which he had sung for him a year before. Vidić responded
with a much longer version of the earlier song. In another case, Halil
Bajgorić sang a shorter version of his song because, Lord (1960:116)
explains, 'the singer was in a hurry to finish and depart, since he had
been called by the authorities from his work in the fields'. It seems
likely that Bajgorić's haste is a symptom of poor bonding between
Bajgorić and Lord, between the artist and his audience, while Vidić's
longer song reflects a desire to embellish a song so pleasing to an
audience that it has been requested a second time. In both situations,
the unusual context of the performance affects the very nature of the
song. Both performances would have been different if they had been
sung under more normal circumstances in a coffee shop.

The effect of audience upon the artist's performances is most dramatically shown by Basgöz's remarkable experiment with Mudami, who is asked to sing 'the same song' on successive nights, once with a typical audience in a coffee house and a second time with high village officials in a school house. The change in environment and in audience has a measurable effect on Mudami's performance. In the coffee house Mudami develops closer ties with his audience, while in the school-house he sings a much shorter song with fewer traces of interaction with a less responsive audience.

All of these examples illustrate the difficulty of recording and pre-serving the full flavour of an oral performance in a natural context and show that any text of an oral performance can be only an approximation of the actual event. Even the most careful transcriber may overlook subtle ties between audience and performance, as Basgöz (1975: 155) notes in his description of yet another performance by a Turkish asik:

> *Aṣik* Murat, a young singer thirty years old, was performing folk songs in Kars in 1967 to an ordinary coffee house audience. A shift took place during his performance as the aṣik suddenly began to sing exclusively *uzun hava*, which can be translated into English as 'blues'. This pattern continued until the end of the session. I did not understand the reason for this sudden change from the pleasant to the tragic. At the end of the session the singer explained to me that a rich and noble person who had lost his wealth following a tragic event had entered the coffee house and sat at one of the tables. His life tragedy was known to all present, including the singer, so that he is treated with extreme tenderness and respect. No one wants to injure his pride or his feelings. The singer considered it disrespectful to sing joyful songs before a person struck with such tragedy. Consequently, he selected songs which he believed pleasing to this guest. This person's presence in the audience entirely dominated part of the session. This would have remained unnoticed had the singer not related to me the impact of this person's presence.

Several important points emerge from this event. First of all, there is the singer's attempt to fashion a performance appropriate to a specific member of his audience. Then there is the close bond which exists within the community of the oral artist, a bond which allows unspoken communication and understanding among members of the community. Finally, there is the difficulty of the outsider to key into this com-munication.

This bond between artist and audience is inevitable in any oral performance and can radically affect the nature of the performance. Yet the literary transcription cannot preserve the dynamic beyond the period of the performance. Even if such transcriptions contain a de-

tailed list of members of the audience and their biographies,
much would still go over the heads of outsiders to the community.
Therefore, we must recognize the innate limitations of our sources
– and the centrality of the audience – for any discussion of oral
performance.

The oral artist's sensitivity to the audience is thus of paramount
importance and can affect both the length and the content of the
performance. Most performances in literate cultures have a predeter-
mined beginning and an end. While it is impossible to ensure that the
audience will not be bored by the proceedings, there is a definite
understanding that they will listen politely and, if they leave, will choose
a suitable moment to do so, causing as little disturbance as possible. In
oral culture, things proceed more flexibly. Lord (1960:14), for instance,
notes that the Yugoslav guslar's audience is always 'coming and going,
greeting newcomers, saying farewells to early leavers'. Crowley
(1966:20–1) describes a similar situation in Bahamian story-telling:
'People move in and out of the room, sign language is used to send
messages back and forth, conversations break out in whispers, girls
giggle and boys nudge each other.' Since such disturbances could
interrupt or even curtail the performance, the audience's instability has
a direct effect upon the length of the artist's composition which expands
and contracts according to the audience's attention span.

In most cases, artists expand and embellish their performances to
meet the expectations of attentive audiences. The Rajasthani *bhopo*
Parbu, for example, explains to Smith (1989) how he adjusts the length
of his performance in response to the interest of his audience: 'When
the men seated in front of me are interested, they have to listen to the
couplets and they know that I cannot escape reciting them. But when I
see that John Sahib [the researcher] has no interest in the matter, then I
recite five or six couplets instead of ten.' In at least one case, however,
brevity is the mark of success. The narratives of Athabaskan native
Americans are essentially an extended sequence of riddles (Scollon and
Scollon 1981). Story-telling of this kind clearly depends on a close
understanding between the narrator and the audience and, at the
slightest mention of a particular narrative theme, the audience will
complete the reference. When all the themes have been suggested the
story is completed. The best telling is therefore the briefest and can
only happen when the teller is in tune with the audience. On occasions,
however, when the understanding of the audience is low, these Athabaskan stories can become extremely lengthy. When the narrator begins
and evokes no response from the audience, he expands his original
exposition; in so doing, however, he risks diluting the narrative impact
and may still fail to evoke a relevant response. Sometimes other themes

may be tried and fail. Finally, the whole enterprise may be abandoned, even in mid-narrative.

Another aspect of the audience which the performer needs to take into account is its variability. This factor is almost too obvious: the individuals who make up an audience will vary from one performance to the next. So to what extent does a different audience necessitate a different performance? One way in which the artist can consciously respond to an audience is by choosing themes which will please those present. So, in a performance of *Sunjata* attended by one of us in Mali, the singer made a special point of making reference to an ancestor of the interpreter for the group. (See Plate 3). A similar example of such manipulation occurs in Dembo Kanuté's performance of *Sunjata*, sung in honour of a man called Seni Darbo. In this version, an ancestor of the Darbo clan shoots the arrow which defeats Sunjata's antagonist, Sumanguru (S_3:956–80). In no other published variant is this deed performed by a Darbo. The singer has clearly varied the plot to please his host.

Performances of *Sunjata* show other ways in which the audience influence the oral artist. In Bamba Suso's performance, which took place in a town called Brikama in The Gambia, for instance, the audience consisted primarily of school children gathered especially so that they 'would have the opportunity to hear an outstanding griot telling them something of the history of their people' (Innes 1974:37). This performance pays particular attention to the foundation legends of towns in the regions surrounding Brikama, none of which is mentioned in other published versions of the epic.

The guslar Stjepan Majstorović also shows striking sensitivity to the needs and preferences of his audiences. According to Lord (1960:19),

> he sang his songs according to the company he was in, since he had to please his audience or else expect no reward. Thus, when he was with Turks he sang Moslem songs, or his own songs in such a way that the Moslems won the battles. When he was with Serbs, whose company was more congenial to him, he sang their songs.

While Majstorović's contradictory songs can be explained both by improvisation-on-the-spot and by separate Christian and Moslem traditions, their differences may also be due to a conscious process of selection and omission on the part of the singer in order to please his audience. Radloff (1885:xviii–xix) describes a similar phenomenon in Mogul epic poetry. The akyn, or singer, would adapt his song to the audience in such a way that, when he was performing among nobles, he would integrate their genealogies and the deeds of their ancestors into his song. However, when he sang among the lower classes, the akyn would make derogatory comments about the same ancestors and their wealth in order to please his audience. So, too, Smith (1989) notes how the Rajasthani bhopo Parbu adjusts the narrative to the composition of his audience: 'If the Rebaris in his audience were anxious to hear the story of their caste-fellow Harmal's exploits in Lanka, he would hurry through the intervening stories of Gogo's wedding and Kelam's message by "reciting five couplets instead of ten," i.e., by restricting each theme to the absolute minimum necessary . . . '

All these observations suggest that the performance may be controlled not only by the singer, but also by the audience.

Audience Evaluation of the Performance

In the examples outlined above the performers show clear sensitivity to the composition, orientation and needs of those present. Equally powerful in shaping the performance, however, are the ways in which either individual members of the audience or the audience as a whole express their pleasure or dissatisfaction with the performance.

We have already discussed in chapter 1 the relationship between material rewards and the social status of the performer: Odysseus shares meat from his table with Demodokos; the Mongolian princess rewards the akyn with the gift of her cloak; Sunjata cuts off a slice of his thigh to save his starving griot; food and drink are offered to Yugoslav and Turkish performers; offers of room and board are made to itinerant Eastern European Jewish preachers; appreciative members of the audience present Japanese story-tellers with money and other gifts. All of these examples show clearly the high prestige attached to accomplished performers within their communities. But material rewards are also a vital ingredient in the interaction between audience and performer. By expressing their approval and pleasure with the artist in such a tangible way, the audience is clearly spurring the good talker on to maintain or even improve the level of performance.

However, remuneration is just one way in which an audience may evaluate a performer. Material reward is widespread but by no means universal and is more likely to be associated with 'sweet talkers' who carry the seal of approval of the community, than with 'broad talkers' who explore forbidden territory with licentious themes and talk. In all cases, the audience have the ability to make their feelings known. Sometimes they show approval by offering the performer the type of absolute silence and attention which a group of Turks displayed during the performance by a singer in the BBC television series *The Search for Troy*. At the other extreme is the direct participation of African audiences in many performances. Biebuyck and Mateene (1969:13), for example, describe the many ways a Nyanga audience expresses this involvement:

> The percussionists and members of the audience sing the refrains of the songs or repeat a whole sentence during each short pause made by the bard. In this capacity, they are called *barisïÿa* (those who agree with ...; those who say yes). Members of the audience also encourage the reciter with short exclamations (including onomatopoeia) and handclapping or whooping.

Similarly, Innes (1974:10) mentions that in The Gambia an audience of *Sunjata* may sing along with the well-known refrains of songs and 'an expert story-teller will often have a friend in the audience who will utter "*Namu*" or some other expression of approval and support after virtually every sentence'.

Both the Nyanga and Gambian examples include variations on the phenomenon of call and response, a pattern or exchange between performer and audience which allows oral artists to test the water as they go. Thompson (1974:28) refers to this mode of organization as 'perfected social interaction' in which performer and audience are part of a single organic whole. Often discussed in relation to African oral culture, call-response is by no means uniquely African. It is also a well-developed aspect of Afro-Caribbean performance. Sermons in the traditional Black churches of the Caribbean, the United States and Britain provide particularly good examples of the interactive nature of oral artist (the preacher) and audience (the congregation). All of the preacher's calls, or statements, are punctuated by responses from those present. The more competent the preacher, the more enthusiastic are the reactions of the congregation. Audiences thus help to shape and evaluate the performance.

Take the following extract from a sermon delivered by the Reverend C. L. Franklin of the New Bethel Baptist Church in Detroit (Sithole 1972:78–89). Encouraged by the audience's responses, he builds skilfully on a theme of Jesus as a living force:

PREACHER: Son of Man,
CONGREGATION: Yes my Lord
Yes my Lord
Oh yeah
PREACHER: I wish you could hear him say that,
CONGREGATION: Oh yes
Ahah

	Go ahead
	(*desk drumming*)
PREACHER:	Son of Man,
CONGREGATION:	All right
	Yeah — (*hummed*)
	My Lord
	Ahah
PREACHER:	Can these bones live?
CONGREGATION:	Yes my Lord
	Go ahead
	Yeah — (*hummed*)
PREACHER:	That son of man seems to be reminiscent,
CONGREGATION:	That's right
	My Lord
	Yes! Yes!
	Yeah — (*hummed*)
PREACHER:	Of man's limitations,
CONGREGATION:	All right
	Yes! Sir!
PREACHER:	Reminiscent of man's finiteness,
CONGREGATION:	My Lord
	Yeah —
	Yes Lord
PREACHER:	Man's humanity,
CONGREGATION:	Yes Lord
	Yes Sir
PREACHER:	Son of man,
CONGREGATION:	Yes Lord
	My Lord
	(*six drum beats on deak*)
PREACHER:	Son of man you are a scholar
CONGREGATION:	Yes!
	Ahah!
PREACHER:	You are an educator,
CONGREGATION:	Yes Sir
	Yes Lord

At this point the preacher, spurred on by the approving cries of the congregation, begins to draw together past and present by making comparisons between the Saviour and contemporary figures who receive widespread acclaim. The combined effect of the catalogue of attributes is impressive and produces a crescendo of support from the congregation:

| PREACHER: | Son of man, you are a scientist, |
| CONGREGATION: | Ahah |

	Yeah—(*hummed*)
	My Lord
PREACHER:	Can these bones live?
CONGREGATION:	Ahah
	Yes
PREACHER:	Son of man, you are an engineer.
CONGREGATION:	Yes
	Show the light
PREACHER:	Can these bones live?
CONGREGATION:	Yes
	Yeah—
	All right
	Oh—(*hummed*)
PREACHER:	Son of man you are a heart specialist
CONGREGATION:	Ahah
	Alright
	Yea! Great
	Yes
PREACHER:	Son of man you are a geologist,
CONGREGATION:	Yeah
	Yes! Lord
	Preach
	Take your time
	Come on up
PREACHER:	You are a botanist
CONGREGATION:	Yes, my Lord
	Yes Lord
PREACHER:	You, you are a specialist
CONGREGATION:	Ahah!
	Yes
PREACHER:	In various phases of the human body,
CONGREGATION:	Woo—
	Yes Lord
	Go ahead brother
PREACHER:	You are a psychologist and psychiatrist
CONGREGATION:	Ahah
	Yea—
	Yes my Lord
PREACHER:	You know all about drives and reactions and responses and tendencies
CONGREGATION:	Yes my Lord
	Come on
PREACHER:	I want to know with all of this knowledge, can you tell me, *can these bones live?*
CONGREGATION:	Oh Yeah!
	All right
	Yes my Lord
	Yes Lord

Come on
Ha, ha, ha, ha, ha
(*cascading laughter*)
Yeah—(*prolonged and hummed*)
Look out now
Go ahead
(*Long extended pause, etc.*)

A preacher with less developed oratorical skills would be greeted in a very different way. As Smitherman (1977:151) remarks, 'you ain't done no preaching if don't nobody shout'.

Patterns of verbal response are by no means restricted to sermons. Audience evaluation is, for instance, a critical element in the ritual invective discussed in chapter 6, and found throughout the world in societies as diverse as Black America, South Asia and the Arab world. The audience express approval—or disapproval—as each insult is delivered. Critically, these interventions also help define the ritual nature of the event, for without the control of an audience, ritual insult could easily become transformed into genuine abuse and degenerate into fighting.

The options open to the audience for showing their displeasure with the performer are as varied as their ways of expressing approval. On the level of both the individual and the group, it is possible to indicate disapproval by criticizing or even refusing to listen to a particular performer. Sometimes the audience express displeasure with the particular theme an artist has chosen rather than with the individual artist. Thus at *Odyssey* I:337–44 Penelope rebukes Phemios for the pain his songs cause her and she requests that he change the subject of his song. Frequently, however, the choice of an unpopular theme is closely associated with the inadequacies of an unskilled performer. Thompson (1974:28) for instance, treats this question in the context of the Tiv of Northern Nigeria in the following terms:

> The poor devil who starts a tale without proper preparation or refinement will find the choral answering to his songs becomes progressively weaker until they ultimately reform about a man with stronger themes and better aesthetic organization. He is soon singing to himself. The terror of losing one's grip on the chorus is a real one in some African societies, a poignant dimension of social interaction.

The same pattern can be observed in toast and story-telling sessions in Afro-American and Afro-Caribbean communities. In this way, the audience control many aspects of the performance, including its length, its pace and even who performs. Crowley (1966:21) describes one such example in the context of Bahamian story-telling. A narrator had been telling a story made up of a series of motifs which followed each other in a very disconnected way. When the performance had lasted for almost half an hour, other more popular story-tellers were waiting for their turn and the audience were becoming inattentive and were losing interest. At this point, the story-teller with the best reputation in the group suggested 'kindly but forthrightly that the story was getting pretty long and that the narrator should finish'.

Oral performers in more 'broad talking' contexts are particular prey of audience disapproval. Protagonists in ritual invective meet with jeers or silence if they fail to better the previous jibe. And in situations where one player is not only hesitant but also consistently fails to match the invective of the other, it sometimes happens that a member of the audience steps in to take the place of this player.

Expressions of audience disapproval for an artist have been documented for a very wide range of oral cultures. They do not always extend to the replacement of one performer by another, but can be equally blunt. There is an abundant literature, for instance, on the United States Old Southwest frontier circuit riders and preacher-farmers which suggests that the expectation of the congregation was a powerful hell-fire oratory. Those who departed from this expectation by being too formal or too uninteresting were subject to ridicule and criticism. Fowler (1968:52), for instance, retells the story of the divinity student who read a carefully prepared sermon to a frontier audience and then made the mistake of asking a member of the audience what he thought of his performance.

> 'Well,' said the brother, 'as I see it, it has just three faults.'
> 'And what were they?'
> 'In the first place, you read it. In the second place, you read it badly. In the third place, it wasn't worth reading.'

The response to an incompetent preacher in Eastern European Jewish communities was equally unambiguous. In his recollections of life in the town of Tyszowce at the beginning of the twentieth century, Shtern (1950) describes the reception such a preacher would receive in the following terms:

> There was a noise in the *besmedresh*, an uproar. Everyone did what he pleased: talked, chatted, argued, and *kheyder* boys played. And so the preacher preached to himself. If this preacher . . . had a habit of stutter-

ing or mumbling and at the same time used to bring forth examples which were not coherent, then *besmedresh* boys, jokers used to listen to this preacher . . . . Then they really had something to mock and imitate. (Shtern 1950, translated in Kirshenblatt-Gimblett 1977:299)

Japanese audiences are no less disparaging in their criticisms. The atmosphere, for instance, in a kodan theatre where serial stories are related is an intimate one: members of the audience tend to come regularly and to have their own special places. Some place their elbows on the stage. Some listen stretched out on the floor and even take a snooze in the course of the performance. Hrdličková (1969:193) describes the critical commentary often heard in the kodan theatre in the following terms:

> Listeners have their favourite story-tellers. On their entry, the ones who have been dozing wake up and sit so that they can hear well. The 'regulars' are, however, also strict critics; and, if they are not satisfied, they do not hesitate to shout out, 'Couldn't you recite something that would not disturb us from the sleep?'

It is important to recognize, however, that audiences do not express approval and disapproval in the same way in every culture. Williams (1972:105–6), for example, studying the different ways that White and Black audiences use body language to respond to speakers, observes how an Afro-American audience uses 'variable eye focus of different members of the audience checking out the "haps" (happenings) else-where even as they listen *attentively* ... Black cultural norms for attentive listening do not require eye contact', while in a White audi-ence 'attentive listening is manifested not only by being within hearing distance but through direct eye contact with the speaker. Variable eye focus ... would signal *inattentiveness* to a white speaker.'

Magnetized Performance

Sometimes individuals in an audience can affect the actual form and content of the performance. On several occasions in the *Odyssey* mem-bers of the audience determine the themes which the artist performs. For example, at *Odyssey* VIII:487–98 Odysseus asks Demodokos to sing about the Trojan horse and, shortly afterwards, Alkinoös asks Odysseus a series of questions which determine the subject of the song which follows. An even more powerful intervention by an audience occurs at *Odyssey* XII:328–76, when Odysseus, believing it too late in the evening, attempts to end the narrative of his adventures. At this point he meets with protest from the audience, in the person of King Alkinoös, who refuses to let Odysseus end his performance. At the same time, Alkinoös goes even further and suggests a new direction for the narrative by asking that Odysseus sing no longer of mythical personages but of the dead companions with whom he spoke in the land of the dead. Modern fieldworkers, assuming the role of the traditional audience, have also requested particular performances from oral artists in both Yugoslavia (Lord 1960:113 and 116) and West Africa (Innes 1974:142).

A similar occurrence takes place in Bamba Suso's version of *Sunjata*. Under normal circumstances, the accompanist adds to the performance no more than affirmative sounds, usually referred to as 'yes-saying', but on this occasion, when the epic is being sung for the education of school children, he interrupts several times with questions or comments. These interjections may be seen as attempts to ensure that the singer give as full an account as possible to the students. At one point during this performance, however, when Bamba has abandoned his narrative and has become involved in praise passages, the accompanist interrupts with the following question: 'At that time was [Sunjata] preparing to wage war against Susu Sumanguru?' (S_1:594). He asks this question not so much to solicit a full account but to reorient the straying singer. This accompanist's contributions appear to go beyond the desire for full narration and can be seen as attempts by a listener to control the form and content of a song.

On some occasions, members of the audience cross the boundary between spectator and artist and actually take part in the performance. In the Bahamas, for instance, individuals listening to a story-telling performance will often complete the narrator's song and even function as characters in the story (Crowley 1966). This kind· of audience intervention in performance quite clearly assumes an intimate knowledge of the themes and personae of traditional tales which would appear to be a widespread feature of oral culture.

Audiences of *Sunjata* display a similar familiarity with the material of the performance and also share expectations with the oral artist. In several versions of this epic, the birth of the hero is announced to his father by a messenger who sits down to eat prior to giving her message. Consequently the birth of another son is announced by a second less hungry messenger and the hero loses his birthright. At this point in one version of this episode (Johnson 1986:205) refreshments are brought in by members of the audience and the singer reacts by announcing an intermission in his performance. In fact, he actually interrupts his narrative at the very point where the messenger sits down so that he, too, can take his refreshment. In this case, both the audience and the artist have shared the expectation that the refreshment theme in the narrative is an appropriate occasion to break off the performance and the audience themselves initiate the intermission.

The audience's bond with the performer is further illustrated when this performance resumes and the artist skips over a significant portion of the story. The post-intermission narrative is picked up, not where it left off with the arrival of the first messenger, but further along, after the second messenger has made a report. Thus the intermission in the performance affects the progression of the narrative and narrative time continues to pass during the intermission. It is significant that the audience are not disturbed by the omission and can follow the artist's truncated performance without difficulty. This would not be possible if audience and artist did not share a common core of material and if there were not an ongoing bond between them during the performance.

The picture which emerges from the many examples of audience interaction both in the present and in the recent past clearly has implications for our reconstruction of periods for which documentation is incomplete. All that remains from many ancient civilizations such as Greece are texts which literate individuals will inevitably be tempted to interpret through literate eyes. The possibility that Greek authors such as Homer were heavily influenced by oral culture has only emerged as a discussion point in relatively recent times. Lord's fieldwork on Yugoslav guslars has drawn attention to very obvious parallels with the ancient Greek aoidoi in the *Odyssey* and the *Iliad* and has finally placed the issue of oral composition very firmly on the classicist's agenda. Various writers, including Havelock (1963;1982) have examined oral features of Greek literature, including drama and history, down to the time of Plato. While the recurrent aspects of oral art, the repetition, the formulae, the metrical frame, and the use of clichés and metaphors which fit into this frame, are all to be found in the works of Homer and other early Greek poets, the one dimension which cannot be resolved on the basis of extant evidence is the role which audiences may have played in moulding both the shape and the content of the Homeric texts. Although it can never be possible to do more than speculate on this question, contemporary examples of oral performance point very clearly to the ways in which those present would have been likely to exert their influence.

The relationship between a poet and his audience is captured memorably, for instance, in the description put into the mouth of Sokrates by Plato in the dialogue *Ion* 535e−6a:

> Then do you know that the member of the audience is the last of those
> rings which I described as getting power from each other through the

magnet? You the reciter and the actor, are the middle ring, and the first is the poet himself; but God through all these draws the soul of men whithersoever he will, by running the power through them one after another. It's just like that magnet! (Translated by Rouse 1956:20)

Contemporary examples of audience control over the performance suggest that the magnetic force also runs in the opposite direction, from the audience to the poet and that, to a certain extent, the audience, too, draw the soul of the poet wherever they will.

Giving Witness

The new importance attached to the central role of the audience in performances of all kinds is a landmark in the developing consciousness of oral culture on the part of literate observers. The audience are rarely passive during an oral performance. The competent performer responds sensitively to the needs and preferences of those present; by the same token, the audience have many different strategies for making known their feelings. Sometimes listeners will offer material rewards in the form of gifts or money; on other occasions they will register their approval–or disapproval–by their shouts or by their silence. Successful artists shape performance–pace, length, content–by paying close attention to the expressed wishes of those present. Those who fail to respond soon find themselves replaced by more competent performers.

Part II

Caught in the Web of Words

In telegraphic sentences, half nodded to their friends,
They hint a matter's inwardness—and there the matter ends.
And while the Celt is talking from Valencia to Kirkwall,
The English—ah, the English! don't say anything at all.
Rudyard Kipling, *The Puzzler*

In this part of the book we shift the focus from performance to the social factors which mould it. These social factors are often very different in oral and literate contexts. In societies which attach great importance to the written word, interaction outside the family is, for the most part, large-scale and centrally organized and individuals tend to form loose-knit social networks which are able to exert control over behaviour only impersonally and indirectly. Middle-class city dwellers, for instance, can deal with a dispute with a neighbour either by recourse to legal power based outside the immediate community or by avoidance tactics. Rarely do they speak directly to their neighbour face-to-face about a problem. In the communities which make up oral cultures, however, the structure tends to be more intimate and interpersonal. In this case, a neighbour might well be a relative or workmate—or both—and more direct action is often required for the lubrication of social relationships.

One of the consequences of this different emphasis in social organization is the tendency of oral performers to include all sections of the community in their performance. They make extensive use of what we have chosen to call 'oral referring', the act of drawing individual members of the community into performance through various acts of allusion, reference and direct address. Whether these individuals are addressed by name or spoken of only in the third person, allusions of this kind ultimately unite all members of the community, both present and absent, living and dead, in a referential web of words.

In 'Praising' we look at acts of oral referring in which the performer makes positive or negative references to other individuals based on reality or fact. Other forms of oral referring are more poetic or exaggerated. In 'Boasting' we discuss performances in which good talkers often abandon the bounds of truth in favour of fiction, and direct the act of praising or blaming to themselves rather than another. Finally, in 'Abusing' we turn to invective or ritual abuse, in which the act of fictional exaggeration is directed at specific members of the community.

Oral referring thus encompasses several kinds of performance. While praise, blame, boasts, self-deprecation and ritual abuse may at first appear to be very different phenomena, in practice the dividing line between categories can be a very hazy one. Praise is often tinged with blame and forms part of a single continuum of behaviour, whether directed towards another or, as in the case of boasting or self-blame, to the speaker. The step from praise of self to derision of another is a small one. Thus, any discussion of these oral events will move almost imperceptibly from praise to blame to boasting to invective. The inter-relationships between these various kinds of performance are such that they can be treated as part of a single process of oral referring.

Acts of oral referring, even more than other forms of oral performance, need to be located within particular social settings. In order to be able to understand a referential act, the observer needs special knowledge of the interpersonal relationships which operate within the community in question. The literate outsider's difficulty in understanding oral referring is further compounded by minimal personal experience of this process. When forced into a literate mould and approached out of context, a boast or an insult may appear quaint, odd, or even childish, and sophisticated functions served by performances of this kind are likely to be misinterpreted. Viewed in a particular social setting, however, oral referring begins to make sense, even from the limited perspective of the literate outsider. As we demonstrate in the following chapters, referring fulfils a vital role: it underlines the social values of the oral culture, by making clear which patterns of behaviour are acceptable and by applying pressure to non-conformists.

4

Praising

If a leaf falls from a tree and nobody praises it, the leaf must praise itself.

Nupe Proverb

The focus of this chapter is not only praise but also blame. In one sense, the act of blaming is the opposite of praising. Nagy (1979:222–42), for instance, has noted the fundamental opposition of praise and blame in Indo-European societies and particularly in ancient Greece. In another sense, however, blaming and praising are near neighbours and can exist side by side as part of the same speech event. Oral performers have it in their power, for instance, to tinge a praise passage with recriminations; conversely, they are able to transform blame into praise. Laments illustrate this subtle blend of praise and blame, for while there is clearly a desire on the part of the performers to honour the person who has died, there are often signs of anger on the part of those who are left behind. In a dirge sung by the Ghanaian Akan, for instance, lament for a dead father is sung directly to the dead man (Yankah 1983:385):

> Father alas!
> Grandson of the valiant one!
> Father of the morning rain with noble looks!
> The *okyereben* snake with a pretty neck ...
> Son of the Asona clan
> I am lonely.

Here we see the uneasy alliance of praise of the dead man as the 'grandson of the valiant one' and blame for causing the singer's loneliness in the same referential context. In a similar way the funeral of Hektor in the *Iliad* includes a formal lament by the women in the family. Hektor's widow Andromache leads the lamentation by addressing her husband in this way:

> My husband, you were lost young from life, and have left me
> a widow in your house, and the boy is only a baby
> who was born to you and me, the unhappy
>
> (*Iliad* XXIV:725–7)

Here, too, praise is tinged with blame as Hektor is rebuked for leaving his wife and infant son.

By the same token, blame can be transformed into praise. This uneasy relationship emerges clearly from West African griots' treatment of Sunjata's retreat in battle. On one occasion, Sumanguru, Sunjata's greatest adversary, takes a bow and shoots at the hero (S_1:671–7). Sunjata simply shakes the arrows off his gown. Implicit in this action, however, is the hint that Sunjata is able to escape unscathed only because he has run so far away from Sumanguru that the shot has lost its force. The singer asks Sunjata whether he was afraid and gives him the name '*Kubang Kubang*', a phrase which he explains outside the performance as meaning 'to run slowly' (Innes 1974:123). Although such a label might be considered insulting because of its reference to the hero's fear, the singer in fact describes 'Kubang Kubang' as *too dima*, 'a pleasing name, a pleasant name'. He has thus added to Sunjata's praise names an epithet which recalls the hero's flight in battle, and in the process, this blame name becomes praise.

On some occasions, praise is unambiguously praise, a quite separate performance serving a distinctive function. If the aim is to ensure good relations, for example, praise, not blame, is the order of the day. On other occasions, blame is unambiguously blame. Thus, for the performer who wishes to urge a subject to behave in a more acceptable way, blame, not praise, is required. Most often, however, the two co-exist in tension and fulfil the same range of social and aesthetic roles.

Good Relations

Praise and blame are not, of course, restricted to oral cultures. In societies where the written word has highest status, there are certaintly many occasions on which praise is permissible: the funeral oration; the presentation of an award; the introduction of an invited speaker. Blame can also be a feature of the political harangue and of satire. None the less, there are qualitative differences between oral and literate communities in the treatment of praise and blame performances.

In oral culture, praise and blame become an art form in their own right irrespective of the social distance between the performer and the subject. Good talkers make use of elaborate and often archaic language to develop their themes. On some occasions praising and blaming find expression through poetry; on other occasions, they find expression in oratory. In more literate communities, performances of this kind tend to be reserved for subjects who are socially remote: the guest speaker is likely to be unknown to the majority of those present; the political satirist has probably never met the object of his satire. Thus the oral practice of focusing so formally on members of the immediate community is often dismissed as obsequious in the case of praise and ill-considered in the case of blame.

One well-documented example of such cross-cultural misunderstanding concerns the contact between European planters in the Caribbean and West African slaves. The views of Bryan Edwards (1793: 78–9) on the oratorical skills of the slaves were typical of Europeans of the day:

> Among other propensities and qualities of the Negroes must not be omitted their loquaciousness. They are as fond of exhibiting set speeches, as orators by profession; but it requires a considerable patience to hear him throughout; for they commonly make a long preface before they come to the point; beginning with a tedious enumeration of their past services and hardships. They dwell with particular energy (if the fact admits it) on the number of children they have presented to Massa (Master) after which they recapitulate some of the instances of particular kindness shown them by their owner or employer, adducing these as proofs of their own merit; it being evident they think no such kindness can be gratuitous. This is their usual exordium, as well when they bring complaints against others, as when they are called upon to defend themselves; and it is vain to interrupt either plaintiff or defendant. Yet I have sometimes heard them convey strong meaning in a narrow compass: I have been surprised by such figurative expressions, and (notwithstanding their ignorance of abstract terms) such pointed sentences, as would reflect no disgrace on poets and philosophers.

From the perspective of the European, then, the oratory of the West African slaves appeared inappropriate for person-to-person communication, regardless of the social distance between the two parties. The use of extravagant words and elaborate formalities for praise and blame gave rise to feelings uneasiness and embarrassment and were usually explained as an imperfect attempt to reproduce the verbal practices of the master. European travellers and plantation owners failed to understand that the West African was operating within a different behavioural system in which such flowery language is the sign of the speaker's high verbal skill and of the complex social code shared by the oral community.

In any small-scale society, the performance of praise ensures smooth relationships between individuals, between families and between neighbouring communities, a function seldom recognized by those who form part of larger, more anonymous and less accountable wholes. Parkin has emphasized the strict linguistic and social rules which operate between two individuals during a meeting in Africa. For example, among the Girama 'the one who is moving must greet the one who is stationary' (Parkin 1980:49) and brother greeting brother should use a singular pronoun rather than the plural reserved for other generations (Parkin 1980:51–2). By showing due respect for the other party, each individual plays an important part in maintaining the social equilibrium. As Parkin notes (1980:52) for a brother 'to initiate with the plural is offensive, for it is like denying brotherhood'.

The need for cooperation between families also gives rise to performances of praise. Marriage is a case in point. In nearly every society, special rites and ceremonies ease the transition from one family to another. Marriage provides for the strengthening of existing ties between two families and the forging of new links and requires delicate social handling. It generates a great deal of tension and anxiety. As we will see later, some societies dissipate this tension with displays of ritual abuse. Just as frequently, however, marriage is taken as an opportunity for the smoothing of relationships through the singing of the other party's praises. In ancient Greece, for instance, songs called *epithalamia* were sung by choirs of young men and women, especially as the bride was carried in procession to the home of her bridegroom. The following fragments are found in the corpus of Sappho:

> Happy groom, the wedding took place
> and the girl you prayed for is yours.
> Now her charming face is warm with love.
> My bride, your body is a joy,
> your eyes soft as honey,
> and your love pours its light
> on your perfect features.
> Using all her skill Aphrodite
> honored you.
>   (Translated by Barnstone 1972:78)

The narrative introduction to the song sung at the wedding of Sunjata's parents in S_7:85–6 may also provide some insight into the psychological context of marriage songs in cultures, like those of West Africa or ancient Greece, where marriages are arranged:

[The bride] was forcing herself to smile, but it was a feeble sort of smile. The oldest of the female griots—called Tuntun Manian—in an attempt to alleviate the sadness in which Sogolon felt herself suddenly plunged, began intoning a chant in honour of Sogolon's future husband. Almost at once the assembled guests took up the refrain of this chant:

> *When he looks at me,*
> *His eyes painted with the Sarakollé pastel crayon*
> *Looking at me,*
>
> *When he lays his hand upon me,*
> *His hand with its fine rings is laid upon me,*
> *How great an event!*
>
> *When he lays his head upon me,*
> *His head with its white skull-cap is laid upon me,*
> *How great an event!*

While in ancient Greece praise of the married couple is sung by choirs and in West Africa the guests join in the griot's song, praise is voiced by an individual in this extract from a wedding toast from Nevis in the Caribbean:

As I stand on this happy occasion giving my best wishes to all Mr. Bride and Mrs. Bride—when I look around at this domicile it make me feel *Homa Doma* which is to say it makes me feel like a new girl. Mr. and Mrs. Bride, this feast reminds me of the feast of Belshazzar. Belshazzar made a great feast before a thousand of his lords and he drink wine before the thousands. Belshazzar while he drink wine he commanded a man to bring his gold and silver vessels, which his father, which was Nebuchudnezzar had taken out of the temple which was in Jerusalem. Mr. and Mrs. Bride, I will not take up any more of your precious and valuable time. Ima dance *pasear de boca* come and take—a kiss from the lips all time touch the heart. (Abrahams, 1970a:524)

To demonstrate her knowledge, the orator makes a wide range of allusions, often to the Bible, and draws on Latin or latinate expressions to create a similar effect. The setting is very different but there is a striking similarity in approach and sentiment between praise offered to the bride and groom in ancient Greece, and in present-day Nevis.

A Force for Change

The values promoted in praise and blame change not only from one society to the next, but also within the same society at different times.

The Nigerian writer Chinua Achebe (1980), on the one hand, gives one of his characters the praise name 'Amalize the Cat' in recognition of his traditionally-valued wrestling skills. Present-day Igbos, on the other hand, are likely to give higher praise to success in school examinations, and Egudu (1975) talks of someone who 'killed people by his writing' (*O degbue madu*), that is, someone who produced an excellent examination. Notwithstanding these differences in emphasis, performances of praise and blame are linked essentially through the social role which they perform. Both establish the values for a community and lay the ground rules for acceptable behaviour. In the same way that praise can be used as a social lubricant by emphasizing the desirable qualities of the subject, blame plays an important role in maintaining this same social order by persuading or shaming individuals into conformity with community ideals. It serves as an insurance of proper conduct and as a goad to action. Many Afro-American sermons, for instance, are based around the theme of humankind's unworthiness to enter the kingdom of God. The preacher enumerates human vices—cruelty, greed, destructiveness, licentiousness—before exhorting the congregation to repent so that they, too, may enter the kingdom. As Holt (1972:191–3) points out, a typical strategy is to begin with a statement about sin:

PREACHER: Husbands gettin' money and ain't comin' home wit it . . . Hunh?
AUDIENCE: (Usually female response here. Men will begin to fidget, shift arm positions, stare straight ahead, lean forward slightly, or lower the head): Yes? Let's go, alright now!
PREACHER: Gettin' Hogs (Cadillacs), booze, etc. Can I get a witness? Ya'll know what I mean?
AUDIENCE: You know it is. You got a witness. Oh yes! Yes, Jesus.
PREACHER: Dressin' it up when they children don't have shoes to wear and decent clothes.
AUDIENCE: (*Females will react with anger and glee in responding*): Keep goin', go on, you tellin' it. Preach! Lord, yes!
PREACHER: Don't you think they got a *right* to what you earn?
AUDIENCE: Yeah, Preach, take yo time now, awright, awright now!
PREACHER: Don't you think they got a *right* to—
AUDIENCE (*louder*):   Yeah!
PREACHER: Don't you think they got a *right* to yo love? Y'all wit me?
AUDIENCE (*shouts*):   Yeah! Eesy! Awright now! Tell it, tell it right, Come on! He's on the road now. Preach!

In reaching the climax of his message, the preacher shifts his attention to the women in the congregation, since both men and women may be guilty of the same sin:

PREACHER:	Wives playin' around. Just as bad as the husbands ... Hunh?
AUDIENCE:	(*male responses come strong and loud*) Tell the truth!
PREACHER:	Talkin' bout I love you and not having no dinner ready when the man comes home from a hard day's work, and he got to wait. Let the church say A-men.
AUDIENCE:	A-men! (*May be repeated several times with varying degrees of intensity*)

Finally the preacher goes on to suggest a solution for both sides, male and female. He advocates forbearance and mutual responsibility:

PREACHER:	To make the man do right—what would *God* have him do? Let the church answer A-men.
AUDIENCE:	A-men.
PREACHER:	To make the man do right you got to do yo part. Do I hear a witness?
AUDIENCE:	Tell the truth! Tell it! Talk!
PREACHER:	You got to get up early in the morning when your eyes still heavy and you limbs still weary.
AUDIENCE:	Come on now. Tell it right. Tell it like it is.
PREACHER:	You got to smile over tears, you got to make the man feel good like a *man*—when he's been kicked and tossed like a dog and a feather. You got to soothe his brow, tend his comfort, and *let him see* you love. You ain't got to talk 'bout yourself all the time.
AUDIENCE:	Come on now!
PREACHER:	And you got to smile—radiant, like the stars of heaven.
PREACHER:	We hear ya; Go ahead! Go brother! I hear you!
PREACHER:	You got to love ... hunh? (*Meaning 'Am I right', or 'You ain't listening to me'*) You got to persevere ... hunh? You got to give yo' all ... hunh? You got to be long suffering ... hunh? You got to do right! And things will be better by and by! Will you do it? Will you *try*?

The theme of self-purification and the strategies for ridding oneself of sin have grown slowly but powerfully out of the recriminations and blame.

Blame and praise are also found side by side in the apae addressed to the Akan leaders of Ghana. Although apae are, in the main, songs of praise, performers often introduce elements of criticism. The same concern. The same concern to modify behaviour which is the hallmark of the Afro-American sermon can also be detected in the apae. Take, for instance, the following lines addressed to King Bediako (Yankah 1983:396):

> Bediako!
> You play with children,
> Yet you are not the equal of children,
> You lower the full palm tree for children to play on it,
> And you jerk it suddenly.
> Yaw the stumbler,
> It's you who stumble for heads of children to go crashing against the
>   stone.

Here the king is confronted with his brutality and the unexpressed hope is that he will be able to modify his actions in the future. His undesirable actions adversely affect other members of society, in this case childern whose heads are metaphorically dashed. The singer's aim is to promote a greater sense of social responsibility.

On some occasions, it is difficult to draw the line between praise and blame; on others, there is no room for ambiguity: the speaker's intention is clearly to indict someone who has behaved in an unacceptable way. At *Iliad* III:39–42, for instance, Hektor berates his cowardly brother, Paris, for his unwillingness to fight Menelaos:

> Evil Paris, beautiful, woman-crazy, cajoling,
> better had you never been born or killed unwedded.
> Truly I could have wished it so; it would be far better
> than to have you with us to our shame, for others to sneer at.

Hektor fears that Paris' shame will fall not just on his shoulders but on the entire community. The misdeed of one member of an oral community has ramifications for the community at large; conversely, the community can exert pressure on its deviant member. Thus Hektor's use of blame with his brother is successful and Paris does eventually meet Menelaos' challenge. In this case, as in the case of the Afro-American preacher and his flock or the Akan apae singer, blame has the power to persuade people to modify their behaviour.

Blame thus functions as a way of manipulating group action to achieve what is considered to be socially desirable behaviour and to assert the speaker's moral – and verbal – superiority. Significantly, it can work just as effectively in the political as in the moral arena. Thus, Kallinos of Ephesos uses poetry to rouse his fellow Ionian Greeks against an enemy in the seventh century BC:

> When will you show some courage, you comrades?
> How long will you lie back and do nothing?
> Lazing in shabby peace on our land bled by war,
> have you no shame before the neighboring townsmen?
> (translated by Barnstone 1972:37)

Similarly, Alkaios addresses his audience about Pittakos, the tyrant of Lesbos, in this way:

> ... We must
> forget our anger and cease these pitiful
> clashes between brothers. Only a god
> could have maddened our people into war
> and so give Pittakos his bit of glory.
> (translated by Barnstone 1972:62)

The same political use of blame is to be found in Akan apae. Take the case of the singer who announces his opposition to the recent inaction of his chief (Yankah 1983:396–7):

> Bediako!
> Nana, that was not your word!
> It was your word that after the festive Sunday,
> You would order me on Monday to kill the prominent chieftain;
> But why have I waited so long?

Political references of this kind can be explained by the inherent power of such poetry to control the actions of the subject. Thus Kallinos goads the Ionians into action, Alkaios hopes for the overthrow of Pittakos, and the Akan singer for less hesitation of the part of his leader. The same function can be seen in songs of the Jamaican artist Bob Marley; 'Concrete Jungle', for instance, is an expression of the frustrations of former agricultural people about the international leaders of modern cities. This blame function was also clearly discernible in Marley's Jamaican Peace Concert, which urged a truce between the violent supporters of the political leaders Manley and Seaga.

The Social Responsibility of the Performer

In a society which has no writing and no history books, the only way in which individuals can achieve immortality is for their words and deeds to be enshrined in the praise or blame of the singers, orators and poets of their own and subsequent generations. Not all such performances serve this particular function. None the less, the role of praise and blame in ensuring a place for the subject in the collective memory would seem to be widespread. In ancient Greece, for instance, poets frequently composed *epinikia*, or victory odes, for specific individuals following athletic contests such as the Olympic or Pythian Games. Thus, for example, Pindar praises Telesikrates, the winner of the race in heavy armour at Delphi in 478 BC:

> My desire, with the deep-girdled Graces aiding,
> is to sing Telesikrates, proclaiming him
> Pythian conqueror in the race with the brazen shield,
> a blessed man and a garland upon Kyrene, mistress of chariots ...
> (Translated by Lattimore 1959:81)

The fact that Pindar does not directly address Telesikrates would suggest that the victor need not have been present at Pindar's perform-ance and that the poem was intended to be performed on more than one occasion. The skilful use of both the third person and the present tense creates a sense of distance, timelessness and permanence. What is more, Telesikrates is not the only recipient of this praise; the people of his home town of Kyrene are also garlanded and thus share in the reflected glory of their fellow citizen.

In a similar vein, Fa-Digi Sisòkò, the West African singer of *Sunjata*, praises Modibo Keita, the first president of Mali, even though he was not present at the performance. The president's family name associates him directly with the hero, Sunjata Keita. Fa-Digi's song not only lists some of Modibo Keita's immediate ancestors but also commemorates him for performing deeds which would have been beyond even Sunjata, such as taking advantage of modern aviation and travelling widely as president of Mali:

> But Sun-Jara did not have the wind as shoes
> To travel far and wide upon.
> But that was done by Modibo.
> (S_6:830–832)

As we have already seen, those individuals who conspicuously fall short of community ideals—the Akan king whose ruthlessness and inaction are a cause for concern, or the cowardly Paris who refuses to meet Menelaos' challenge—are just as likely to be ensured of a place in posterity as those who conform more closely to the ideal. Outside of performance the recitation of such blame might well invoke the risk of physical retaliation. It would seem, however, that the positive features of the blame performance have the potential to override the negative potential of blaming as an act of criticism. When individuals are addressed in blame passages this can be a signal that they are so important that whatever they do matters to society. The fact that they are mentioned is more important than what is said.

The oral artist's role in this process is openly acknowledged. The Gambian griot, Bamba Suso, for instance, says at the end of a performance of *Sunjata* that

> When Sunjata's reign came to an end,
> There were kings in the east,
> Because his territories were numerous, and there were kings there,
> But none of these are kings whose names have been preserved,
> Except that a griot who was associated with the kings in any particular
>   country
> Would know those kings.

$$(S_1:1270-1275)$$

A similar pattern is found in ancient Greece. While the poet Theognis, who lived in Megara in the late sixth century BC, works through the medium of the written word, his poetry retains oral elements. For instance, he uses praise functions which ensure that particular members of society will be remembered in song after they are dead. As he points out to Kyrnos, one of the subjects of his praise:

> ... And even after you pass to the gloom and the secret
>   chambers of sorrow, Death's house hidden under the ground,
> even in death your memory shall not pass, and it shall not
>   die, but always, a name and a song in the minds of men,
> Kyrnos, you shall outrange the land of Greece and the islands,
>   cross the upheaving sea where the fish swarm, carried not
> astride the back of a horse, but the shining gifts of the dark-wreathed
>   Muses shall be the force that carries you on your way.
> For all wherever song is you shall be there for the singers.
>   So long as earth endures and sun endures, you shall be.

(Translated by Lattimore 1960:27)

Like Bamba, Theognis builds his poetry around direct address and personal reference, and, in so doing, shows a consciousness of his role as praiser, as the preserver of the good name of his subject.

The performance of praise and blame carries with it heavy responsibilities. Licence to overstep the boundaries of normal social interaction carries with it many limitations. Thus, poorly skilled individuals, or those who choose to praise and blame in situations where this behaviour is clearly inappropriate, risk ridicule and shame. The Greek oral tradition, for instance, insists that good words be applied to good men and bad to bad; to do otherwise would entail disruption of the social equilibrium upon which the exchange of words is based. For example, when his athletic abilities are questioned on the island of Phaiakia, Odysseus responds to the unskilled blamer with the following rebuke at *Odyssey* VIII:166–85:

> Friend, that was not well-spoken; you seem like one who is reckless.
> So it is that the gods do not bestow graces in all
> ways on men, neither in stature nor yet in eloquence;
> for there is a certain kind of man, less noted for beauty,
> but the god puts comeliness on his words, and they who look toward him
> are filled with joy at the sight, and he speaks to them without faltering
> in winning modesty, and shines among those who are gathered,
> and people look on him as on a god when he walks in the city.
> Another again in his appearance is like the immortals,
> but upon his words there is no grace distilled, as in your case
> the appearance is conspicuous, and not a god even
> would make it otherwise, and yet the mind there is worthless.
> Now you have stirred up anger deep in the breast within me
> by this disorderly speaking, and I am not such a new hand
> at games as you say, but always, as I think, I have been
> among the best while I still had trust in youth and hand's strength.
> Now I am held in evil condition and pain; for I had much to suffer:
> the wars of men; hard crossing of the big waters.
> But even so for all my troubles I will try your contests,
> for the word bit in the heart, and you have stirred me by speaking.

Odysseus informs his abusive challenger that 'his words lack grace'; in other words, the speaker has abandoned the blame structures expected within the community and replaced them with 'disorderly speech'; he has said bad things about a good man, namely Odysseus. Nevertheless, these bad words have a positive effect and rouse the reluctant Odysseus to compete successfully in the games. The blame stirs both the good and bad to action.

In a similar vein, Nagy (1979:231) notes a traditional Irish tale in which the bad performer is punished more seriously. In 'The Second Battle of Mag Tured', the hero Dagda is oppressed by a blame poet named Cridenbel who greedily demands a third of Dagda's food ration

(Cross and Slover 1969:31–2). Implicit in the poet's request is the threat of abuse which will follow the hero's failure to comply. The hungry Dagda eventually puts gold coins in the meat and the singer perishes from the intestinal effects of his unjust wealth. Like the Phaiakian, Cridenbel used blame against a good rather than a bad man and was punished as a result.

Contests of Praise and Blame

Praise and blame are not always necessarily one-sided affairs. While it is true that they often form the focus for performances by individuals they can also be part of more competitive behaviour. The tea meetings on the Caribbean islands of St Vincent and Jamaica, for instance, are essentially festivals of oratory. Performers compete not only with one another but with the chairmen who preside over the proceedings. There is an expectation at these meetings that speeches will begin with an address in which the orator makes a series of comparisons with great men. The following extract, reported by Abrahams (1972a:25–6), was delivered by an advanced student of speechmaking preparing for a tea-meeting performance:

> Mr. Chairman, fellow citizens, ladies and gentlemen, including these ceremonial judges. Admitting Mr. Presenter and choir. Wishing the audience a happy and joyful evening. Mr. Presenter, sir, while listening to yourself and choir, I think it was Mr. Tennyson's choir singing in the St. Paul's Cathedral. Then sir, to whom must I compare you? I must compare you to the great man George Frederick Handel, now, the German composer. You are greater. I must now compare you to Admiral Collingwood, Lord Nelson's second in command at Trafalgar. He was born in 1750. He completed his excellence of Cape St. Vincent in 1797. As for you Mr. Chairman, it is in island spread that you are a Biblical and classical presiding officer. Then, sir, to whom must I compare you? I must now compare you to that great man John Ephilopótus who reckon the first King Syria after Alexander the Great.

Praise is not the only focus for these speeches which proceed to develop other themes and strategies. None the less, it is an essential part of the address, as each orator attempts to outdo those who have come before and those who will come later with increasingly elaborate references.

The same competitive framework which marks West Indian speech-making is also to be found in Maori rituals of encounter (Salmond 1977). *Hui*, or ceremonial gatherings, take place in the *marae* complex which consists of a carved meeting house and courtyard for orators fenced off from the rest of the settlement. Local people and each group of visitors have their own 'side' of speakers, the most distinguished orators going first and last. On the Northern and Eastern coasts, visiting orators speak *en bloc*; elsewhere they alternate. Although there is a basic structure to be followed, each side attempts to use this structure to its own advantage. In any *hui*, a ritual response must be matched to the relative prestige and social distance of the other group: the greater the prestige the more ritual should be offered. It is possible to score points over the other side by producing a particularly elaborate or appropriate response. One such example was provided by a Governor General of New Zealand who was very interested in Maori culture and who won the amazement and approval of the audience by using an ancient form of reply to the ceremonial challenge.

Another strategy is to manipulate the other side into making a mistake. Thus, if a visiting speaker's *tau*, or chant, can be anticipated, it may be possible to put him off his stroke. The same Governor General who replied to the ceremonial challenge delivered a magnificent *tau* at a state occasion in Auckland. However, he found that at the next *hui* he attended, the opening speaker proceeded to use the same *tau*. To everyone's great amusement, the Governor General, who knew no other *tau*, had to admit defeat. Manipulation of the rules in ways like these lends considerable drama to the occasion. The audience takes careful note of each victory or loss of face. For the most part, the proceedings are good-humoured, although occasionally participants show signs of agitation. A well-placed intervention sometimes revives old rivalries or even leads to the development of new ones. When one side scores a victory over the other, this will form a topic of conversation for months afterwards.

The St Vincent tea meeting and the Maori *hui* are examples of contests which centre on praise. It is not uncommon, however, for the competitive focus to change from praise to blame. One such case is Guyanese women's *busin'* (from English *abusing*) which takes place when one participant considers that the other is guilty of 'eye-pass', or disrespect for the social rights and privileges of a person. If no apology is forthcoming the offended person feels the need to bring pressure to bear so as to restore the social equilibrium. Busin' can be triggered by a wide range of undesirable behaviour including disrespect for property, disrespect for parents' authority over their own children, disrespect for person and personal space, promiscuity and the bearing of illegitimate children.

Edwards (1978:201) describes the situation of Johnson, Millicent and Joan. Johnson and Joan had lived in a common law marriage until a week before his marriage to Millicent. Joan sought a court order to make sure that Johnson supported the child of their union. She understandably felt bitter about Millicent who, she believed, had stolen Johnson away from her. The busin' took place in the yard with Joan and Millicent surrounded by relatives and neighbours.

JOAN: Why don't you keep out, yu red [i.e. light skinned] whore yu . . .

MILLICENT: But look at she, coming up me step to call me whore. Who is more whore than you?

JOAN: Shut yu mouth, yu red whore yu.

MILLICENT: Who is more whore than you, yu lang-mouth pig. Big hard-back woman like you gat every little boy swelling yu belly. You en gat shame, yu nasty lang-mouth whore yu. Why yu don't go and look for them others and summons them; only de pestering the man. Yu want he, but yu en gon get he, because he en want you, yu nasty whore yu. Calling me whore.

JOAN: Shut up you red whore yu.

MILLICENT: What me colour gat to do with you, yu fool yu.

JOAN: Yes, yu whore. Them two [children] yu gat iz where yu get them from?

MILLICENT: When I get them I was married. I get them legal. And these I gat here, they know their father. He en gat no doubt bout them. You don't even know the father for them you gat. Why you don't leave the man alone and look for you size, yu ole hard-back thing yu.

JOAN: I don't want your f . . . man. He is a nasty whore just like you. The night before he married you he sleep with me. I don't want your f . . . husband.

MILLICENT: Why you don't shut up, yu rally-card whore yu. Every man that pass around does take a punch. Yu liard thing yu. You think I en gat the letter you write he. Yu old bitch Yu! If you din want he, what you writin he letter for. You had he but he en want you. Why you don't go and look for you size, yu lang-mouth fool yu.

JOAN: Yu jealous because he sleep with me.

MILLICENT: He en want yu else he wud a deh with you. I en mad an stupid like yu. Why yu don't go to the mad house? Yu mad fool yu. If yu want support, tek yu children them and mind them.

Millicent's insults, focusing on Joan's age, suspected madness and promiscuity are especially effective: Joan was ten years older than Johnson; she had a reputation as a loose-living eccentric. The most important feature of *busin'* is therefore its truth value. While the elaborate and formal language of much praising and blaming is not a feature of these exchanges, the vivid imagery and the considerable verbal dexterity of the participants—and, in particular, Millicent—are beyond dispute.

The presence of an audience of relatives and neighbours who know the background to the dispute is extremely important in preventing the busin' from degenerating into a physical fight. The aim is to air grievances–to assert the rightness of one's own position rather than passively to accept the judgement of other people–and the audience ensures that this aim is achieved. The busin' can end in a number of ways. Often observers will intervene by leading the busers off in different directions with reassurances that they have made their point. Sometimes a third party, reminding them that they are neighbours who should cooperate rather than hurl abuse, gives both sides the opportunity to stop without actually surrendering. On other occasions, one participant may feel so embarrassed that she has to appeal to the audience. Edwards (1978:208) sums up the function of this behaviour in the following terms: 'Eye-pass presupposes the existence of rules for social living which are valued by members of the community. Infringement of these rules must be inveighed against publicly so that the law breakers could be brought to the attention of other members of the community.'

Blaming contests of this kind are by no means restricted to Afro-Caribbean communities. A series of verbal challenges also appears in a traditional Irish folktale called 'The Story of MacDatho's Pig' (Cross and Slover 1969:199–207) in which Cet mac Matach of Connacht claims the right before all comers to divide the pig as he sees fit. The scene consists of a series of challenges and refutations in which each man rises to announce that Cet will not divide the pig and is effectively dismissed by Cet's reply. To each challenger he responds not with blows but with shameful words which in one way or another illustrate the challenger's inferiority. In one encounter, Cet tells how he had easily defeated the father of one challenger in battle and therefore asks 'What should bring the son of such a man to contend with me?' Cet's words force the young man to sit back down.

A Question of Perspective

Praise and blame are frequently misunderstood by literate observers who interpret them through their own cultural matrix and fail to see the important underlying rationale. The examples we have chosen illustrate the fine distinction which exists between blaming and praising and the ways in which good talkers can move freely from one to another. Both kinds of performance draw attention to the social values shared by the community as a whole. In praising, oral artists reinforce community ideals and ensure good relations with their neighbours; in blaming, they goad their subjects to more acceptable forms of behaviour. The Akan apae singer, the Manding performer of *Sunjata*, ancient Greek poets and choruses, West Indian busers—all reinforce the social values of the group and ensure that these values are complemented. They have the power to modify the behaviour of individuals and groups.

Praise and blame fulfil other functions as well. They ensure a place in the collective memory for individuals, virtuous or otherwise, in those cultures which recognize the staying power of commemorative performance. At the same time, elaborate language and imagery elevate many such performances to the level of an art form. This is the case not only for the individual performer, but also in competitive contexts. In this way the performance provides entertainment for the audience. The good talker who outpraises or outblames a competitor demonstrates a high degree of verbal agility and wit, qualities which win the respect—or awe—of audiences and the community at large. Thus the act of praising or blaming has collective results. Praise and blame fall not only upon the person who is mentioned in the performance but also upon the performer.

5

Boasting

Jones likes to mix.
So I'll let it go six.
If he talks jive,
I'll cut it to five.
And if he talks some more,
I'll cut it to four.
Muhammad Ali, before his match with Doug Jones,
March 1963 (Torres 1971:112)

There are obvious links between praise and blame on the one hand, and boasting and self-deprecation on the other. In both instances, we are dealing with a continuum of behaviour. In the last chapter we dealt with praise and blame, contexts in which the performer refers to somebody else. Thus the ancient Greek praise poet, the Akan apae singer or West Indian buser all focus their attention on specific members of the audience or the community. In contrast, the present focus is the self rather than another: performers and subject merge into one when boasters or self-blamers proclaim their own virtures or weaknesses for the benefit of an audience.

We have already noted how observers often misinterpret performances of praising and blaming, dismiss them as obsequious and inappropriate, and fail to see the great power of words to affect action. The literate response to boasting and self-blame is couched within a similar cultural perspective. Like praise and blame, boasting has frequently given rise to serious misunderstanding. In most North American or European contexts, the unacceptability of boasting behaviour is neatly captured in such derogatory comments as 'blowing your own trumpet'. Similarly, self-deprecation summons up the image of Uriah Heep's ingratiating 'I am a very 'umble man' and all its unfavourable associations. Yet in other milieux, this same behaviour is viewed highly favourably, as speakers consciously use the spoken word like a physical weapon. The boast can be used as a way of legitimately asserting oneself; it can be used to win social approval and to establish oneself in the pecking order; it can be used to defuse difficult situations and provide defence against criticism or attack; it can be used as a source of humour and entertainment.

Self-assertion and Self-defence

In the Caribbean, for instance, boasting is a kind of assertive behaviour which steers a difficult course between the serious and the humorous. This is apparent in a wide range of different performances, including the calypso. Take the following example from the great calypso singer, Mighty Sparrow:

> Is me the village ram
> I don't give a damn
> If any woman say that I
> Leave she dissatisfy
> She lie, she lie, she lie.
> (Reisman 1977:117)

Boasts provide an opportunity for speakers to show themselves off to best effect. An Antiguan known as 'The Champion of Champions', for instance, used to march to the podium in oratory competitions reciting verses such as:

> I am the champion of champions
> From my head to my toes
> I must remain a champion
> Wherever I goes.
> (Reisman 1977:117)

In boasts of this kind, there is more than a small element of self-presentation which may well have some substance in fact. Yet, at the same time, no-one loses sight of the humour of behaviour which is essentially a subtle combination of the expressive and the rhetorical.

The Greek lyric tradition preserves a series of elaborate boasts concerning the power of poetic skill. Several poets, for example, associate their performative abilities with the flight of birds. The following boast comes from the poet Alkman, active in Sparta in the late seventh century BC:

> I know the tunes
> of every bird,

> but I, Alkman, found my words and song
> in the tongue
> of the strident partridge.
>   (Translated by Barnstone 1972:46)

At other times, the ability to use performance as a weapon can become the subject of a boast, as when Archilochos, another seventh-century Greek lyric poet, asserts

> One big thing I understand:
> I know how to spit back with black venom
> against the man who wrongs me.
>   (Translated by Barnstone 1972:34)

Boasting is clearly a form of self-assertion. Equally important, however, is the way in which boasts fulfil a vital psychological function as a form of defence against criticism. The person who responds to a challenge or a tease with a boast is engaged in a show of strength far more effective than replying in kind. This reaction is exemplified in the autobiographies of Afro-American figures like H. 'Rap' Brown (1969; 1972) and Dick Gregory (1965), who show, for instance, how they developed verbal strategies as a means of coping with the harsh realities of street life. These tactics encompass self-aggrandizing boasts, such as the one described here by H. 'Rap' Brown (1972:205):

> A session would maybe start by a brother saying, 'Man, before you mess with me you'd rather run rabbits, eat shit and bark at the moon.' Then, if he was talking to me, I'd tell him:

> > Man, you must don't know who I am.
> > I'm sweet peeter jeeter the womb beater
> > The baby maker the cradle shaker
> > The deerslayer the buckbinder the woman finder
> > Known from the Gold Coast to the rocky shores of Maine
> > Rap is my name and love is my game.

The advantage of this boasting behaviour is that it will often prevent the situation from degenerating into a fight.

Boasting in an Afro-Caribbean context is taken at face value and there is no expectation that the boaster will necessarily enact the boast. White observers, however, have often interpreted such behaviour literally. The boasting of Muhammad Ali, for instance, often provoked a negative reaction. The verbal declaration of his own superiority which regularly preceded boxing matches – 'I am the greatest' – caused considerable discomfort for many White Americans and Europeans who interpreted this behaviour as an example of severe narcissism. One feature of these boasts passed largely unnoticed: Ali's predictions of how he would achieve his victory were usually delivered in verse, a device which set the boast apart from normal everyday speech. (See, for example, Ali's boast before the Jones fight quoted on page 100.) The

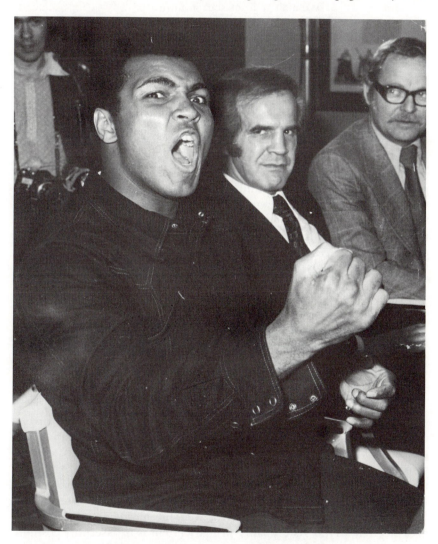

Plate 7   *Muhammad Ali in boasting pose, behaviour which has frequently given rise to misunderstanding among literate observers. Photograph: Hulton-Deutsch Collection, Hulton Picture Company.*

narcissistic label clearly grew out of one cultural tradition imposing its
own interpretation on another.

Very often boasts consist of bravado plus challenge. This can be
seen, for instance, in the following Mighty Sparrow calypso:

> We young and strong
> We ain't fraid of soul in town
> Who think they're bad
> To meet them we're more than glad
>
> I've got my gun
> And Pardner I ain't making fun
> If you're smart clear the way
> And if you think you bad
> make your play
>
> (Reisman 1977:117)

The same combination of bravado plus challenge is to be seen in a wide
range of oral cultures, past and present, though the seriousness with
which the boasts are made would appear to vary a great deal. Homeric
warriors, for instance, sometimes link physical combat with boasts of
their lineage and might. Thus at *Iliad* XXI:153–60 the Trojan Asteropaios boasts to Achilleus in this way:

> High hearted son of Peleus, why ask of my generation?
> I am from Paionia far away, where the soil is generous,
> and lead the men of Paionia with long spears; and this for me
> is the eleventh day since I arrived in Ilion.
> For my generation, it is from the broad waters of Axios,
> Axios, who floods the land with the loveliest waters.
> His son was Pelegon the spear-famed; but men say I am Pelegon's
> son; now, glorious Achilleus, we shall fight together.

Asteropaios gives Achilleus a straightforward account of his divine
origin. His boast contains no falsehood, yet Homer concludes the
passage with the phrase 'so he spoke challenging' (*apeilesas*), a verb
someone from outside Homeric culture would not necessarily expect in
this context. Adkins (1969) has shown that the Greek verb *apeilein*,
variously translated into English as 'to boast', 'to brag', 'to threaten' or
'to challenge', is essentially informative and means 'to make one's
presence felt'. Thus Asteropaios' primary intent is to assert his position
in Homeric society. Yet, at the same time, this assertion is a challenge
to Achilleus' own status and leads inevitably from verbal duelling to
physical combat. Achilleus does not respond to this boast by the son of

Pelegon with words; he raises his ash spear and the two warriors lock in battle. Only after Achilleus has killed his opponent does he respond with his own genealogy. Words and deeds are here bound together in the act of boasting.

Similar boasts are spoken in *Sunjata* when men volunteer for difficult missions by self-confidently affirming their invincibility or inevitable success. In Dembo Kanuté's song, for example, Faa Koli, the hero's chief lieutenant, challenges Sumanguru's generals with the following boast:

> I have sworn an oath by all the men and women of Manding that
>   tomorrow
> Tomorrow when we meet at Kaya –
> Great Jibirila, Sumanguru's senior commander,
> Has among his followers ten men.
> He has ten followers who are learning to acquire supernatural powers;
> Those ten men are his followers;
> Those who are his followers,
> Tomorrow I will catch every one of them with my bare hands.
> I will not take an arrow, I will not take anything.
> I will not take a sword, I will not take anything,
> I will punch them all with my fist,
> And kill the lot of them.
>
> $(S_3:663-73)$

The Hyperbole of Boasting

While Faa Koli's boasts are deadly serious, many Afro-American boasts achieve a similar effect by injecting an element of humour, as in the following exchange of words between youths on street corners:

> If you don't quit messin' wif em, uhma jump down your throat, tap dance on your liver, and make you wish you never been born.
>
> Yeah, you and how many armies? Nigger, don't you know uhm so bad I can step on a wad of chewing gum and tell you what flavour it is.
>
> (Smitherman 1977:79)

The same humorous exaggeration is to be found in the absurd claim made by an Afro-American known only as 'Kid':

> I'm so fast. A girl told me one time, she said, 'Kid, now if you can get some cock 'fore my mother get back home, and she's coming 'round the corner right now, you can have it.' So I said, 'Lay down.' She layed

> down, I pushed the light switch, got undressed, jumped in bed, busted
> two nuts, got dressed and got outside the room before that room got
> dark. (Kochman 1981:64, quoted from Abrahams 1970b)

Both 'Kid' and his audience know that his sexual prowess is exaggerated in this story but both derive pleasure from the absurdity of the
situation and from the verbal dexterity of the speaker. To a certain
extent, such exaggeration is part of every boast, even the deadly serious
one of Faa Koli in *Sunjata* (S_3:663–73) where the warrior vows to slay
not one, but ten powerful opponents barehanded. Certainly, the audience of *Sunjata* gets as much pleasure from hearing Faa Koli's boast as
'Kid''s friends did from his. The critical difference between the two
boasts, however, lies in their accountability. Faa Koli must back up his
claims with action while 'Kid' has already done what he had set out to
do: to prove himself a good boaster.

In the same way that oral artists must target their performances of
praise and blame at suitable individuals, boasting behaviour is also
subject to strict limitations. When people live up to the image they are
creating in the boast, they are likely to meet with appreciation. In
Antigua, for instance, the audience tends to respond to boasts which
tally closely with reality with approving remarks like 'He just feels he's
set' or 'He just feels he's good' (Reisman 1977). Boasting is thus an
important element in the presentation of self, and, in some situations,
can be used to devastating effect. *Iliad* VIII:147–50, for instance,
illustrates the effect which a boast may have on opponents even off the
battlefield. Diomedes imagines what the Trojan Hektor might justly say
were he to reach the Greek ships:

> But this thought comes as a bitter sorrow to my heart and to my spirit;
> for some day Hektor will say openly before the Trojans:
> 'The son of Tydeus, running before me, fled to his vessels'
> So he will vaunt; and then let the wide earth open beneath me.

The verb 'vaunt' is a translation of the same Greek verb *apeilein* which
Homer used in reference to the boast of Asteropaios discussed above.
Diomedes thus projects his own death as the consequence more of
public boasting by his enemy than of physical defeat.

When a boast has no substance, however, audience reaction varies
from one culture to the next. In an Afro-Caribbean situation, it can be
perceived as a form of humour, though, in this case, at the expense of
the person who makes it. Reisman (1977:118) cites the example of the
claim made by East Indians in Trinidad that their political leader, Dr
Capildeo, was the world's greatest mathematician. The boasting of the

Midnight Robbers of Trinidad, who make speeches to passers-by, also falls into this category. Their aim is to inspire awe and admiration–and some small financial appreciation–and invariably they make the audience laugh:

> For at the age of five, I, this dreaded monarch, was sent to school, but the schooling was not drastic enough for me, for I was a downright dunce. But anything too mathematic was alwys a puzzle to my brains, but when it came to snatching children faces, ringing their ears, biting off piece of their nose, I, King Korak, was always on top. . . . At the age of two I drowned my grandmother in a spoon of water. (Crowley 1956: 271–2)

In other situations, however, the tension between claim and reality has more serious consequences. Thus, in ancient Greece the boast could only be carried so far. Identification of self with the gods was considered an act of *hybris*, of excessive pride for which the boaster would suffer divine punishment. Disgrace is also the inevitable outcome of an untrue boast in *Sunjata* when the hero's ally, Faa Koli, swears the oath that he will defeat with his bare hands Sumanguru's ten commanders. This boast, intended to counter the great occult strength of the enemy, all of whom 'are learning to acquire supernatural powers', stakes the speaker's personal disgrace and isolation upon the fulfilment of the boast. Faa promises Sunjata that

> If that vow is not kept, then I will put on the loincloth of an uncircumcised boy,
> And may every man and woman in Manding spurn me.
>
> $(S_3:677-678)$

The potential consequences of a false boast are thus twofold: the lowering of status suggested by the wearing of a child's clothing and rejection by the rest of Manding society.

Self-blame

So far the discussion has focused on performances of self-praise. In many cultures and many contexts, however, self-blame can be used to achieve a very similar effect. In the same way that praise and blame can be seen to form part of a single continuum, so too can boasting and putting oneself down.

It is interesting to note, for instance, that Afro-Americans engage not only in self-aggrandizing but also in self-deprecatory boasts. We have already shown how performers make use of exaggerated, highly metaphorical language to make extravagant claims about what they might do to an opponent. Yet the same people who boast about their speed, strength or 'badness' are just as likely to dwell on how hungry, lazy or tired they are:

– My stomach is so empty it thinks it's married to my backbone
– So low that I could crawl through a crack in the floor
– So slow you can see the dead lice falling off
– I am so tired my ass is dragging my tracks out

(Halpert 1951:passim)

The mechanisms for scoring points over the other side will vary a great deal from one society to another; the net effect, however, is essentially the same.

Sometimes self-blame is actually intended to be an indirect boast, an ironic transformation of feigned self-criticism into self-praise. Thus the Greek performer creates an impression of self-deprecation by assiduously attributing the beauty and skill of the performance to an outside force, the Muse or goddess of poetry, rather than to innate ability. In a similar way, the Black preacher may admit to the congregation that 'I am a sinner like you'. From the perspective of the audience the speaker's modesty can thus transform an act of self-blame into praise. Both Greek singer and Afro-American preacher indirectly praise themselves for their self-knowledge and for their role as divine representatives in the community. There are obvious parallels between these examples and the cases of praise and blame discussed in the last chapter: the personal reference to the singer is, in many ways, more important than the type of statement which is made.

Fighting Fire with Fire

Sometimes boasting or self-blame is sufficient in itself to stem any further criticism or challenge. On other occasions, one boast will lead to another and a battle of wits develops between two or more protagonists. The power of words as weapons can be clearly seen, for instance, in verbal encounters between Sunjata and Sumanguru. In scenes prior to the battle, the antagonists confront each other with words and assert their own power and superiority over the other. At one stage Sumanguru expresses his occult power in a series of dangerous metaphors. Thus, he calls himself, in succession, a wild yam, a poisonous mushroom, a red-hot cinder and a mighty silk-cotton tree (S_4:60). Sunjata replies in kind with antidotal metaphors: he is a rock shatterer;

a ravenous cock immune to poisonous mushrooms; a rain which exting-
uishes cinders; and the strangling creeper that can wrap itself around
the tallest tree. In each case, Sunjata demonstrates his ability to surpass
his opponent on the level of verbal debate and occult power. Just prior
to his fight with Joe Frazier on 8 March 1971, Muhammad Ali wrote
the following poem in which he sounded just like Sunjata:

> Joe's gonna come out smoking
> And I ain't gonna be joking,
> I'll be pecking and a-poking
> Pouring water on his smoking.
> This might shock and amaze ya,
> But, I'm gonna re-tire Joe Frazier.
> (Ali 1975:227)

West Indian women and Cet mac Matach of Connacht use blame to
devastate an opponent; Sunjata and Muhammad Ali achieve similar
effects with boasting.

A boasting contest takes place without the threat of physical violence
in a choral poem by Alkman, a Greek poet of the seventh century BC.
In this poem, a *parthenaion* or 'maiden song', boastful words become
playful weapons as two groups of young girls, competing at a religious
festival, debate in song the physical qualities of their leaders, Hage-
sichora and Agido. At one point the two women are compared to
racehorses:

> Look and see. That other is
> Like a Venetian courser,
> but the tresses of my cousin
> Hagesichora! They blossom
> into gold without alloy,
> and her face is pale like silver.
> Must I tell you this so plainly?
> There is Hagesichora.
> Loveliest after Agido,
> she will still run,
> Lydian horse with Scythian racer
> close together.
> (Translated by Lattimore 1960:34)

The Arab *Mufakhara* and *Munafara*, or contests of honour, could also
be described as boasting competitions (Huizinga 1949). The *Mufakhara*
were held at fixed times of the year, at fairs or after pilgrimages. Each
side was represented by a *sha'ir*, a poet or an orator, and the contest

could centre either on individuals or the group as a whole. The *Munafara* was a similar kind of contest in which two parties would set out their claims for honour before a judge, supported by witnesses acting under oath. Both sides agreed upon a theme, such as who is of the noblest descent, and competed for the prize of one hundred camels.

In many oral cultures contests of self-praise give way to displays of self-deprecation. In China, for instance, *iang* (or yielding to another) allows one to demolish one's adversary by demonstrating superior manners. A similar value set can be observed in the Malagasy of Madagascar. Here, in verbal contests, the more accomplished the performer, the more indirect the criticism will be. Malagasy speakers, aware of the need for subtlety, go to great extremes to avoid causing affront. Comments on this question offered to Keenan (1977:130) when studying this particular community included:

> In the *kabary* [formal speech] it is not good to speak directly. If you speak directly the *kabary* is a *kabarin-jaza* (child's *kabary*) and there is no respect and honour.

> Speakers are not afraid to explain to one another, to answer with wisdom. But the censurer must be careful not to dishonour or mock or lower in public that speaker, because this was *fady* (taboo) for our ancestors.

The way in which Malagasy speechmakers set about offering criticism is therefore very carefully considered. It is fundamental to preface any negative remarks with compliments:

> Thank you very much, sir. The first part of your talk has already been received in peace and happiness. I am in accordance and agreement with you on this, sir. You were given permission to speak and what you said gave me courage and strength. You said things skillfully but not pretentiously. You originate words but also recognize what is traditional. But as for myself I am not an originator of words at all but a borrower. I am more comfortable carrying the spade and basket. You, on the other hand, have smoothed out all the faults in the speech; you have woven the holes together. You have shown respect to the elders and respect to the young as well. This is finished. But ... [Criticism begins]. (Keenan 1977:129)

Boasting and self-blame can thus be seen to be very effective forms of behaviour with a wide range of possible applications. It does not seem to matter whether boasters are better or worse, stronger or weaker, prouder or more humble than their audience. The essential quality of boasting is that the performer has more of whichever attribute is important in a particular setting at a particular time. Boasts can be used as a means of self-assertion, either playfully as in the case of West Indian calypso singers or the ritual choruses of ancient Greece, or to more serious effect in the challenges of heroes in Homeric and West African epics. They are also a useful form of self-defence and can be a great deal more effective–and less painful–than physical retaliation when emotions are riding high. Those performers who respond to taunts with boasts which clearly have no substance become the butt of their own humour; but, in so doing, they have the power to defuse an explosive situation. Boasting, whether playful or serious, is a force to be reckoned with.

6

Abusing

'Are you going to let him say something like that about your mother?'

from an Afro-American 'sounding session'
(Kochman 1972:258)

Maledictio autem nihil habet propositi praeter contumeliam quae si petulantius iactatur, convicium, si facetius urbanitas nominatur.
Cicero, *Pro Caelio* III, 6

'The only object of slander, on the other hand, is to insult; if it has a strain of coarseness, it is called abuse; if one of wit, it is called elegance.'

Translated by Gardner, in *Cicero: The Speaches*

The step from ritual self-praise, or boasting, to ritual invective of an adversary is a very small one, so it is not at all surprising to find that verbal duelling, like ritual praise, is a feature of diverse societies, both past and present. Even more than the forms of oral referring which we have already discussed, invective is open to misinterpretation by literate observers who, all too often, take such performances at face value, accept the verbal abuse as sincere, and fail to recognize both the ritual nature of such performance and the range of social functions which it serves. Only a member of the community in question can fully appreciate the degree to which such invective crosses the boundary of truth and marks the subject of abuse in a special way within the performance.

The Universal Bite of Satire

Joking and repartee are, to a certain extent, features of all societies, both literate and oral. As part of the verbal repertoire of both adults and children in literate societies they have been well documented. The

Opies (1977:65), for instance, have shown how children engage in strategies such as 'having the last word':

FIRST BOY: If I had a face like yours, I'd put it on a wall and throw a brick at it.

SECOND BOY: If I had a face like *yours*, I'd put it on a brick and throw a wall at it.

However, while the 'banter' which functions in more literate societies tends to rely on a limited number of set routines and focuses on a smaller number of topics, the ritual invective in oral cultures is broader and more formalized and ranges over a wider variety of forms and topics than its literate counterpart.

Oral cultures with a well-developed tradition of invective generally establish set patterns of behaviour for such abuse. Radcliffe-Brown (1940; 1952), for instance, has drawn the attention of ethnologists to formal joking relationships based on family and marriage ties in Africa and other parts of the world. Thus Dogon men have joking relationships with their wife's sisters and their daughters; and among the Manding certain griot families have joking relationships with a group of trading families known as *jula* (Innes 1974:322). For this reason Dembo Kanuté can tease his *jula*-host by associating traders with sexual adventures at S_3:859–862. The restrictions on who can joke with whom reflect the power of such abusive words, which are, with good reason, both privileged and special.

Even in cultures where such joking relationships are either less socially delineated or do not exist at all, the destructive power of abusive words is often strongly expressed and invective is used only sparingly. In the following example from Old Irish folklore, for instance, the power of abuse is deadly serious. When a poet is asked by the chieftain in 'The Second Battle of Mag Tured' (Cross and Slover 1969) what power he can contribute to forthcoming battle, the oral artist replies: 'I will make a satire upon them. And I will satirize and shame them, so that through the spell of my art they will resist the warriors.' The poet thus claims the ability to defeat the enemy by the very power of his satirical song.

A similar awareness emerges on occasion in *iambos*, the Greek form of poetic abuse. This form of blame poetry developed in close association with a particular metrical form, the iambic [$\cup$ —]. While most scholars would agree that the term 'iambic' is derived from its links with the poetic genre, the etymology of *iambos* is more controversial. Various writers, including Huizinga (1949), derive *iambos* from its function and understand it to mean derision. Others, however, such as Dover (1964:189) and Nagy (1979:243–52), believe the word to refer to the type of occasion for which this genre was appropriate. In either case, the close link between the metre and the genre emphasizes the restricted form and context for abuse in the Greek tradition.

The early seventh-century BC poet Archilochos of Paros, for example, was hurling a poetic tirade of abusive Greek iambics against the Lykambid family who had broken off his engagement to their daughter Neobule, when he made the boast, quoted in the previous chapter, that he knew how 'to spit back with black venom against the man who wrongs me' (Barnstone 1972:34). As Burnett (1983:60) notes, Archilochos' reference to himself as a reciter of abuse reveals the intense 'consciousness of function' also seen in the claims of the Irish poet. Within the poetic frame, both poets maintain the role of someone who can with justice respond to bad actions with bad words. Unlike the Phaiakian whose unjust questioning of Odysseus' athletic skills leads to his verbal ridicule and athletic defeat by Odysseus in *Odyssey* VIII, both Archilochos and the Irish poet can expect better results from their abuse because they know how to use their words to best effect.

In Archilochos' mind, it is perfectly reasonable to respond to the unfair actions of Neobule and her father with abusive language: abuse, like the boasting and blaming we considered earlier, has the ability to challenge wrongful action effectively. The power of Archilochos' poetry is further strengthened by the tradition that Archilochos' abusive attacks drove the Lykambid family, both father and daughter, to commit suicide. The potential death which Diomedes imagined as the result of Hektor's boasts in the *Iliad* becomes a reality for Neobule, who loses both life and reputation as a result of her former suitor's verbal abuse.

Archilochos' abuse, however, is different from the boasts discussed in the previous chapter in that it is blatantly and consciously false. It allows the poet, for instance, to use obscenity and to identify his former fiancée with a prostitute. In the so-called 'Cologne Epode' Archilochos refers to Neobule in this way:

> . . . Count on this! Neobule no!
>   Marry her somebody else! Good god! By now she's overripe,
> her girlhood bloom has withered and dropped off,
>   also the grace of before: she's never yet kept down her lust –
> a randy slut that's shown her woman's prime.
>   Out to the crows! Keep her off! May never he who rules the gods
> decree that I–possessed of such a wife–
>   stand as a neighborhood butt . . .
>
> (Translated by Van Sickle 1975:2)

Neobule is an overripe fruit suitable only for the birds.

While the theme of revenge against the Lykambids maintains the appearance of deadly seriousness throughout the extant fragments of Archilochos, there is nevertheless a scholarly suspicion that the entire tradition is a poetic fabrication, a game the poet is playing to demonstrate the power of words to the audience. Thus Nagy (1979:242) and others have noted the linguistic links between the name Lykambes and *lykos* (the Greek word for 'wolf') and *iambos,* and have suggested that Archilochos' victim is actually a poetic stock character representing the dishonourable victim of skilled abusive poetry. In this interpretation, Archilochos' invective has been composed for the pleasure of an audience of revellers at symposia, the drinking parties at which such poetry was regularly performed; its primary function is not revenge.

This tension between apparent seriousness and underlying playfulness is an important aspect of verbal abuse which distinguishes it from the true-speaking of blame and protects the speaker against the dangers of free speech. Archilochos' abuse can be spoken only at the symposium. Spoken on the street, the poet could expect a totally different, and unpleasant, reaction from his audience.

Verbal Abuse as a Poetic Contest

In may oral cultures abuse takes the form of a competition between two sides. For instance, *Mufakhara* and *Munafara,* the contests of honour of the pre-Islamic Arabs which we have described in the previous chapter (Huizinga 1949), often degenerated into *hidja*: as each side boasted of its own superiority and excellence, the boasts slipped all too easily into abuse and derision of the adversary.

Such competitions are also found in Northern European contexts. Old Norse literature contains examples of *mannjafnaðr*–the comparing of men–as part of the Jul-Feast. The Old French, Old English and Old Erse traditions refer to similar speech events. Emblematic is a tale from the Old Germanic tradition (Huizinga 1949). During the course of a banquet offered by Turisina, king of the Gepidae, shortly after the death of his son, one of the royal princes subjects the Langobard chieftains to a series of insults ranging from 'White mares' to 'You stink'. The guests retaliate with 'Go to the field of Asfela where you will surely learn how valiantly those mares of yours can put about them, where your brother's bones lie like an old nag's in the meadow'. Significantly, this is not a signal for physical violence. The King restrains the verbal adversaries, and the banquet is brought to a merry end.

Verbal duelling of this kind is by no means a thing of the past. It is an essential element, for instance, in the oral culture of Afro-Americans where it is known variously as 'sounding', 'screaming', 'joning', 'signifying' and 'playing the dozens', depending on geographical location and the precise form of the duel. In the activity most commonly known as playing the dozens, insults are delivered in rhyme. Changes in pitch, stress and syntax can provide the signals for the contest and help maintain considerable symbolic distance between this speech event and other kinds of verbal interaction. Thus ancient Greeks tended to restrict their abuse to a special poetic metre. Similarly, the player of the dozens maintains a reservoir of abusive couplets and the winner of the game is the person with the largest store of couplets, the best memory and, perhaps, the best delivery. Although the original composers of these rhymes may have shown great skill and verbal ingenuity, nobody would expect duellers to be able to manufacture them in the heat of the moment. While there is little opportunity for improvisation or creativity when playing, judgement is required in fitting one insult to another, and good players are those who are able to follow with rhymes which build on and improve on themes introduced by the previous player.

When insults are rhymed, sheer memory will do. But in sounding, another form of Afro-American verbal duel built this time on unrhymed exchanges, the requirement that the reply must be appropriate, well-formed and built on the specific model offered is even more important. There is thus a considerable degree of improvisation and creativity. Players who are good have the special skill of being able to turn what their opponents have said back on them. A particularly good example is contained in Labov (1972:296):

DAVID: Your father got brick teeth
BOOT: Aw your father got teeth growing out his behind!
DAVID: Yeah, you father, y-got, your father grow, uh, uh, grow hair from, from between his y'know.
BOOT: Your father got calluses growin' up through his ass and comin' through his mouth.

The power of Boot's performance derives from the fact that both sounds feature the same attribute (odd appearance) and the same target relative to the speaker (their father). They also preserve the same form. However, Boot's new theme is particularly successful because it manages to combine anal interest with absurdity.

Verbal duelling is also found among West Indians, where it is known variously as 'rhyming', 'making mock', 'giving rag' or 'giving fatigue'. It is well-documented in its original cultural context by Abrahams (1970c;

1972b); and the presence of West Indian settlers in the United Kingdom since the mid-1950s has given opportunities for study of the same range of phenomena in a British setting. It is interesting to see that the same tradition of verbal duelling has been maintained by many second- and even third-generation British children of Afro-Caribbean descent. For instance, the *Santley Lookout*, a magazine produced by children in a London primary school (V. Edwards 1979:50), includes the following ritual insult:

> Hush you mouth
> Why should I?
> Cos it's closing time
> But I ain't a shop, so!

> I said, shut you mouth
> Why should I?
> Cos you lip long like frog.
> You don't talk about you own lip do you?
> You mouth favour the dog.
> A dog can eat off a frog! So!
> But a frog can jump over a dog! So!
> Take a mash and don't come flash! Take the shame and don't complain!

In actual recorded sessions with the same children (Edwards 1982a), the fixed routine element is much less obvious, though there is a similar desire to transform and outdo the other participant's insult while preserving the surface form. These insults are by no means random. They call for quick wit and a high degree of verbal dexterity which can be seen in the following extract from an exchange between two ten-year-olds:

	Exchanges	*Commentary*
B:	Right, then, look pon you eye. You haven't got pupils in you eye. You can't see. Take the shame, don't complain!	Initial insult
A:	I got dirt in my eye. I got dirt ina my eye, bogey nose you. You clean out you nose . . .	Transformation of *eye* into *nose*
B:	You big nose. When you breathe the same nose . . .	Nose theme sustained
A:	You stretch neck large, you! When you breathe you nose come up big as a saucer	Nose theme sustained

B: You see any puff head, you got puff head . . .	Attempt to change theme
A: Just shave you teeth, shave you teeth	Successful change of theme
B: I can't shave my teeth man	Challenge of logic
A: Well cut them	Transformation of *shave* into *cut*
B: Me can't cut them	B claims victory of logic
A: You can	
B: If I cut them I have no teeth. Me have to go like this (noises). Take the shame, don't complain!	Concluding formula

With the concluding formula, 'Take the shame, don't complain', speaker B declares victory in the debate because his opponent has spoken illogically. As in Sunjata's debates with Sumanguru, or the busin' of Millicent and Joan, the winner is the one who shows the better control of words.

An audience is an essential part of duelling. The exchange of insults assumes the presence of friends and bystanders who can appreciate the skill of the duellers and even participate in the exchange. Thus members of the audience can often act as catalysts for competition with so-called signifying remarks like

'Are you going to let him say something like that about your moma?'

or

'He's talking about YOUR mother so bad
He's making ME mad'.

As the contest proceeds, the audience is actively involved, showing approval or disapproval for each exchange, and if one of the players is clearly outclassed, a member of the audience may step in to replace him.

Sometimes an individual rather than a group acts referee. Turisina's intervention in the verbal exchange at the banquet is one of many examples which point to the need for an impartial referee. This role is performed by the king not only in Germanic contexts, but also in Greece. For example, in the conflict between the Phaiakian and Odysseus it is Alkinoös, king of the Phaiakians, who intervenes and ensures that the two men do not come to blows as a result of their verbal exchange. Whether this role is performed by an individual or the audience as a whole, the presence of an arbitrator is yet another indication of the social controls imposed upon verbal abuse.

How Far Can You Go?

The Black British examples of ritual abuse come from pre-adolescents and, although they often contain the same preoccupation with the mother found in Afro-American duels, they fall short of being obscene. The same cannot be said for the duelling rhymes of adolescent Turkish boys. Like Afro-American exchanges, the imagery is real and explicit; even the seasoned student of abuse is left reeling. Challenge and reply are linked through content. Turkish adolescents, like their Afro-American and Black British counterparts, take up and develop the theme offered by their adversary. The goal is always to force your opponent into a passive role. There is also a formal requirement that the reply rhyme with the challenge. Opening sequences include:

A: *Ibne*. ('Passive homosexual')
B: *Sen ibneysen bana ne?* ('What is it to me if you are a passive homosexual?')
(Dundes et al. 1972:147)

Strategies may be both direct and indirect: insults may be focused on the adversary himself, or on his mother or sister. Effective Turkish duellers, like players of the dozens, are those with a large store of traditional retorts. The failure to reply in rhyme is likely to invite scathing comments from the other party. More serious still is the failure to reply at all, since this is felt to be an admission of the receptive role.

The main difference between the Afro-American and Afro-Caribbean traditions on the one hand, and the Turkish tradition on the other, lies in the Turkish preoccupation with homosexuality. This is by no means a unique focus for abuse. The distinction between active and passive homosexual roles in which scorn is thrown only on the passive role has been described, for instance, in the *albures*, or verbal duelling of rural Mexico (Ingham 1968).

There has been a great deal of discussion of the obscenity of adolescent verbal duelling and, in particular, the way in which it centres on the alleged sexual exploits of the opponent's mother and grandmother. Many insults are indeed obscene and the dueller searches for exchanges that will be considered as disgusting as possible. With long familiarity, however, the vividness of the images fades and it is possible to argue that they are far less powerful for the duellers than for an uninitiated audience.

Various explanations have been put forward to explain the obscenity associated with ritual invective. Dollard (1939), for example, has suggested that playing the dozens provides an outlet for Black people's anger and frustrations at their treatment by White people. This explanation, however, fails to take into account a wide range of similar behaviour in many other societies. The preoccupation with female members of the family is also a theme in Turkish boys' duelling rhymes and is a widespread feature of African ritual insult. Mayer (1951), for instance, reports 'Eat your mother's anus', 'Copulate with your mother', 'Look at your mother with three corns in her vagina' and 'It is your mother you abuse, not me' as typical West African Gusii invective. It seems, therefore, that we cannot explain Afro-American ritual invective simply as an outlet for displaced racial aggression (Levine 1977).

Abrahams (1962), in contrast, argues that this phenomenon is a male ritual which reflects the tensions caused by the allegedly matriarchal 'absent-father' household of many Afro-American families. In view of the evidence from studies in Africa, and indeed elsewhere, this explanation is, at least superficially, more attractive than the racial steam-valve argument. The obsession with insults to the mother and other female relatives has been noted, for instance, in many parts of the Middle East and South Asia (Dundes et al. 1972). Although these societies are by no means matrifocal, strict segregation of the sexes means that boys have relatively little contact with their fathers before puberty. The same observation could be made about family life in Turkey.

Family life in ancient Greek society offers a similar pattern. While interpretation of the evidence, which mostly comes from literary sources, remains controversial (Pomeroy 1975:58–60), it would appear that the Athenian family also suffered from the absent-male phenomenon (Slater 1968). The public life of the Greek male which kept the husband out of the home for much of the day, and strict segregation of the sexes at meals and elsewhere, meant that Greek boys, raised almost exclusively by their mothers, rarely had contact with an adult male or with women outside their immediate family until adolescence. Further, Greek marriages were arranged according to the financial needs of the family rather than the compatibility of the couple, and the typical union was between a male of thirty and a female of fifteen. Under such circumstances, many married males apparently viewed their wives merely as incubators and sought sexual satisfaction outside marriage. The evidence suggests that Greek males often visited prostitutes and even kept concubines, both practices which would entail great financial and emotional strain on the resources of the family.

As with Afro-Americans, obscenity appears to have been an important weapon of insult among the ancient Greeks. Although few examples have survived the vagaries of time and censorship, some indication of the Greek use of poetic obscenity can be obtained from Archilochos, who, admittedly, lived not in fifth-century Athens but in early seventh-century Paros. Sexual activity with a prostitute is the particular focus of his verbal abuse. One whore named Pasiphile ('Lover-of-All') is celebrated for her promiscuity with mild invective in this fragment:

> As the figtree on its rock feeds many crows,
> so this simple girl sleeps with strangers.
>   (Translated by Barnstone 1972:30)

Burnett (1983:79) argues that the prostitute herself, albeit the symbol of sexual excess, is not the only butt of Archilochean blame. It is possible that the poet is criticizing her clients even more than the girl. In this culture which values guest friendship highly, the rights and obligations of both host and guest are clearly defined. Neither should give or take too much. Therefore, while the girl's name ironically associates her with sexual hospitality towards strangers, her companions are compared metaphorically to gluttonous crows, that is, to bad guests. This abusive reference to sexual activity outside marriage can be seen to include an element of social criticism, a warning of the risks of excess on the part of both males and females. It may be that Archilochos' abusive language—like the language of the dozens, West African invective and Turkish boys' verbal duels—reflects the structure of family experience. Behaviour of this kind can perhaps be explained in terms of a larger set of rituals through which young men try to assert a masculine identity and independence from the female members of the family for the benefit of their peers.

However, this explanation of obscene insults must be qualified by several observations. While most of the accounts in the research literature on Afro-American verbal competition focus on young males, a closer examination of the sources suggests that young women also play the dozens with the same sort of verbal dexterity and sexual innuendo used by males. In *Die Nigger Die!*, for instance, H. 'Rap' Brown (1969) recalls that some of the best dozens players were girls; and in *Tomorrow's Tomorrow* Joyce Ladner (1972) writes about Kim, a charming and well-mannered ten-year-old, who was also a competent player of the dozens. Kochman (1972:244) describes the following skilled repartee between and Afro-American female and her male counterpart:

> A man coming from the bathroom forgot to zip his pants. An unescorted party of women kept watching him and laughing among themselves. The man's friends hip [inform] him to what's going on. He approaches one woman–'Hey baby, did you see that big black Cadillac with the full tires ready to roll in action just for you?' She answers–'No mother-fucker, but I saw a little gray Volkswagen with two flat tires.'
>   Everybody laughs. His rap was *capped* [excelled, topped].

When such material is combined with evidence of obscenity in certain *gali*, or wedding songs, sung by some North Indian women (Henry 1975), it is clear that those elaborate psychological theories discussed above and formulated to account for playing the dozens by Afro-American males have to be re-evaluated. While the Afro-American woman's use of sexual language to put her male interlocutor in his place may be seen to result from the women's liberation movement of the 1960s and 1970s, it is more likely that playing the dozens and related speech events have always been more than a male activity and that, as with the female Scottish story-tellers recorded by Goldstein (1964), insufficient attention has been given by fieldworkers to contexts in which women would engage in behaviour of this kind. From this point of view, playing the dozens is more than an assertion of a masculine identity; it is an opportunity for any individual to assert personal identity.

It is worth nothing, too, that figures other than the mother and the grandmother feature prominently in ritual insult. A closer look at invective in a wide range of societies, including those where the mother is a prominent butt of the abuse, also shows other figures on the receiving end. A common thread which runs through duelling activities is the licence to focus on the generational split and to impute that older members of the community are not beyond reproach. Such figures include fathers (as in the example with Boot and David above), brothers and preachers. Take the following quatrain from a rhyming session recorded in Nevis by Abrahams (1970c:231):

> I went up the lane
> I met the parson kissing Jane.

He gave me a shilling not to tell,
An' that's why me suit fit me so well.

Invective, obscene or otherwise, would thus appear to be directed at any member of the community who exercises a degree of social control over its members. The particular circumstances of a given group will undoubtedly influence the focus for ritual abuse. None the less, any attempt to interpret the precise significance of obscenity in a given context is fraught with difficulty.

The tension of seriousness and playfulness inherent in ritual abuse is further illustrated by the use of invective in religious contexts in ancient Greece. An essential element in the worship of Demeter and Dionysus was the public procession in which participants were subjected to abuse and ridicule by spectators (Fluck 1931). There was also a strong element of obscenity in Dionysian processions in which gigantic decorated phalloi were carried in honour of the god. So, too, did Roman soldiers shout licentious verses (called Fescennine verses) as they marched in triumph through the streets of Rome.

While surviving sources are insufficient to form a clear picture of the form and function of verbal abuse in these ceremonies, several observations can be made. First of all, the practice is divinely sanctioned. In the *Homeric Hymn to Demeter* (lines 200–4) the goddess herself was apparently subject to abuse when Iambe used jokes and jests in an attempt to bring a smile to the face of the grieving goodess. Such abuse serves to mark participants in these religious ceremonies as the focus of attention. It may also serve as a magical attempt to avert the evil eye: bad words are better than bad luck. So apotropaic phrases were whispered into the ears of victorious Roman generals as they rode triumphantly through the city. In its fullest contexts, then, verbal abuse can be viewed as a social balancing act, as a combination of jealousy and admiration for the powerful, in which violent words are used to prevent violent actions against the socially successful and prominent.

Wedding Invectives Past and Present

The abuse connected with Demeter and Dionysus is only indirectly documented in ancient Greece. The ritual use of insult in Greek *epithalamia*, or marriage songs, however, is easier to examine. The praise function of these songs has already been discussed. There are other aspects of this speech event, too, such as the humorous invective of the few fragments which survive from Sappho's *epithalamia*. In one she mocks the big feet of the door-keeper whose function in the Greek ceremony parallels the prominence of the modern best man.

> The doorkeeper's feet are fourteen
> yards long.
> Ten shoemakers used up
> five oxhides to cobble each sandal
> (Translated by Barnstone 1972:79)

This friend of the newly-weds may well have worn larger-than-average shoes, but the exaggeration of the passage transforms into ritual humour what, in other contexts, would be personal insult. Similarly another fragment alludes to the height of the bridegroom, perhaps with a tinge of sexual innuendo:

> Raise the ceiling and sing
> Hymen!
> Have carpenters raise the roof.
> Hymen!
> The groom who will come in
> is tall like towering Ares.
> (Translated by Barnstone 1972:78)

This passage is thus an ambiguous blend of praise and abuse in which height is both a sign of greatness and a cause of trouble.

Because of its geographical isolation, Cyprus has remained, in many ways, linguistically and culturally closer to ancient Greece than to the modern mainland (Papadaki d'Onofrio and Roussou 1990). It is especially on this remote island that the ancient custom of marriage invective still thrives in much the same way as it did in the time of Sappho. As a result, Cypriot songs provide valuable evidence for the continuing tradition of Greek marriage invective and the context of its performance. Adult male duellers come together in the wedding festivities to sing from their repertoire of rhymed insults. These Cypriot insults (Markou, personal communication) are learned over a period of time before the competition and there is little creativity during the actual performance. There is, however, considerable skill in finding a suitable couplet to lead on from the last and to go one better.

A: Oh let whoever has the ability come out and duel
    But he must take off his hat and salute me.
B: I will come out here under your orders
    To hear what you will say and see your dexterity.

A: Oh I fired two shots and my gun became empty.
　　Oh I asked for a madman and here he comes.
B: Oh you! What can you deduce from my looks?
　　You should go to the priest first and take Holy Communion.

Note how the other dueller picks up the reference to communion in his reply:

A: You take Holy Communion when you are about to die
　　Therefore I'll murder you [verbally].
B: You say that you can duel but I am doubtful
　　For I can't find your name on my list.
A: Oh I need seven dozen understudies like you
　　To clip you on the ears and make sparks fly.

The power of abuse is acknowledged in the next pair of couplets, in which speaker B first announces his intention to drive his opponent home through his verbal duelling, and speaker A counters with an affirmation of invulnerability to such attack.

B: Oh I will make you run back to the village.
　　Oh you will run so fast your heels will strike your bottom.
A: Oh I am a black rock which does not take wedges.
　　You strike me but no chips come off, only sparks.
B: I will put dynamite into the black rock.
　　It will become a nice plot and I will plant okra . . .

The firing of one verbal weapon is followed by another. The entertainment value of such exchanges is high; good singers attract large audiences and are thus the focus for considerable prestige. While the ancient Greek *epithalamia* were known to have been sung by multiple choirs, there is little evidence that these choirs exchanged verbal insults in the way that Greek Cypriots do today. However, in both Greek traditions, poetic exaggeration appears to be an essential feature, directed in the ancient tradition towards the wedding party but in the Cypriot context towards the other singer. The result in the Cypriot song is a series of boasts and attacks similar to the exchanges between Summanguru and Sunjata. Both the Manding and the Cypriot duellers speak metaphorically of their own invulnerability or of their ability to pierce that of their opponent.

Ritual insult is also practised at nuptial banquets in Galicia in Spain where the taunts are begun by individuals who have not been invited to the celebration. The people who have been snubbed in this way time their arrival to coincide with the end of the banquet, stand outside the house and petition in song for tobacco. Tolosana (1973:283) quotes the following example from the village of Zanfoga:

> May God in heaven be my witness
> My name is not Navarron,
> I request the bridegroom
> To give me a cigar.

This quatrain is a challenge directed towards the bridegroom and other male participants in the celebration. Refusal to provide the requested gift leads to a verbal duel in which each side improvises graceful retorts in order to ridicule the other. The wedding group can be accused of stinginess and the outsiders of discourtesy. The whole village may gather to witness the exchange which lasts until the outsiders are finally awarded tobacco. Both the song and the gift mark the wedding as a special event. Within the process of ritual abuse, both sides benefit: the wedding group gains the extra attention of the village while the other group is compensated for their exclusion by the gift of tobacco.

While ritual abusing is a male domain in modern Cyprus and Galicia, women are highly proficient ritual duellers in many other cultures. In *Sunjata* (S$_7$:87) there is reference to the custom that the bride's future sisters-in-law make fun of her on her wedding day. Among the Hakka-speaking refugee peoples of Hong Kong abuse-filled laments were still being sung at weddings in the 1970s. While not part of the formal marriage ceremony, these laments, a traditional expression of the bride's feelings and reservations about her impending marriage, contain abuse directed towards the groom, his mother, the marriage broker and even the bride's parents (Blake 1978:16–18). The following verse directs towards the match-maker scatological abuse stronger than anything Archilochos hurled at Neobule:

> My match-maker,
> You have such feeling;
> By the roadside lie dog feces,
> They are eaten all.
> My match-maker.
> You are so full of feeling;
> By the roadside lie dog feces,
> With which your teeth are cleaned.
> (Blake 1978:26)

Another example of this skill is the singing with which women accompany various aspects of the marriage rites throughout Northern India, and possibly other areas of the country. There is an ancient tradition of verbal duelling in song and rhyme which can be traced back to Sanskrit court poetry and on which wedding songs draw heavily (Huizinga 1949). Although known, passively at least, by the entire community, wedding invective is essentially a female domain. The women in certain families have a reputation for being good singers. Their skill is defined both in terms of their voices and the extent of their repertoires. An accomplished woman is likely to have daughters who follow in her footsteps. These good talkers fulfil the role of chorus leaders in weddings and less confident women will deliberately place themselves near the leaders. Most often tunes are either traditional or taken from popular films, so the words are the most important prop provided by the leader.

Sometimes Indian weddings are the scene for power struggles between two good singers. A British Gujarati (Edwards and Katbamna, 1989:164) comments on such a situation in this way: 'If there are two chorus leaders in the wedding they'll probably try to outdo each other. Sometimes one chorus leader starts and the other also starts, but the one who's got the louder voice carries on and the other one joins in. Then she'll probably lead the next one.' Nor are the social implications of choosing a leaders–both in terms of the prestige attached to this position and in the manipulation of relationships to one's own advantage–to be underestimated: 'Sometimes women are represented to further your interest. Someone might suggest a woman from your family as being very good at singing because they want to appear nice in your family for some reason. Maybe they've got a daughter to marry or something. There's a lot of politics that goes on.'

There are clearly many differences from one society to another, but fieldwork on Gujarati Hindu communities in Britain suggests that there are two main occasions for ritual invective, the *sanjina geet* or independent gatherings of the bride's and groom's parties on the evening before the wedding, and the *fatana* or songs of insult sung during the actual ceremony up to the critical part where bride and groom walk around the fire and are considered man and wife. The main function of the songs at the *sanjina geet* is to emphasize family identity–to draw in the various members, particularly those related by marriage, to heal any rifts in family relations and present a united front as the bride's *jan* (party) or the groom's *jan* ready for the actual wedding ceremony on the following day.

Many of the tensions generated by the wedding preparations find their expression in songs which make fun of both parties. A typical *sanjina geet* song for the groom's *jan* is the following (Edwards 1982b:32):

Place some roses in a vase,
Sprinkle kum-kum and print the invitations.
Send them to all four corners of the world,
Send the first invitation to Rajkot.

Next the singers insinuate that the bride's family are not well off because they do not even possess a bullock cart, a very basic form of transport:

'Lakshmiben, come early to our festivities,
Bringing all the young and old of your household with you'.
But Amarsi, son-in-law, is in want of a bullock cart
And here we are getting ready for Vinodbhai's wedding.

It could well be the case that this family actually owns a Mercedes and has no need of such a cart. It is all an exaggerated jest.

The invective becomes considerably keener in the *fatana*, when nothing is safe from the taunts of the singers as each side portrays the other as mean, weak, lowly, unsophisticated, stupid and unattractive. Typical insults include:

Bridegroom, why is your best man like this?
If you look at his nose you see a jewel.
If you look at his ears you see earrings.
If you look at his mouth he stammers.
If you look at his hands you see bangles
If you look at his feet you see sandals.
If you look at his legs he seems to be lame.

(Edwards 1982b:51)

These insults parallel in an uncanny fashion those found in the fragments of Sappho and leave little doubt that the description is based on exaggeration rather than fact. There are actually many clues as to the ritual nature of the abuse in wedding songs. Take, for instance, the following insult, offered by the groom's side and rebutted by the bride's side:

Sir, what have you done, what have you done,
What have you done? You have got an artifical pearl.
You brought up your daughter with so much love and affection,
Educated her and made her sophisticated, and then you gave her away to
a stupid man.

Sir, you have done well, you have done a
kindness, you have a real pearl.

You brought up your daughter with so much love and affection,
Educated her and made her sophisticated, and then you
gave her away to a clever, intelligent man.

(Edwards 1982b:46)

The fact that it is the groom's side which calls the groom 'a stupid man' shows that the abuse is all in jest. The parallel structure and themes of these two songs also reflect the polish and control which the singers must maintain over their songs, as stanzas are constructed around contrasts between the real and the artificial, the intelligent and the stupid.

It is not difficult to understand why invective should have developed in the ritual setting provided by marriage in various oral cultures. The tensions which surround weddings are strong. The social pressure on the girl to get married and on families to find suitable partners is considerable. Weddings provide many opportunities for displaying wealth and forging new links which enable a family to consolidate or improve their position in the social hierarchy. However, opportunities of this kind also bring with them great anxiety and worry. Either party could withdraw up to the last minute. Guests may be invited to the wedding but until the day arrives there is no way of knowing whether the occasion will be sufficiently important or well-managed to merit their presence. If key figures are missing or relatively few people arrive, the effect on the social standing of all concerned could be disastrous.

The bride, in particular, has very ambivalent feelings about her transition from a family where she has been loved and cherished to one where her status will be low and where she will meet with varying degrees of hostility. This ambivalence is particularly evident in Chinese wedding songs in which daughters hurl abuse at their mothers for treating them as disposable assets like vegetables or livestock. In the following verse, the prospective mother-in-law is described as the 'bitch' and her son as the 'runt':

People know how livestock are sold,
Everyone chooses the cow by its foot;
My mother has no way of choosing,
Much less knowing if the bitch is evil or not.
People know how livestock are sold,
Everyone chooses the cow by its low;
My mother has no way of choosing,
Much less knowing if the runt is naughty or not.
People know how livestock are sold,
There are several months to look them over;

My mother would sooner die,
Much less take a month to look over the new key to hear it jingle.

(Blake 1979:94)

Like other occasions when joking behaviour functions under strong disjunctive and conjunctive forces (Radcliffe-Brown 1952), weddings are a time of tension. On the one hand, it is very much in the interest of both parties to bring about the marriage successfully in order to fulfil religious obligations to their children and to enhance their own social standing; on the other hand there are many potential conflicts—expectations of the various parties are high and the failure to meet these expectations is likely to be interpreted as a slight. The teasing and taunting of wedding songs offsets the anxieties felt by both sides and thus acts as a very important release valve.

Ritual or Reality?

The critical difference between ritual abuse and blaming is the truth value of what is said. It is vital that any insults should be blatant exaggerations: abuse which has some basis in truth is likely to provoke retaliation. Thus, in Richard Wright's *Lawd Today* (1963:80), one character absurdly imagines that the grandmother of his listener overreacted to her lack of wiping material:

> I remembers when my little baby brother was watching with slobber in his mouth, your old grandma was out in the privy crying 'cause she couldn't find a corncob ...

As if any farm ever suffered a shortage of corncobs! While obscenity, scatology and sexual prowess are important themes in these exchanges, accusations must remain in the realms of the imagination. As Smitherman (1977:133–4) points out, 'The "insult" hurled must not represent and accurate statement of reality, or a battle ... will ensue'. This very widespread pattern of performance would certainly add weight to the argument that Archilochos, in his attacks upon the Lykambids, was like the modern player of the dozens, functioning in the realm of poetic exaggeration to demonstrate his verbal prowess to his audience.

In a similar vein, South Asian wedding singers are careful to ensure that insults contained in *fatana* are ritual, not real. Any song which contains a blatant element of truth in relation to the other party is likely to cause offence. For instance, songs which criticize the harsh treatment of the new bride by the senior daughter-in-law are likely to be avoided in the wedding of a second son. And where feeling is sufficiently strong over some aspect of the other side's behaviour, such as the standard of catering, the party on the receiving end is likely to react very strongly.

The course between ritual and real abuse is often a difficult one to steer. Bad judgement on the part of the performer has potentially dangerous consequences. This is illustrated very clearly in the case of the *regueifa* contests held in rural Galicia in Spain. Prizes of loaves made of flour, eggs and sugar are given to the winners of verbal duels which are held on several occasions including house-building and weddings. These duels are often based on formal reply in verse, beginning with the last word of the challenger's quatrain. In one instance, a *regueifa* singer points to someone in the audience who held the position of *paritixeiro*, or overseer of the division of inherited lands and goods, and sings:

> This man apportions a lot of land
> The world is wont to say
> Through many of his deceits
> The man manages to live.
> (Tolosana 1973:286)

While the playfulness of this abuse is underscored by competitive and ritual context, there is always the danger that such verbal blows will turn physical. Tolosana (1973:283) describes in the following terms the *brindis* ('toasts') and *loias* ('quatrains') sung during Galician carretos, or the house-building event in which all neighbours share: 'Usually what started in the morning as a manifestation of neighborly solidarity becomes a ceremonial gathering of neighbors in the evening and ends at dawn with deep resentment among several of them; even personal physical aggression between some of the participants is not unlikely.' Yet within each of these invective types exists a tension between truth and exaggeration, between reality and poetry, between praise and abuse which ensures the proper use of words within oral culture. At one end of the spectrum is the truth-based abuse of the Galician singer and at the other is the playful exaggeration of the player of the dozens. Binding the two together is a spirit of playfulness, a temporary dismissal of seriousness which negates the danger inherent in the use of the spoken word as a weapon.

Ritual invective can take a number of different forms. It can be performed by an individual as in the biting poetry of Archilochos; or it can take the form of a contest either between two parties, as in the case of the Afro-American dozens, or between two choruses as in the weddings of present-day South Asia. Although at first sight the obscene abuse of adolescents may have little in common with the more elegant wedding invective, several common threads run through both kinds of performance. Smitherman's (1977:131) description of the Afro-American dozens as 'a competitive oral test of linguistic ingenuity and verbal fluency' applies as much to the wedding songs of Greek Cypriot men and South Asian women as it does to adolescent exchanges on street corners. Ritual invective in both settings is a source of real entertainment, a role which deserves due recognition. It also provides valuable opportunities for the training of the oral artist.

Ritual invective, like other forms of oral referring, sets out the values and expectations of society. Performers are given licence to focus on those qualities and behaviours which are considered socially undesirable. By looking closely at the insults which are offered it is possible to build up a very clear picture of community ideals. Sometimes invective is the province of 'sweet talkers' who embody the qualities most highly valued by the community: the language and comportment of Greek Cypriot verbal duellers or Gujarati women, for instance, is beyond reproach. On other occasions licence is given to 'broad talkers' to use obscene language and to pillory the authority figures around whom the community revolves. Yet in neither case does the skilled performer of abuse threaten the existing social order. By focusing on the important structures and personalities, the oral artist relieves the tensions from outside and within society.

7

Drawing Together the Web

The tunes that we sing
The uninitiated ones cannot understand them.
from *The Mwindo Epic* (Biebuyck and Mateene 1969:71)

So far in this part of the book we have shown how oral performance often creates a web of praising, blaming, boasting and abusing into which members of the oral community are drawn. This is a web uniting the good talker, the audience and the community at large by what may be called the referential aspect of orality. At first sight, these various kinds of performance may appear very different; yet they all draw specific members of the community into the performance by some form of direct address or personal reference. The oral artist singing the praises of the bride and groom in ancient Greece or the present day West Indies; the Akan *apae* singer reproaching his leader for inaction; the Trinidadian calypso singer or the epic hero challenging opponents with a boast; the Afro-American or the Turkish adolescent hurling verbal abuse at an adversary–in all these cases we are dealing with a referential structure which binds members of the oral community into the performance and creates a dialogue.

In this chapter we draw together the common threads which run through the various forms of oral referring. These points of similarity are both linguistic and functional. On the one hand, the language and context of oral referring set it apart from everyday speech. Good talkers are thus insulated from the very real dangers which follow in the wake of performances where the subject may not be flattered by the nature of the reference. On the other hand, personal allusions and direct address make for a conversational tone which binds together performer and audience into a single referential whole. The whole thrust of oral referring is thus to maintain the social equilibrium under extraordinary circumstances.

Playing with Fire

One of the threads which runs throughout oral referring is the potential for violence which surrounds the performance. The performer who oversteps the boundaries and unjustly blames a good person is likely to provoke an angry response. Thus Odysseus hurls scorn on the Phaiakian who questions his athletic prowess; and Dagda replies to the threats of the Irish blame poet, Cridenbel, by poisoning his food. Similarly the boaster who makes claims that clearly cannot be supported will be the subject either of humour, as in the case of the Afro-American rapper who wants to deflect the aggression of an adversary, or of contempt, as in the case of Sumanguru who was forced to retract his claims of physical superiority over Sunjata.

When the insult comes a little too close for comfort, ritual performance can easily spill over into unpleasantness and even violence. South Asian women, for instance, avoid making reference to the poor treatment meted out to junior daughters-in-law in the marriages of second sons for fear of causing offence. Galician *regueifa* singers, who exercise less prudence, can find themselves confronted with a physical response, suggesting a similar potential in every performance.

The whole thrust of oral referring is thus necessarily directed at preserving the social equilibrium and defusing potentially explosive situations. The three levels of structure—textual, contextual and social—outlined by Bauman (1975) provide a useful framework for this discussion. While originally intended to be applied to a wide variety of performances, the vital role which they serve in setting performance apart from everyday speech becomes especially important in the context of oral referring.

Three Levels of Referring

In 'Thinking On Your Feet' we looked at the recurring textual features of oral performance, including the use of rhyme, tempo and pitch; archaisms; and formulaic language. Each of these features marks the performance as an extraordinary event, one which functions outside the realm of everyday communication and social intercourse. The special language which a performer uses informs the audience that the normal rules are temporarily set aside and the group can operate under a different set of guidelines.

Thus the ancient Greeks generally restricted blaming to a special iambic meter and expected blamers to use archaic and poetic rather than everyday vocabulary; and the West Indian 'buser' makes use of the indigenous Creole, associated with familiarity, rather than more standard English speech which would have a distancing effect. Similarly, boasting and invective occur within a formal rhyming or thematic structure: boasts are delivered in rhyme by the Trinidadian calypso singer; the Galician *regueifa* singer follows a very strict poetic form which requires direct response to the words of an opponent; and Greek, Black and South Asian invective all operate under similar rules restricting the performance to fabricated rather than accurate abusive material in which metaphors, exaggerations and, sometimes, obscenities combine to set a particular speech event apart from normal communication. As long as performers stay within these textual limitations, there is no danger of offence or physical response, since both performers and audience know that reality has been temporarily suspended.

Just as referring is carefully marked by its textual structure, so, too, is performance restricted by what Bauman calls 'event structure', but which we prefer to call 'contextual structure'. This contextual structure affects two main aspects of performance. The first relates to the fact that oral referring takes place only on special occasions which, like the textual features of oral referring, helps to create a special communicative frame. The second concerns the question of the oral artists' skill. Not everyone has the verbal wit required for oral referring and the audience has a keen appreciation of what constitutes good and bad practice in this area.

Thus blaming and abusing, and even praising and boasting, occur in oral cultures only under specifically defined social circumstances. Greek blame poetry, for instance, is performed at symposia, weddings and religious festivals. West Indian busin' takes place in the presence of neighbours and relative who are able to evaluate the validity of each party's claims and counterclaims. Whether in the ritual context of heroic confrontation or in the playful activities of Trinidadian Midnight Robbers, boasting, too, requires a critical audience to achieve the desired effect. Even Galician invective occurs on specific, extraordinary social occasions, such as weddings and house-building ceremonies. The same insults spoken in other contexts might produce quite different results.

The referential performance, in particular, cannot succeed without an audience psychologically prepared for such an event. Not only are members of the audience vulnerable themselves to potential references in these performances, but they are also expected in some oral cultures to become active participants. Thus in the Galician *regueifa* and Afro-American sounding, the audience not only accompany the performance with verbal and physical reactions such as shouts, laughter, applause and catcalls, but also often serve as referee or even judge of the performers. Similarly, in ancient Greece spectators at processions in honour of Demeter were encouraged to shout abuse at participants.

The second important contextual restriction for referential events is the skill of the performer. Incompetent performers are often rapidly replaced by others who feel they can do better; thus, not every Black youth would dare to play the dozens and players choose their opponents carefully. In many cultures and contexts, a similar fate awaits boasters who are unable to fulfil their claims. Questions of skill play an important part not only in establishing the status of the oral artist in the community but also in political manoeuvres. The choice of a particular woman as a chorus leader in Asian weddings, for instance, may be overlaid both with considerations of prestige and with the desire to manipulate social relationships to one's own advantage. If one family wishes to make a good impression on another, they may choose to put forward the name of a good singer from the other family rather than their own.

Bauman's third level of performance structure, dealing with the social organization of the event, emphasizes especially the 'emergent' nature of the performance in which the social relationship between the performer(s) and the audience is determined. One aspect of this structure affects the performer, who, as noted above, is either praised as a good talker or blamed as a bad one. The audience's opinion can ultimately emerge, however, only during the performance.

Another, more basic, emergent aspect of referring affects the community at large and concerns the social function of the performance. Indeed, the audience's judgement of the singer is based, to a large extent, on how well the oral artist performs these social functions. Although the precise form of referring activities changes in varying degree from one community to the next, the many points of similarity in function are far more striking than the differences in form. The entertainment of the audience; the development of the verbal skills of oral artists; the enacting, on the one hand, of the social values of the group and, on the other hand, of anti-community feelings–these are the functions which are observed time and again in oral referring in many different oral cultures.

The first and foremost function of such events, however, is to entertain. Praise, blame, boasting and abuse take place with an audience keen to evaluate performance and to enjoy their skills. Performance is dependent on interaction between oral artists and their audience: an enthusiastic response encourages the performer to continue and embellish; derision or lack of interest leads to a rapid conclusion or the replacement of one performer by another.

Very often oral referring is couched within a competitive framework. Beidelman (1989), for example, has shown agonistic, i.e. competitive exchange to be the chief way by which an individual is defined in the society of Homeric Greece. Such a contest can heighten the entertainment value of oral referring. But it can also play a vital role in providing a training ground and model for the development of verbal facility in societies where the spoken word plays a very important role. Oral artists put their skills to the test in the presence of an audience: they are able to learn valuable lessons when they find themselves pitted against more polished performers and to gain in confidence when they outclass a performer less experienced than themselves. This observation quite clearly applies as much to ceremonial duelling in India or Cyprus or ancient Greece as it does to adolescent duelling on street corners. In all situations expert duellers enjoy considerable prestige and are valued members, in some cases, of their peer group and, in other cases, of the wider community.

A very different use for invective has been proposed in the context of marriage ceremonies. From this point of view the newly-weds are in an unusual and dangerous position of social prominence. Society reacts to the vulnerability of these individuals by ridiculing them with violent words in order to avert more serious consequences, such as violent action. This abuse is found in other religious contexts; we have already described how it was hurled at initiates in the worship of Demeter in ancient Greece. But oral referring is by no means restricted to religion: the blaming of kings in the Akan apae may serve a similar purpose. Socially condoned negative reference to the successful may avert physical reaction on the part of other, less successful members of the community, acting out as it does agreed community values.

Oral referring lays out very clearly the agreed social order for any given community. The Afro-American preacher alternately praises and blames his congregation as he shows them the kinds of behaviour which will lead them to salvation; the Akan apae singer attempts to modify the unreasonable behaviour of his leader; Hektor berates his cowardly brother for his unwillingness to fight Menelaos; South Asian women pillory stinginess, weakness and effeminacy. In any community there is a recognized order. This order has a deeply felt sense of logic about it, no doubt because it provides both comfort and control to those who share the same world view. None the less, everyone at some time feels tensions and contradictions, from both outside and inside the system. One way of handling this shared tension is to get together and ceremonially re-enact or recite in its most basic terms the conditions and the genesis of the world's order. Another way is to provide licence to members of the community to impose a new sense of order on the world, an order which is so different from that of the everyday that it produces laughter.

Sounds Familiar?

In our earlier treatment of the audience, we showed how interaction of performer and audience create an organic whole. The essentially intimate process of referring which draws other members of the community into the oral event is an important thread in this process. The performance is ultimately an open conversation shared by the entire community.

Most frequently the subject of the reference is a member of the audience. A dialogue – sometimes explicit, sometimes implicit – is created between the performer and those present. It is interesting in this respect to note that prayer, a very early form of ritual communication, is intrinsically referential, with direct address to the deity by name. Thus the basic Christian prayer begins with the vocative phrase, 'Our Father who art in Heaven' and is filled with second person addresses or imperatives to the deity, such as 'lead us not into temptation'. The same conversational style underlies oral referring performances of all kinds. Thus, Greek and African praise singers usually address their subject by name and in the second person, and South Asian wedding songs allow the singers to insert the names of the bride, the bridegroom and members of their families.

On other occasions reference is less specific. Attention is directed at particular individuals because of the role which they are performing. A West Indian wedding toast, for instance, may be addressed not to a named couple but to 'Mr and Mrs Bride'. Similarly, speechmakers at tea meetings will begin with an address to 'Mr Chairman, fellow citizens, ladies and gentlemen, including the ceremonial judges. Admitting Mr President and the Choir'. However, as we have seen, the subject of the performance is not necessarily present. For instance, the President of Mali does not have to be present for a West African griot to sing of his achievements. Nor was the victorious athlete celebrated in Pindar's victory ode always present at every performance. The reference can even cross the boundaries of the living and the dead, especially in laments where the deceased is often addressed as a living and hearing member of the audience.

The act of referring is thus not restricted by temporal and spatial boundaries. Any member of the oral community, present or absent, living or dead, can become the subject of the performer's reference, which becomes an important unifying force within the community. There is therefore a tension between the more formal aspects of referring, in which the normal rules of interaction are suspended, and the strangely intimate atmosphere which is created in these same performances. Audience involvement is evident even in the Homeric epics, where the personae of the singer and his audience emerge from the linguistic barrier of the third person narrative on at least some occasions. In addition to various invocations, in which the Muse, the goddess of poetry, is addressed in prayer in the second person, Homer occasionally speaks directly to a character in the narrative, as he does while describing Menelaos' miraculous escape from death at Troy in *Iliad* IV:127–9:

> Still the blessed gods immortal did not forget you,
> Menelaos, and first among them Zeus' daughter, the spoiler,
> who standing in front of you fended aside the tearing arrow.

A second-person verb creates a similar conversational tone at *Iliad* IV:223–5, where the poet speaks directly to his audience:

> Then you would not have seen brilliant Agamemnon asleep nor
> skulking aside, not in any way a reluctant fighter,
> but driving eagerly toward the fighting where men win glory.

These Homeric addresses spread the referential web even wider. Divinity and mythical hero, performer and audience, are all part of the oral community in its fullest sense.

These common threads which run through oral referring often form no part of the experience of literate observers, or else are used in ways very different from their use in the oral community. We are therefore dealing with a potential minefield of cross-cultural misunderstanding which we will explore in greater detail in chapter 10. Those who live in small-scale communities depend to a very large extent on the good will and cooperation of those around them. Social relations need to be mediated in a very direct and sometimes confrontational way. In contrast, in societies where the written word plays a more important role, it is possible to achieve a far greater social distance and to live without direct dependence on immediate neighbours. The kind of personal allusion which runs through oral referring inevitably makes for a certain discomfort in observers who often go to great lengths to avoid unwanted 'interference' from those outside the immediate family.

Oral referring holds still further potential for misunderstanding because it is so closely intertwined with the social values of the community: without a knowledge of those values, it is very difficult to appreciate the power of oral reference or the part which it plays in the life of a given society. South Asian wedding songs, for instance, are permeated with the importance of strength, courage and dominance for males and of grace, gentleness and submission for women. Afro-American invective is replete with the values of the counter-culture: cunning, ruthless-ness and worldly wisdom.

It is very easy for literate observers to misunderstand performances of oral referring: praise can be interpreted as obsequious; blame as ill-considered; self-deprecation as an indication of a poor self-image; and abuse as outrageous. Such a construction of reality, however, fails to take into account the social values of the communities in question and underestimates the considerable power of personal reference to in-fluence and change behaviour. Words are weapons and are recognized as such.

Preserving the Social Equilibrium

Yankah's (1983:382–3) redefinition of praise poetry as referential poetry is not enough, for the referential nature of oral performance extends well beyond the boundaries of what is usually called praise poetry. Its conversational tone draws together oral artist, audience and subject into a referential web uniting all members of the community both living and dead, present and absent.

Inevitably, personal reference carries with it the risk of retaliation. The structure of the text in oral referring and the special circumstances under which it takes place create an expectation in the audience that the rules for normal social interaction will be suspended. Oral artists focus attention on the social values which are important for a commun-ity and evaluate the ways in which individuals achieve or fall short of society's standards in both real and imagined ways. In a true-life situation, they would be exposing themselves to the risk of physical retaliation. Only the carefully constructed performative context insu-lates them from this very real risk.

Oral referring needs to be discussed within this social context. Observers whose life is mediated by the written word are able to maintain a far greater distance from those around them and sometimes balk at the direct confrontation which marks most performances of oral referring. In doing so, they demonstrate an insensitivity to the social roles performed by the various referential performances and seriously underestimate the power of spoken words.

Part III

The Tapestry of Words

But Themistocles made answer that the speech of man was like embroidered tapestries, since like them this too had to be extended in order to display its patterns, but when it was rolled up it concealed and distorted them.

Plutarch's *Life of Themistocles* XXIX:3
(translated by Perrin 1914:79)

So far in our stepping into the oral world we have observed the special characteristics of performer and audience. We have also examined the social forces which create a web of words into which all members of the oral community are drawn. In this portion of the book we consider several other important verbal threads woven into the fibre of the performance and into the cultural heritage of the community.

In 'Spinning the Threads', we look at the various strategies– elaboration, repetition, exaggeration and metaphor–which are part of the shared expectations of oral communities and which run through performances of many kinds. These elements, essential to the aesthetic of oral culture, are often evaluated very differently by literate observers.

'The Web That Binds' provides a cross-cultural survey of the contexts and functions of oral performance and shows how a wide range of speech events, from riddles and proverbs to 'Them and Us' tales and 'Then and Now' tales, help to create social cohesion by reinforcing the shared values of the oral community. In particular, we look at multigeneity in oral performance. Speech events as diverse as the Homeric epics, the Afro-American toast and the traditional Black sermon can all be shown to be highly complex constructions in which narrative, dialogue and description form part of an integral whole, and in which metaphor and boasts are as much a part of the tapestry of words as proverbs and riddles, or genealogies and folk etymologies.

8

Spinning the Threads

CHILD 1: *Knock, knock.*
CHILD 2: *Who's there?*
CHILD 1: *Banana.*
CHILD 2: *Banana Who?*
CHILD 1: *Knock, knock.*
CHILD 2: *Who's there?*
CHILD 1: *Banana.*
CHILD 2: *Banana Who?*
CHILD 1: *Knock, knock.*
CHILD 2: *Who's there?*
CHILD 1: *Orange.*
CHILD 2: *Orange Who?*
CHILD 1: *Orange you glad I didn't say banana?*

(a child's joke)

The repetition inherent in this 'Knock-knock' joke is not peculiar to children. Rosenberg (1970a and 1975) has shown how such repetition is also a basic tool of the Asian *akyn*, the Yugoslav guslar and the American folk preacher. This device can affect the performance in three distinct ways: agonistically, as a means of building a crescendo of involvement; retrospectively, as a means of helping everyone remember what has been said; and prospectively, as a kind of pause which gives performers time to think ahead to what comes next. In chapter 2 we concentrated on the prospective use of repetition and other techniques which help the process of composition in performance. In this chapter we take things one step further by looking at some of the building blocks of performance from other perspectives. The various techniques which we explore–verbal elaboration, digression, repetition, refrains, cata-logues, lists, metaphor and exaggeration–are all important elements in the armoury of the good talker. But such techniques also function retrospectively and agonistically. The oral artist's ability to draw on familiar resources such as these assists the audience's ability to under-stand the performance in real time. In addition, shared knowledge of these techniques establishes a feeling of solidarity between speaker and audience, and draws them together as one organic whole. As such, these threads which run throughout performance become part of the aesthetic of oral culture.

The end product of oral composition often departs dramatically from literate expectations. Once again we must put aside some literary pre-conceptions about structure and adjust our aesthetic values. The radical difference between literate and oral perceptions of structural unity can be illustrated by comparing the sonnet with the sermon of a Black preacher. While in the sonnet every word and every line fit a tightly knit, economic form, in the sermon cohesion is based upon a looser, more expansive structure, which fits Ong's definition of oral language (1982:37–41) as 'redundant or copious', 'aggregative rather than analy-tic', and 'additive rather than subordinate'. In the sonnet nothing can be redundant or aggregate. In the sermon and other kinds of oral art, repeatable forms like formulae, proverbs and riddles form an essential part of the communal basket of threads from which the oral perform-ance is woven. Thus the structural unity of the written word is analytic and creates unity by trimming the excess and irrelevant, while in the oral world structural unity is essentially synthetic, a constant elaboration of elements added to the fibre of the web of words.

Evaluation of oral narrative has long been affected by literate mis-understanding of oral performance. From the literate perspective, the typical oral narrative is considered to have a simple structure because it pits together in a single scene only two characters, a good one and a bad one (Olrik 1919). Yet such a narrative is not simple when seen in the context of the repetitious language and recurring character conflicts in which the narrative takes place. Not only *can* you 'say that again' in oral narrative, you *must* say that again.

Verbal Elaboration

The many scrupulously detailed descriptive passages found in oral performances are certainly not part of a 'simple' structure. Such elabo-rate descriptions are often used for objects of great significance, includ-ing Achilleus' shield in *Iliad* XVIII or Odysseus' scar in *Odyssey* XIX, or Jibirila's special arrow, which receives the following notice in *Sunjata*:

> But great Jibirila had an arrow,
> And if he took that arrow like this and put it into his hand like this,
> He did not even put it in the bow and pull the bow and fire it;
> He just said to it, 'Go!',
> And on its way it would kill seven men,

And on its return it would kill seven more,
Then it would come and lie down in the quiver;
His hand never touched it, all being done by supernatural power.

$(S_3:709-16)$

In all three cases the descriptions significantly interrupt the narrative flow of the performance. The description of Achilleus' shield draws on a series of vignettes from Greek daily life based upon scenes decorating the shield. The descriptions of Odysseus' scar and Jibirila's arrow include stories-within-the-story, narratives explaining the origin of the scar and the special powers of the arrow.

Afro-American toasts are also noted for descriptive passages. Typically, toasts have an exciting introduction, packed with picturesque detail which sets the scene. For example, Abrahams' (1962:9–10) version of the 'Monkey and the Baboon' begins with this description:

Deep down in the jungles, way back in the sticks,
The animals had formed a game called 'pool'. The baboon was a slick.
Now a few stalks shook and a few leaves fell.
Up popped the monkey one day, 'bout sharp as hell.
He had a one-button roll, two-button satch.
You know, one them boolhipper coats with a belt in the back.
The baboon stood with a crazy rim,
Charcoal grey vine, and stingy brim,
Hand full of dimes, pocket full of herbs,
Eldorado Cadillac parked at the curb.

Such elaboration is also found in sermons. For example, a sermon given by an American preacher in 1967, outlined here by Rosenberg (1975:79), includes a description of King David of Israel:

LINES	SUBJECT
1–3	Scripture
4–22	Digression on preaching
23–35	Digr. on self and fishing
36–44	Digr. on liars
45–48	David's experience
49–60	Digr. on St. Paul
61–67	Description of David
68–81	*David's anointing*
82–107	*Fight with Goliath*
108–140	*David's flight to cave*
141–161	David as shepherd
162–218	*David saves lamb*
	(and recitation of Psalm)
219–260	Digr. on selfishness
278–330	Four Horsemen

The description of David expands the sermon in the same way that the description of Achilleus' shield expands the *Iliad* or the description of the monkey and the baboon expands the toast. But the structure of the sermon is also elaborated in another way, through the addition of digressions. Rosenberg describes several sections of the sermon as 'digressions', apparently because their personal commentary does not fit the general theme of a sermon about David. Yet for the preacher and the congregation these sections are not digressions at all but an integral part of the performance. Commentaries interspersed in this way have the effect of personalizing the discourse for speaker and listeners alike.

Digression is also an important feature of epics in ancient Greece and in West Africa. The entire tenth book of the *Iliad*, sometimes called the 'Doloneia', relates a Greek incursion into the Trojan camp which has little to do with the main plot of the epic. While it has sometimes been suggested that the 'complexity' of the Homeric epics is the result of literate input into the oral form (Lesky 1966:38), even a more traditional epic such as *Sunjata* cannot be characterized as simple. Literate bias against oral structure is, in fact, notable in Innes' versions of *Sunjata*, which are preceded by plot summaries containing no reference to the many and lengthy non-narrative sections of the epic. Digression is particularly conspicuous in the last portion of Bamba Suso's version of *Sunjata*, where historical events unconnected with the story of the hero are related. While this 'digression' consumes more than a third of the entire performance, its subject matter is not included in Innes' plot summary (1974:37).

Innes' incomplete summaries of *Sunjata* are, unfortunately, not unique. Any analysis of an oral performance based only on plot summaries would suggest a simpler structure than is found in the actual performance. Part of the difficulty is that most extant narratives are literary paraphrases of oral performances in which digressions and other 'irrelevant' elaborations are omitted by the editors.

As soon as we move away from literate attempts to reduce performance to a series of lifeless plot summaries and consider speech events in their performative and cultural contexts, the overwhelming body of evidence points in the direction of the structural complexity and sophistication which can be noted in Scheub's (1977:69) description of the story-telling performance of the Xhosa oral artist, Nongenile Musithathu Zanani:

> Performing an average of six or seven hours each day, this great performer produced a unified narrative that ultimately totalled a staggering one hundred hours, a narrative that imaginatively incorporates Xhosa origins, with such ethnographic data as fully detailed marriages, circumcision

ceremonies, and women's purification rituals, but with imaginative narratives forming the basis of the performance. She introduced images from the ancient art tradition, exploring three generations of characters, each with a woman at the center, developing their activities against a single traditional narrative which she boldly and competently opened, so that a large number of other Xhosa narratives and narrative segments could be worked in and locked to the basic core of images. The performance was never allowed to become a mere series of loosely connected stories.

But sermons and epics are lengthy and elaborate speech events, complex in range and structure. What about more economical and pithy oral forms like proverbs? Even these oral events are not linguistically 'simple'. Proverbs make use of poetic devices such as balanced phrasing, rhythm, rhyme, metaphor and assonance which create a sophisticated combination of wit, wisdom and dramatic effect. Thus, the proverb 'Beauty is in the eye of the beholder' is only superficially simple in structure. Behind the wit and assonance of this proverb lies an elaborate web of related phrases like 'Beauty is only skin-deep' and 'Pretty is as pretty does' which imply multiple standards of beauty inseparable from the proverb's tradition. Indeed, the literate observer of this proverb or of any oral performance must remember that 'Complexity is in the eye of the beholder' and that we, as literate observers of the oral art, must remain aware of the difference between literate and oral conceptions of structural unity. Otherwise we may see only disjointed or unfinished aspects of an oral performance, where the orally wise listener recognizes a familiar and coherent verbal pattern. Any analysis of the structural pieces of an oral performance, including this one, creates a distortion of cultural reality by taking apart the threads which are meant to be woven together. When the literate tool of analysis is applied to an oral context, a disequilibrium is created between the medium and the message.

Repetition in Oral Performance

Another basic structure of oral performance is repetition. While the literate author repeats specific words and phrases only for a limited and designed effect, various forms of repetition are part of the essential armoury of the oral artist. We have already considered several forms of repetition woven again and again into oral performance: these include the formulaic repetitions discussed in the chapter on 'Thinking on Your Feet' as well as other verbal threads of referring, such as direct address in the form of vocatives, imperatives and second-person references, which we discussed in 'Drawing Together the Web'. But oral performance uses repetition in other contexts as well; in the case of proverbs, which must be repeatable in order to be successful, the entire proverb is repeated. To say 'Beauty is superficial' instead of 'Beauty is skin-deep' destroys the proverb, even if the meaning of the two expressions is the same.

Other patterns of repetition have been observed by Rosenberg (1975:82) in the speech of American folk preachers, where certain words and phrases recur throughout the performance. In a sermon entitled 'God is Mindful of Man' Rev. Brown of Bakersfield, California, said:

> I want to say to the deacon board
>   I want you to be mindful
> I want you to be mindful how you serve as a deacon
> Because the Lord doesn't have to use you
> I want to say to you brother preachers be careful how you preach
> Because the Lord didn't have to have you to preach.

Similar repetition of key phrases can be seen in other oral cultures, such as a singer of *Sunjata* who says that

> Sunjata became master of both countries.
> He did not have any enemies,
> He did not have any rivals.
>   (S$_1$:914–6)

The use of repetition thus serves as a kind of pause which gives the performer, who is thinking on his feet, time to look ahead to the next thought. It also helps the audience to remember what has just been said.

Yet the need for a pause does not entirely account for the prevalence of repetition in oral performance. Smitherman (1977:137–45), for example, notes the use of repetition as an important feature in the talk-singing of Afro-Americans, such as the following lyrics from 'Mighty Love' sung by the Spinners:

> Just giiiiiiiiiiiive me yo looooooooove ... [cadenced 'preaching']
> miiiiiiiiighty, miiiiiiiiighty, miiiiiiighty, miiiiiiiiighty, miiiiiighty, miiiiiighty,
> miiiighty, miiiighty, hear what I say, saaaaaaaay, now, now, now, now,
> baby ...

Smitherman's observations suggest that repetition in oral performance is not just a stall tactic, but a basic aesthetic value which could be compared to the stylized and repeated patterns of waves and spirals often used in weaving or on a geometric Greek vase (see plate 2). That is, oral language, by its very nature, is redundant. When Helen of Troy, describing the Greeks to the Trojans from the walls of the city, says

> . . . And I see them
> all now, all the rest of the glancing-eyed Achaians,
> all whom I would know well by sight, whose names I could tell you . . .
>
> (*Iliad* III:233–5)

her repetitious language reflects an essentially oral form of speech in performance. Repetition provides both performer and audience with a basic and familiar pattern for the web of words.

A specific form of repetition is the refrain, a phrase or stanza repeated at intervals during a performance. The narrator's task is to make a skilful choice of images and of refrains which reinforce those images. Such refrains allow those present to focus on what has been happening in the story and also to provide a commentary on events. The use of repetition, and particularly repetition in the form of a song, serves to heighten emotions and to make a powerful impact on the audience. West African singers, for example, often use refrains in the form of specific tunes and lyrics associated with a character or a theme. The following refrain, which has its own melody and is one of the most popular tunes associated with the hero, is used to commemorate the great deeds of Sunjata:

> Thatching grass, thatching grass, thatching grass,
> Other things go underneath thatching grass,
> Thatching grass does not go underneath anything.
>
> (S$_2$:1360–2)

Another common refrain in *Sunjata* is based upon a theme of lamentation:

> Don't you know that death spares no one at all,
> Don't you know that Makhang Sunjata is cold;
> Their day is past.
>
> (S$_2$:1129–31)

The power and versatility of the refrain emerges very clearly in the story-telling performances of the Mende people of Sierra Leone, whose narrative is punctuated by songs in which a chorus responds to the lead of the soloist. Such choruses are often marked by internal repetition, repetition of initial words in end positions and the repetition of intital and ultimate words in medial position. Such a choral structure has the effect of creating a stable backdrop against which the soloist can perform.

Plate 8   *Story-telling in Sierra Leone. The performer, Lεlε Gbomba, is supported by a chorus. Photograph: Rebecca Busselle.*

Cosentino (1982:104–5) illustrates the centrality of such refrains in a story called 'The Krio and the Cat' which centres on a woman's logical but over-zealous response when she decides to eat the cat who has swallowed the food she has been preparing. The oral narrative is interspersed with song in the form of solos and choral refrains which play a vital role in the story-telling process. The interaction between the soloists and the chorus is notable both for its complexity and the evident enjoyment which it generates. The main narrator, Macarthy, assumes the persona of the Krio woman; the audience plays the role of the mocking crowd of onlookers.

In the performance witnessed by Cosentino, this call–response is repeated six times before Macarthy once more sings the main song line as a signal that the next chorus should be the final one. Just then, James Vandei, who owns the compound where the performance is taking place, returns from an errand. Reluctant to hear a song which he obviously enjoys come to a close, Vandei pushes the chorus into yet another repetition with his own musical intervention:

He then takes over the role of narrator asking, 'If you had dried that meat very, very well and set it next to the fire, and then if a cat ate it, wouldn't you eat the cat?' This question spurs Macarthy on to start the song again and the chorus to respond with its refrain. At this point Vandei provides a short summary of the story as a prelude to yet another round. The call–response between soloists and chorus is repeated many more times before Macarthy brings the story to an end with a spoken epilogue.

Several aspects of this use of the refrain deserve comment. Call–response of this kind depends on enjoyment of the storyline and a shared knowledge which bind the group together. The refrain also serves a dramatic function as the chorus assume the role of the onlookers. It serves as a platform for a display of considerable virtuosity. Vandei demonstrates an ability to spur on the chorus and the main solo performer; he also shows outstanding musical talent. At one point, for instance, he helps create a choral fugue by starting a new solo line in contrapuntal harmony to the chorus. The refrain is thus not only an essential element in the story-telling process but is also an achievement of considerable interest in its own right.

This Mende example shows the highly complex interaction between Macarthy, Vandei and the chorus and the central role which this plays in the narrative structure of the tale. Refrains may, however, take on many different forms and shades of complexity. On some occasions they are sung; on other occasions they are spoken. Sometimes they contain elaborate repetitions; sometimes they take the form of simple interjections. The shouts by members of the congregation during a Black preacher's sermon, phrases such as 'Praise the Lord' and 'Say the Word', are just as much a part of the process which many observers have labelled call–response as are the choruses which mark Mende story-telling performances.

So, too, is the call–response of the most enduring oral performance in British theatre, the Christmas pantomime. Although the actors work from a written script, a number of features define pantomime as an essentially oral tradition. These include the high level of improvisation which occurs in response to the audience, the well-known structure of the plot and, most significantly for the purposes of the present discussion, audience cries of 'Look behind you!' or 'Oh no he didn't!' countering the performer's 'Oh yes he did!' at various highly predictable points in the action.

Another form of repetition is the catalogue or list, which can be as elaborate as the famous catalogue of ships in *Iliad* II or as simple as this 'shopping list' spoken by the hero of *Sunjata*:

> I don't want anything in Manding,
> Except a son,
> An older sister,
> A wife,
> An attendant,
> A griot,
> And a smith.
>
> $(S_2:1073-9)$

Here it is not the same words which are repeated but the same grammatical structures; that is, the list is a series of direct objects for the verb 'I want'. In S₅:2063–9 the list is clearly repetitious in its prophetic reference to Sunjata's rule over various segments of Manding society:

> If you would rule over the Manden's smiths,
> If you would rule over the Manden's bards,
> If you would rule over the Manden's *funès*,
> If you would rule over the Manden's cordwainers,
> And rule o'er all the warriors in Mandenland,
> When you beat the cane upon the ground,
> Let fresh blood flow out!

Despite the arguments of Goody (1977:53) that listing and categorizing are generally 'more consistent with literate rather than with non-literate forms of communication and tradition', such lists can be found in a variety of contexts of oral performance. The blues singer Frank Stokes (quoted in Levine 1977:326–7), for example, gives the following list of sins committed by Men of God:

> I don't like 'em
> They'll rob you
> Steal your daughter
> Take your wife from you
>   Yeah
> Eat your chicken
> Take your money
>   Yeah

And Homer lists the names of those slain by a fighting warrior:

> Afterwards with Erymas, Amphoteros, and Epaltes,
> Tlepolemos Damastor's son, Echios and Pyris,
> Ipheus and Euippos, and Argeas' son Polymelos,
> all these fell to the bountiful earth in rapid succession.
>
> (*Iliad* XVI:415–8)

The genealogies which form such an important element in many West African oral performances are also essentially lists, such as the following example from *Sunjata*:

> King Nyadu was the father of king Ali,
> Who became king.

> He was the father of king Maalang,
> Who became king.
> He was the father of king Yoro,
> Who became king.
>
> (S$_1$:1160–5)

The repetitious language of the genealogy, aided by the referential features discussed in 'Drawing Together the Web', weaves into the linguistic web members of the oral community, both living and dead.

The catalogue is also a basic structure of teasing rhymes. Take, for instance, the following examples reported by Sutton-Smith (1959:99) as common among English-speakers in Aotearoa but which are also well known in Britain, the USA and, no doubt, in much of the English-speaking world:

> Dan, Dan, the dirty man,
> Washed his face in a frying pan,
> Combed his hair with the leg of a chair,
> Dan, Dan, the dirty man.
>
> Baldy's teeth were long,
> Baldy's teeth were strong.
> It would be no disgrace,
> To Baldy's face,
> If Baldy's teeth were gone.
>
> It's raining, it's pouring,
> The old man's snoring.
> He went to bed to mend his head,
> And couldn't get up in the morning.
>
> Poor old Ernie's dead,
> He died last night in bed.
> They put him in a coffin,
> He fell through the bottom,
> Poor old Ernie's dead.
>
> Little Michael Finnigan,
> Grew whiskers on his chinnagin.
> The wind came along,
> And blew them innagin,
> Poor old Michael Finnigan.

The children offer a list of old men and features of their personal appearance which the children dislike. Several of the stanzas also begin and end with refrain-lines.

Repetition is also used in oral narrative in several ways. In one

European fairy tale called 'The Rich Landlord and the Poor Shoe Maker', repetition takes the form of a series of questions which the story-teller addresses periodically to the audience. Such questions include: 'Why can't they find the shoes?' and 'Well, what's the shoemaker going to do? Is he going to steal that horse?' A similar structure can be noted in the 'Knock-knock' joke cited at the beginning of this chapter. Repeated questions of this kind draw the listeners into the process and reinforce the referential aspect of the performance. The list of questions is thus a variation on the catalogue; the regularity of the questions adds an element of the refrain to the narrative.

Repetition can also serve as the structural basis of an entire narrative. Many long traditional stories are divided into symmetrical and equal episodes. Frequently, the contents of narrative are organized in groups of three: thus three characters perform the same tasks in succession as in the case of 'The Three Little Pigs', 'The Three Billy Goats Gruff', or 'The Three Bears'. Among such Native American societies as the Athabaskans, in contrast, narratives are organized around the pattern number four (Scollon and Scollon 1979).

Such structural and thematic repetition is also a significant feature of the variants of *Sunjata*. For example, tests involving animals, especially dogs, occur throughout the tradition and are to be found at various stages of the narrative, while Sunjata is still in his mother's womb and throughout his childhood and adolescence. A test of trousers whose fit marks the wearer as worthy to rule the Manding at S_1:107–21 operates much like the baobab seed of S_2:850–1083, consumption of which is fit for the ruler alone. All these tests, scattered in the tradition through several parts of the epic, affirm Sunjata's superiority over his antagonists and his inevitable accession to the throne of Mali. The repetition of the tests provides ever-increasing emphasis on the occult power of Sunjata, whose life is filled with sign after sign of his greatness. Such multiple testing is partly the result of a quest for religious certainty; repeated signs from heaven are more reliable than single occurrences. Repetition here is also an aspect of oral composition which favours parallel theme and construction of this sort. Significantly, the tradition allows great flexibility of placement of these signs within the narrative. In a sense, the early life of Sunjata is one long series of signs of the hero's future greatness.

So fundamental is repetition to the process of composition and performance, that it comes as no surprise to find not only that it occurs across time and space, but that it exists even in species other than *homo loquens*. A report in the *Chicago Tribune* of 12 March 1989 (section 5, 4), for instance, suggests that whales use similar strategies in their songs:

After analyzing morethan 500 whale songs recorded during the last twelve years, two scientists detect identical endings in highly organized phrases and rhyming sounds in the whale singing. Linda McGee of the Long Term Research Institute in Lincoln, Mass., and Katharine Payne of Cornell University broke the songs down into units distinguishable by humans and then found phrases, sub-phrases and themes similar to music composed by humans. They found rhyme-like sub-phrases occurring more than one third of the time ... The rhymes are used mostly in the longer, more complex songs, leading to speculation that the whales use them as mnemonic devices to remember the songs.

Repetition, lists and refrains are found in a variety of oral performances. It is worth lingering a while, however, to look at one genre found in many oral cultures, the lament. The following lament from *Sunjata* is a typical blending of all three characteristics in a strong referential context:

> Don't you know that Darama Jallo's Fili is gone –
> Kiliya Musa, Nooya Musa, Wanjaga Musa is gone –
> Darama Jallo's Fili is dead.
> He was descended from Farang Ngaali;
> Fili is gone,
> Futu Nyogo Bula, Sinna Nyogo Bula,
> Bumba Bula Karata Kobila.
> Ah, ah, Darama Jallo's Fili is dead.
>
> $(S_3:11-18)$

There are several forms of repetition here. First of all there is the cry of lamentation 'Darama Jallo's Fili is gone' which is repeated in various forms five times in eight lines. A long series of epithets for Fili make his presence resound in the lines. Then there is an element of genealogy suggested by the reference to Fili's ancestor Ngaali. Finally there is the catalogue nature of this particular lament, which sings not just of Fili, but also of other dead members of the Manding community.

Andromache's lament over the body of her dead husband Hektor exhibits similar features:

My husband, you were lost young from life, and have left me
a widow in your house, and the boy is only a baby
who was born to you and me, the unhappy. I think he will never
come of age, for before then head to heel this city
will be sacked, for you, its defender, are gone, you who guarded
the city, and the grave wives, and the innocent children,
wives who before long must go away in the hollow ships,
and among them I shall also go, and you, my child, follow where I go ...

(Iliad XXIV: 725–33)

Here verbal repetition can be noted in the phrases referring to Hektor's death ('you were lost young from life' and 'you are gone') and in the related idea of going away, which is mentioned successively in reference to the Trojan widows, to Andromache and to her son. Like the *Sunjata* lament, Andromache's plaint is also a catalogue, in this case a list of all the people who have been abandoned by Hektor's death. The repetitive pattern of Andromache's lament is illustrated artistically on the geometric Greek dipylon vase shown in Plate 2.

Andromache's lament can be compared to the *valave* or songs of conciliation performed at South Asian weddings (Edwards 1982b). At the climax of the ceremony, songs performed by the women to taunt and tease the other side suddenly give way to the more serious *valave*. The transition period is over and the time to recognize the couple's newly wed status has arrived. No longer do the women mock and ridicule the other side. Rather, they entreat the bride to behave in a way which will bring honour on her family. There is, however, a tremendous poignancy in these songs which reflects a very real concern about the bride's loss of status as she passes from a family in which she has been loved and cherished to one where she will occupy the lowest rung in the social pecking order:

> Sister, as you go to your in-laws, be careful not to shed any tears.
> Daughters are only held in trust.
> Sister, daughters are like the cow, going wherever they are led.
> Daughters are only held in trust.
> Sister, your father's hand will never caress your brow, never caress your
>   brow.
> The walls of the house where you grew up and played will weep, the
>   walls will weep.
> Sister, no tears can halt the approaching hour to say farewell.
> Daughters are only held in trust.
> Sister, as you go to your in-laws, be careful the papals do not get wet.
> Daughters are only held in trust.
>
>   (Edwards 1982b:55)

As in the laments of other cultures, there are repetitions and refrains, such as 'Sister, as you go to your in-laws', 'Daughters are only held in trust', 'never caress your brow' and 'the walls will weep'. At the same time, these features are more structured in the South Asian song than they are in Andromache's lament. The recurrence of key images, together with the dirge-like quality of the music, is suggestive of the very real emotion experienced at this moment. The evocative nature of *valave* is further underlined by the fact that the women openly wept when singing these songs for the researcher, even though theirs was a performance for the tape recorder and totally out of context.

The lament form is by no means limited to South Asian marriage ceremonies. As a Chinese bride passes from one family to another, her pain and sorrow are so powerful that she feels her mother guilty of a heinous act of betrayal and she speaks of her as if she were dead:

> Mother is with the dead people,
> The talk reaches accord;
> Beef is fried with ginger
> Ginger is fried with sugar.
> Mother is with the dead people.
> The talk is then sweetened;
> Dead people send a one-footed raven,
> To come proclaim life.
> Mother utters one sentence,
> There is approval;
> Dead people send a one-footed raven,
> To come proclaim death.
> Mother utters one sentence,
> There is release;
> The ocean freezes the heart,
> Sand is dashed to the bottom.
>
> (Blake 1979:95)

Like the South Asian lament the Chinese girl's song exhibits a careful structure in which three refrains ('Mother is with the dead people'; 'Dead people send a one-footed raven'; and 'Mother utters one sentence') create a frame for the girl's complaints.

Spinning a Yarn

In Homer, the death of Hektor creates a bridge by which the remaining Trojans will join their dead loved ones. In the Chinese passage, the role of the girl's living mother in arranging the engagement has caused the mother to join the dead in the eyes of her daughter. Both songs contain striking verbal repetitions which link together living and dead. While the South Asian song contains no direct reference to the dead, its images of the wailing wall and the bride led like a cow suggest a fate scarcely better than death. Such heightened language can be found not only in the lament; it is also a basic feature of other oral performances, such as the boasting and invective discussed in 'Caught in the Web of Words', which use metaphoric language to create exaggerated comparisons.

To a certain extent, metaphor, an essential element of language whether oral or written, is an exaggeration which distorts reality and makes identifications between objects which are fundamentally diffe- rent. The building up of powerful imagery is part of the art of the story-teller: the more vivid the image, the greater the impact. Some of Homer's metaphors, such as the well-known 'early-born, rosy-fingered Dawn', are used so frequently that they become part of the repetitive fabric of the performance. The effect of other metaphors comes from an unusual verbal association or turn of phrase. The pathos of the Chinese bride's lament is partly based on the metaphoric association of her mother with the dead. With similar force, Jesse Jackson has described the fate of Afro-American people as like being on the ex- pressway with all the entrances and exits closed off. Another Afro- American speaker expressed his dislike of women who wear wigs by saying that they look like nine miles of bad road with a detour at the end. Smitherman (1977:156) also quotes the following excerpt from a story by 75-year-old ex-slave: 'some of them slaves was so poorly thin they ribs would kinda rustle against each other like corn stalks a-drying in the hot winds.'

Metaphor is one area where oral and literate techniques merge. Both a sonnet and a sermon can be filled with such playful comparisons. In a literate context, a metaphor is a temporary suspension of belief, a poetic form outside the real world. In the oral world, this suspension of belief reflects a readiness to relate anything to anything else. Everything is potentially connected in the web of the oral community, where dawn can have fingers, where the living and the dead are confused, and where a rib is like a corn stalk.

The metaphoric basis of oral performance is particularly strong in proverbs and riddles, which expand the semantic web and mark com- parisons between objects not normally compared. Thus, the interpreta- tion of 'A bird in the hand is worth two in the bush' requires an acceptance of the links between captured birds and seized opportuni- ties, in order to understand the point of the proverb. The following riddle recited by an 80-year-old Maine native in the 1950s and related to us orally by her great-grand-daughter requires a similar suspension of belief:

> Inside a green house a white house.
> Inside the white house a red house.
> Inside the red house
> A whole crowd of little black and white men.

The riddle statement is a cryptic combination of verbal repetition of the word 'house' and a list of colours. The answer, a watermelon, explains the riddle by means of a metaphoric association of the fruit and a three-layered house.

Afro-American toasts also make extensive use of hyperbolic imagery and metaphorical language which often extend over many lines. This passage (Abrahams 1962:10), for example, is based upon the metaphor of cardplaying.

> He said, 'I'ma hold my jacks, spread my queens,
> I'ma do switching in this old—deck the world's never seen.
> I'ma hold my deuces, lay down my treys,
> Get down on your mother—ing—in a thousand ways.'
> He said, 'Now skip Mr Rabbit, hop Mr Bear,
> Look's—, but there's 'leven of them there.'

In a very real sense the tall tales told all over the world by yarn spinners, both past and present, are an extension of the metaphoric language found in proverbs and riddles. Exaggeration and metaphor set these tales apart from normal conversation. They can also be an integral part of the humour of the tale and serve as a comment on human behaviour and appearance. For example, during the American Civil War President Abraham Lincoln is reported to have commented that 'Some of my generals are so slow that molasses in the coldest days of winter is a race horse compared to them. They're brave enough, but somehow or other, they get fastened in a fence corner, and can't figure their way out' (Dorson 1962:97).

Local detail will naturally vary a great deal in tall tales. The traditional story-teller in ancient Greece or along the Atlantic coast of the USA will draw materials from supernaturalism of sea and land, while along the frontier or in communities with frontier characteristics, like the Upper Peninsula of Michigan, heroes will boast of feats of individual strength and daring in the forest or with Indians. Autobiographical sagas of a hair-raising nature are particularly common and illustrate the threads of exaggeration found in both personal sagas and the hero legends. Very often these take the form of contrived stories about unusual events which have elements of truth and which are meant to be taken seriously. For example, there are stories in eastern Minnesota based upon the actual life of Otto Walta, a Finnish immigrant, homestead farmer and occasional lumberjack who died in 1959. Otto's great strength becomes proverbial in the following story (Dorson 1973:171):

> Once he walked three miles across the swamp behind his homestead to the railroad tracks, ripped up an eight-hundred-pound rail with his bare hands, lifted it to his shoulder, walked back to his land, and went to prying

up stumps by ramming one end of the rail in a hole he dug under the stump, setting the rail on a rock for a fulcrum, and leaning on the other end until the stump popped out of the ground like a potato.

A few days later six men from the Duluth, Winnipeg, and Pacific Railroad called on Otto. The rail was tilting against his bachelor's shack, built into a sandy ridge and topped by a rocking chair and lookout platform. They asked Otto who had helped him tote the rail across the swamp. When Otto replied that he had done it alone, they sniggered. Calmly he reached down, took a hold, swung the rail onto his shoulder, and strode around his clearing. Dumfounded, the railroaders beat a hasty retreat. It would have taken a crew of eight to clear a road through the swamp and haul the rail back.

The metaphor of this tale encompasses more than the comparison of the tree stump to the potato. The whole story serves as a metaphoric exaggeration about Otto's great strength.

In the *Odyssey*, Odysseus subjects his own story to exaggeration, like that found in the story of Otto Walta. Having returned in disguise to his home in Ithaka, Odysseus is ever-ready to fabricate new and original autobiographies. First he is a Kretan exile who is left ashore by sailor rescuers (*Odyssey* XIII:256–86). Then, as the bastard son of a Kretan lord, he claims to have fought at Troy alongside Odysseus, to have been shipwrecked, and then to have been enslaved (*Odyssey* XIV:192–359). In these lies, Odysseus acts much like the Afro–American rapper whose aim is to impress an audience with verbal dexterity. Sometimes this will take the form of demolishing a competitor with a superior performance, an essential element of which is exaggerating and 'lying'. Other times the object is to win over a member of the opposite sex via similar techniques. The 'lies' which form the fabric of such raps are not meant to be taken at face value, though as we have already pointed out in our discussion of boasting and self-blame, outsiders often misinterpret the speaker's intentions.

A similar phenomenon is the exaggeration noted in contemporary oral narrative from Maine to Kentucky. A choice selection includes:

Land so poor that fertilizer must be place around the door to get the clock to run.

She is so skinny she can drink a glass of tomato juice and look like a thermometer.

Mountains so steep we planted potatoes on one side of the hill and picked them on the other.

He's so tight that he crawls under the door to save the hinge.

(Halpert 1951:*passim*)

The metaphors found in these proverbs are essentially distortions of reality, which make them very similar to the tall tale and show that in oral cultures 'truth' is not as important as verbal skill, that the adept exaggerator is more valued than a truthful half-wit. Exaggeration extends the truth in the search for the boundaries of human experience and releases the tensions which surround these boundaries.

The Crafting of Songs

This exaggerated and metaphoric structure of oral performance is expressed in several cultural contexts which show a bond between the creative art of the good talker and the technical skill of an artisan. In the *Odyssey*, for example, the link is between words and weaving, and Odysseus, often called *doloplokos* 'weaver of wiles', is a master of tall tales. He is equalled at the loom of words by his wife Penelope, who uses a real loom to deceive her persistent suitors. Hero and wife are thus both weavers who can capture their audience in a deceitful web. Sometimes the Homeric performer is also called a weaver. While the Homeric term for oral artists like Phemios and Demodokos is *aoidoi* or 'singers', in other contexts early Greek artists are described as *rhapsodoi* or 'weavers of songs'. So at *Theogony* 30ff. the poet Hesiod describes himself with rhapsode's staff (*rhabdos*) in hand, and in fragment #357 (Merkelback and West 1970:223) the poet refers to singing with Homer and 'weaving [*rhapsantes*] song in new forms'. While later Greek rhapsodes, like the Ion who gave his name to Plato's dialogue, may have become more reciters than creators of songs, it is clear that early Greek rhapsodes, at least, were considered both performers and poets. As Gentili (1988:7) notes, 'It is obvious that *rhaptein* is a concrete metaphor for the process of composition, describing the operation by which the strands or web of discourse are woven together.' We suggest that this act of 'stitching together a song', found also in the English colloquial phrase 'spinning a yarn', is an appropriate metaphor for the art of all good talkers, not just those of ancient Greek performance. The weaving metaphor affirms an important aspect of oral performances, namely the skilful use of words, and presents the performer as an expert artisan.

It is interesting to speculate further on possible links between the classical rhapsode and the contemporary rapper. In the absence of any documentation on the origins of the term 'rap', we might do a great

Plate 9 *A Greek rhapsode, or reciter of epic poetry, with words issuing from his mouth, on an amphora painted by Kleophrades. Photograph courtesy of the British Museum.*

deal worse than falling back on to folk etymologies (Hardwidge, personal communication). To sustain the imagery of the sub-title of this book, it could be argued that Homer was, in fact, a rhapper!

Another craft-based metaphor for the good talker is contained in an etymology for the name of Homer which identifies the poet with a carpenter. Deriving 'Homer' from the Greek verb root **ar-* 'to fit, to join' and understanding the name to mean 'He who fits [the song] together', Nagy (1979:297–300) not only notes that a form of this Greek verb is used to express a similar metaphor in the *Homeric Hymn to Apollo* (line 164):

So beautifully is their song fitted together.

(Translation by Nagy 1979:298)

but also finds a parallel in the following passage from the *Rig-Veda* (1.130.6ab):

> The sons of Āyu, wishing for good things, have fitted together this utterance,
> just as the skilled artisan (fits together) a chariot.
>
> (Translation by Nagy 1979:298)

In *Sunjata* the skilled craft of the good talker is expressed by yet another technological metaphor, that of smithing. As a blacksmith, Sumanguru, the hero's antagonist, possesses a magical and creative art which often, as in the verbal dual between the two warriors at S_4:60, can be expressed both in the realm of words and in the physical world. Thus, a variety of technical contexts, from spinning to weaving to fitting a chariot to smithing, affirm the craft-based and metaphoric nature of oral performance, in which the song is shaped from various materials, just as thread or wood or metal is used by the artisan.

The structural unity which emerges in the oral tradition from this stitching together of various elements is very different from the end-product of literate composition. A literate discourse structure can be characterized as a sequence of points, planned in advance and ordered in a linear fashion. The underlying structure of oral discourse, however, departs in many important respects from the analytic linearity of literate discourse. The lyrics of Afro-American blues offer an excellent example of the qualitatively different organizing principles of oral composition. The structure of the verse is unvarying: two more or less repetitive lines followed by a line that 'caps' or comments on them. The arrangement of verses, however, does not adhere to the linear sequentiality which literate observers usually expect. Jarrett (1984:156) gives the following instances of adjacent verses from 'Preaching the Blues' by Eddie Son House, a Mississippi Delta singer-composer:

> Well, I love my baby just like I love myself
> Well, I love my baby just like I love myself
>   Oooooooh just like I love myself
> Well, if she won't have me, she won't have nobody else
>
> Well, I'm gonna fold my arms, I'm gonna kneel down in prayer
> Oh, I'm gonna fold my arms, I'm gonna kneel down in prayer
> When I get up I'm gonna see if my preachin' suit a man's ear
>
> Well, I met the blues this morning, walking just like a man
> Ohhh, oh ohhh, walking just like a man
> I said, good morning, blues, now give me your right hand

Within the Afro-American oral community, however, there is no expectation of a linear development from verse to verse. Cohesion is provided by shared knowledge of traditions, by a series of concentric circles and themes, including references to the preacher as an object of humour or the dichotomy between the church and the world of temptation. The oral formulaic language normally associated with the blues and common expectations of what constitutes a blues song serve the same purpose.

Different expectations of coherence can also be detected in oral narrative. One feature which has attracted comment is the tendency for story-tellers to avoid either explicitly stating the underlying point or developing full-fledged propositions. Instead narratives in the New York Jewish community (Tannen 1981) or among the Athabaskan Indians of northwest Canada and the United States (Scollon and Scollon 1981) usually consist of anecdotes rhapsodized or stitched together in a way which many literate observers dismiss as episodic, disconnected and difficult to follow. There is greater emphasis in oral culture on the negotiation of meaning and the general assumption would seem to be that the audience are capable of drawing their own conclusions. Oral discourse seeks to persuade by using vivid and concrete narrative detail rather than by abstract propositions. Successive anecdotes are linked implicitly rather than formally. While some writers, like Ong (1967), have suggested that members of oral cultures avoid abstract propositions because they are incapable of abstract thought, other writers, like Cole and Scribner (1974), argue that oral discourse style avoids such strategies simply because they are less persuasive in face-to-face communication.

You Can Say That Again!

The good talker thus makes use of a wide range of strategies which recur throughout oral performance. These function not only prospectively, by allowing the performer to think ahead to what comes next, but also retrospectively, by helping the audience to remember what has been said, and agonistically, by creating a crescendo of audience involvement. Elaboration gives texture to the performance. Repetition, in the form of refrains, call–response, lists and recurrent themes and structures, is another vital element in the oral armoury of the artist. It is an essential part of the oral aesthetic, spun into the fabric of performance.

These strategies, however, are often evaluated quite differently in oral and literate contexts. Good talkers weave or stitch together the different elements of performance in a way which departs significantly from literate expectations. Whereas written discourse shows a linear progression of ideas, oral discourse can be more properly characterized as a series of concentric circles, designed to achieve the maximum dramatic effect and audience involvement.

9

The Web That Binds

'When a story flourishes in the heart of a folkore, it is because in one way or another it expresses an aspect of "the spirit of the group".'

Fanz Fanon, *Black Skins, White Masks*

In the previous chapter we looked at the ways in which certain techniques help form the building blocks of performance and showed how the very familiarity of these techniques acts as a prop for both good talkers and their audiences. The ways in which these features are stitched together in performance, however, are so varied that no two oral performances by a single artist are ever the same. This variety of performance is true on a larger scale as well. A basic feature of oral performance is openendedness, an ability to include a diverse number of forms. Thus the Chinese bride sings both lament and invective at her wedding and the sermon of an Afro-American preacher blends narrative with personal anecdotes. Yet, behind this flexibility lies a shared perception of the world, a communal well of expressions, social bonds and performative forms which are readily understood by all members of the oral community. Without these common bonds, the Chinese bride's lament would be incomprehensible to her listeners and the preacher's personal commentary would be mere digression from the point of the sermon.

In the last chapter we examined the various techniques on which oral composition draws. We now change the emphasis from technique to genre, from the aesthetic effect created by different discourse strategies to the special functions and meanings contained in distinct forms such as riddles, proverbs and narrative which bind the community together. We do not claim to offer a comprehensive survey of such structures. Rather, our focus is on the way some of these many threads bind the performance into a shared web of words and reinforce the cultural cohesion of the community.

Proverbs

The use of short, witty sayings known as proverbs warrants special attention because of the way that these forms of communication encapsulate the wisdom of experience and are time-tried solutions for recurring moral issues. Proverbs suggest courses of action which sit comfortably with the values of the community as a whole. They also offer the advantage of indirection: it is possible, for instance, to couch criticism in proverbs and to reprove or make a point politely, as in 'People in glass houses shouldn't throw stones' or 'Many a true word is spoken in jest'. Because they allow the speaker to depersonalize what is said, they are often a great deal more acceptable than direct comments. Above all, because proverbs are repeatable, they contain a shared meaning which is immediately understood by members of the community. Proverbs are used for a wide range of purposes. They are used to reinforce the social values of the group and to teach enduring truths about the human condition. Recurrent truths find expression in a startling variety of ways in many different cultures.

In traditional language, it is sometimes difficult to separate the formula from the proverb. For example, Homer puts the saying 'Once a thing has been done, the fool sees it' (*Iliad* XVII:33) in the mouth of Menelaos who is warning his opponent on the field of battle not to be a fool, not to challenge him one-on-one. From the context, the didactic potential of a proverb is clear. While this same expression is quoted as a proverb several centuries later in Plato's *Symposium* (222b), it is impossible to determine whether it had reached the status of proverb in the time of Homer, or whether its use by Homer made it a proverb.

The didactic force of proverbs is also to be seen in *Sunjata*. Examples like:

> A child may be first-born, but that does not always make him the elder.
> $(S_6:2025)$

or

> '. . . Today may belong to some,
> Tomorrow will belong to another.'
> $(S_6:2026-7)$

or

> '. . . As you succeeded some,
> So shall you have successors.'
> $(S_6:2028-9)$

reiterate the claim of Sunjata to future power. They refer not only to Sunjata's relationship with his antagonists, but also to the audience, who are encouraged throughout the epic to emulate Sunjata and become his successors.

While proverbs are used in all societies, the stock of proverbs and the range of uses to which they are put vary a great deal. Oral cultures have particularly well-developed repertoires. As the Nigerian writer, Chinua Achebe (1980:7) remarks: 'Among the Ibo the art of conversation is regarded very highly, and proverbs are the palm-oil with which the words are eaten.' Like other forms of oral expression, proverbs need to be studied in the specific social settings in which they naturally occur. It is potentially misleading to present them as decontextualized texts. For this reason, proverb collections, such as those of Evans (1988) and Burton (1969), consisting of bare texts and offering little information about performative contexts, leave unclear the proverbs' meanings within the culture and tempt readers to impose from their own culture interpretations which may or may not be appropriate. In a collection of Manding proverbs edited by Meyer (1985), however, each proverb is followed by examples of usage, such as the following:

It's no use to wash a tortoise; it will never become a water turtle.

'A foreigner is learning the Manding language; he makes a great effort; the proverb is cited to him to make him understand that, despite all his efforts, he will never speak Manding perfectly because he is not Manding.'

'Diba received a visit from his friend who has always lived in the city; they go together to work in the field but people say the proverb: he will not be able to work well. He is not a farmer like us.' (Translated from Meyer 1985:17)

The examples guide outsiders to understandings of the proverb which are both culture-specific and generalized. The Manding proverb has meaning which is not found in its counterpart in Aesop's 'Tale of the Country Mouse and the City Mouse'. As we translate from Meyer (1985:12), 'the proverb has only meaning situated in a precise human context and situation'.

Proverbs are often used to cross the generational gap and to bind older and younger people together. 'Fire under mus-mus tail, dem think a cool breeze', for instance, is a proverb commonly invoked by older West Indian and British Black children to warn younger children that their behaviour is annoying (Jackson 1986:33). The implication is that those who cannot distinguish between fire and pleasure will find themselves in trouble. While the use of proverbs among age-mates is also common, it would be extremely unusual to find a younger person quoting a proverb to an older person. In order to sanction such behaviour in Yoruba society, for instance, etiquette would demand that the proverb be prefaced by an apology such as 'I don't claim to know any proverbs in the presence of you older people, but you elders have the saying ...' (Arewa and Dundes 1964:79). This apology thus acknowledges the central role which proverbs play in children's education.

The situations in which proverbs are used to train children are many and varied. In Yoruba families proverbs are used in a wide range of situations which reinforce both the children's concept of relationships within the community and expected patterns of behaviour. For instance, when children discuss certain subjects, such as a quarrel which has taken place between the mother and the father, parents will often show their disapproval by saying 'One should not say in jest that his mother is fainting' (Arewa and Dundes 1964:73–4). In Yoruba culture, fainting is a passage from the normal state of life to another state which should not be treated lightly. In the same way, important personal events should not be made the subject of jokes.

There are also situations in which opposing proverbs can be brought into play to argue for different child-rearing strategies. For instance, in a situation where one parent is advocating leniency while another favours more rigid discipline, the father might state his position by saying 'Untrained and intractable children would be corrected by outsiders' and the mother might counter with 'If a man beats his child with his right hand, he should draw him to himself with the left'. The father's proverb implies that if parents fail to fulfil their obligations to give their child a proper education, the community at large will find it necessary to intervene, while the mother's stresses the need for parents to demonstrate their love.

This adversarial use of proverbs is particularly well developed in many judicial systems. In the courtrooms of the Western world, lawyers rely heavily on precedent, citing previous cases to support the validity of their case. In many oral cultures, proverbs are used for the same purpose. Proverbs express meaning vividly and dramatically. By definition, they do not vary. The creative use of proverbs therefore lies in successful application to a new situation. Thus, the person who wins is the one who knows how to apply the proverbs most effectively rather than the one with the largest supply. The Mataco Chaco of Argentina, for instance, conduct their entire adjudication system by trading of proverbs between the opposing parties (Abrahams 1968a:152).

For the Anang people of southeast Nigeria, competence in the use of proverbs is an essential skill widely called upon in settling disputes

(Messenger 1959). In one particular court case a chronic thief was accused of stealing and the plaintiff caused a great deal of antagonism towards the defendant by quoting the following proverb: 'If a dog plucks palm fruits from a cluster, he does not fear a porcupine'. Since a cluster from a palm tree is so full of sharp needles that anyone prepared to handle it would not be frightened by the spines of a porcupine, the plaintiff was implying the equivalent of the English proverb 'Once a thief, always a thief'. Later in the proceedings, however, the defendant achieved his acquittal by offering a different proverb, 'A single partridge flying through the bush leaves no path', which pointed out that the robbery could have been committed by someone else without his unfortunate history, someone who would arouse no suspicion. By drawing attention in this proverb to his isolation the defendant persuaded the judge to look on his case as objectively as possible and to disregard both the hostile audience and his past history. The use of proverbs thus wove together plaintiff, defendant and judge into a shared cultural bond.

Africa is remarkable not only for the use of proverbs in everyday conversation and in the settling of disputes, but also for the use of drums as a channel for communicating proverbs on ceremonial and other public occasions. By moving the left arm which holds the drum, it is possible to vary the shape of the drum and hence the tone. Native speakers are able to identify the proverb by the relative pitch differences and the rhythmic sequence of the drum tones. The choice of channel– speech or drum–depends upon the intended audience and drumming proverbs would be reserved for addressing a large group of individuals or a situation where it was important that the message be made public. For instance, Arewa and Dundes (1964:81) point to the use of:

> It is palm oil that I carry. Person bearing rock, please don't spoil that which is mine. It is palm-oil that I carry.

in a situation where a person's good name is being threatened by an irresponsible young man who envies the other's prestige and seeks to damage it by spreading malicious rumours. The young man therefore risks destroying the honourable man's reputation in the same way that pieces of rock can spoil palm oil, and the offended party seeks redress by the public broadcast of the drummed proverb.

Proverbs also serve other less serious functions. Smitherman (1977:95), for instance, discusses how they can be used as a means of entertainment and are extremely effective in giving point and colour to ordinary conversation. Afro-American 'raps' are sprinkled with familiar proverbs which make a point with short, succinct statements and have the sound of power and wisdom. Many Black proverbs have also become titles or lines in hit songs, such as 'Still Water Runs Deep' by Aretha Franklin and 'Smiling Faces Sometimes Tell Lies' by Undisputed Truth (whose very name is synonymous with a proverb).

Riddles

Riddles have a great deal in common with proverbs. Both are economical, witty and essentially poetical descriptions. There are, however, some differences between the two structures. The referent of a proverb is clear from the context; the riddle must supply its own referent. Furthermore, while both riddles and proverbs have two or more elements in their description, these metaphoric elements behave quite differently in the two genres. The familiarity of the elements contained within a proverb is such that the listener immediately recognizes a pattern. The intent of the riddle, in contrast, is confusion, at least until the answer is provided. Abrahams (1968a:151–2) suggests four different ways in which the riddle can achieve this effect:

> 1. A contradiction is set up between the traits, generally some sort of opposition between them. (What has eyes but cannot see?–a potato. What goes up the chimney down but cannot go down the chimney up?–an umbrella.)

> 2. Not enough information is given in the description to provide a complete *Gestalt* and allow the recognition of the referent. (What is white, then green, then red?–a berry growing.)

> 3. Too much inconsequential or misleading evidence is provided, causing a 'scramble' effect. (As I was crossing London Bridge I met a man who tipped his hat and drew his cane, and now I give you his name. What is it?–Andrew Cane.)

> 4. A false *Gestalt* is created; the traits seem to combine meaningfully, but the apparent referent is not the same as the true referent. This usually leads to a 'catch' situation in which the wrong answer, often obscene, is given by the answerer. The effect is very like that of the trick picture which can be read in two ways. (What goes in hard and smooth and comes out soft and gooey?–a piece of chewing gum.)

Riddles are thus used to entertain by creating a confusion which is eventually resolved by supplying an answer to a question.

The range of forms which riddles take is impressive, and riddles are no more homogeneous than other speech events. Bryant (1983:13–14), for example, has made a distinction between the oral riddle as 'a simple unembellished puzzle which has been passed down by word of mouth and whose solution is usually a familiar object, natural phenomenon, etc.' and the literary riddle 'which has been deliberately crafted around the written form'. The following anonymous riddle about a saw, for example, can function equally well in written or in spoken form: 'What has teeth but cannot eat?' (Bryant 1983:95). But other riddles require a more literate context. The solver must have some knowledge of the alphabet in order to recognize 'Mississippi' as the answer to the following anonymous riddle in Bryant (1983:95): 'What has four eyes but cannot see?' Both riddles are based upon a sophisticated use of words, a metaphorical confusion between teeth in the mouth and teeth on a saw in one and confusion of the homonyms 'eye' and 'i' in the other. While both riddles work equally well in spoken form, only the saw riddle works in writing because the Mississippi riddle depends upon an aural illusion which cannot be replicated in print.

Riddles vary between and within cultures. Thus, in the Somali countryside, children use riddles which have an introductory formula and answers which are usually fixed and unique. However, when adults engage in riddling, the expectation is that the answer should show wit and wisdom, but there is no formalized pattern of question and response (Andrzcjcwski 1973). Similarly, in their discussion of children's lore, the Opies (1977:93–104) observe several types, including true riddles which describe a creature or object in an intentionally obscure manner and resolve the paradox in the answer (What gets wet when drying?–A towel); rhyming riddles (Riddle me, riddle me, what is that, /Over the head and under the hat?–Hair); punning riddles (What runs but never walks?–A river); and conundrums (What is the difference between a warder and a jeweller?–One watches cells and the other sells watches).

While many riddles take the form of questions and answers, other riddles consist of simple statements, such as the following variations on the same Bantu riddle about an egg (collected in Beuchat 1965:187):

It has no door. (Mwera)
Round with no mouth (Makaa)
My house is large. It has no door. (Swahili)
An animal built a house, but it lacks a door, it lacks windows. What is it? (Lingala)

The same riddle is told in the European folk tradition in the following form:

> I have a little house in which I live all alone, Without doors, without windows,
> And if I want to go out I have to break through the wall.
> (Bryant 1983:105)

Another riddle in the form of a statement is the riddle which the Sphinx poses to Oidipous in the Greek tradition:

> There is a thing on earth two-footed, and four-footed, and three-footed, whose name is one, and it changes its nature alone of all creatures that move creeping on earth or in the air and sea. But when it moves supported on most feet, the swiftness of its legs is at its weakest. (*Greek Anthology* XIV:64; translated by Paton 1979:59)

While this riddle about three stages of human life is preserved only in literate sources, such as this collection of Greek verse known as the *Greek Anthology* (Paton 1979), its long oral history is suggested by the central place it holds in the traditional story of the Greek hero Oidipous.

The oral context of Greek riddles is also evident in Plato's reference in the *Republic* (V 479B) to children reciting another riddle in the form of a statement rather than a question,

> a riddle about the eunuch, where they riddle how he shot at the bat, what he hit it with and what he sat on. These sayings also have double meanings, and it is impossible to fix any of them firmly in the mind as being or not being, or as both or as neither. (Translated by Rouse 1956:280)

The riddle to which Plato refers is the following: 'A man not a man (i.e. a eunuch) saw and did not see a bird not a bird (i.e. a bat) sitting on a stick not a stick (i.e. a reed) and hit it with a stone not a stone (i.e. pumice).'

In addition to riddles which are phrased impersonally, sometimes riddles are both dramatic and personal and take the form of first-person vignettes such as these riddles from the *Greek Anthology*:

> If you look at me, I look at you too. You look with eyes, but I not with eyes, for I have no eyes. And if you like, I speak without a voice, for you have a voice, but I only have lips that open in vain (a mirror). (*Greek Anthology* XIV:56; translated by Paton 1979:55)

> If you had taken me in my youth, haply you would have drunk the blood shed from me; but now that time has finished making me old, eat me,

wrinkled as I am, with no moisture in me, crushing my bones together
with my flesh (a raisin). (*Greek Anthology* XIV:103, translated by Paton
1979:79)

Or this West Indian riddle:

I went to town, my face turn to town;
I came from town, my face turn from town.

                                                    −climbing a coconut tree

This sense of the dramatic extends to all aspects of West Indian
riddling (Abrahams 1972c). Participants sometimes leave the house
during a riddle session partly to think up new riddles and partly to time
their re-entry and achieve maximum effect. Clever riddles skilfully
delivered are met with applause and appreciative murmuring.

There are also important differences in the social motivation for the
two genres. The thrust of proverbs is to support group solidarity by
reinforcing the shared values of the group; they occur as part of
everyday speech. Riddles, in contrast, explore ambiguous and disturb-
ing aspects of life which are potentially destructive of community
values. For this reason, they often form part of a stylized performance,
or riddling session, with all the constraints which accompany performances of this kind. The antisocial forces which play an important role in
riddling are thus channelled into a form of expression which is both
creative and psychologically helpful.

Riddles are a very ancient form of word play, no doubt almost as old
as *homo loquens*. The earliest records of riddles can probably be traced
to Vedic lore in India. The hymns of the *Rig-Veda*, still recited to this
day, reflect their original riddle character in their poetic structure. In
the eighth hymn the attributes of the principal gods are described in ten
typical riddles, each of which is followed by the name of the god in
question:

One of them is muddy brown, many-formed, generous, a youth; he
adorns himself with gold. (Soma)

Another descended refulgent into the womb, the wise among the gods.
(Agni)

                                                    (Huizinga 1949:106)

This canonical and liturgical aspect of riddling has received a great deal
of attention from commentators such as Huizinga (1949) and Callois
(1968) who have pointed to the way in which knowledge of riddles is
associated with magical power. In Vedic lore, for instance, heroes

demonstrate their sacred knowledge – and attendant power – by reciting riddles that concern both secret names and the origins of the world. A similar theme emerges in *Sunjata* when the hero creates a visual riddle for another antagonist by laying before him a broken pot, a bush fowl's egg and some old thatching grass. The meaning of these objects is interpreted by a wise man called Makhang Kuu Bee Long (Makhang Know All) who declares:

> What Sunjata has said here
> Is that a day will come
> When he will smash this town of yours just like this broken pot;
> A day will come
> When old thatch will not be seen in this town of yours
> Because he will burn it all;
> A day will come
> When bush fowls will lay their eggs on the site of your deserted town.
> (S_1:427–34)

The riddle repeats the threat of Sunjata's revenge through the series of three objects, which metaphorically suggest destruction of the town. Addition of the refrain 'a day will come' reinforces the effect of this threat. At the same time the cryptic threat, once deciphered, creates a bond of knowledge between the riddler and his antagonist.

The riddle also functions as a dramatic testing device. One of the best-known examples is the divine oracle, especially associated in the ancient Greek tradition with ambiguous pronouncements in dactylic hexameter by Apollo's oracle at Delphi. The following example is part of the oracle reputedly given to the Athenians just before the naval battle of Salamis in 480 BC:

> For when all else is taken that the boundary of Cecrops and the dell of divine Cithaeron contain, a wooden wall doth far-seeing Zeus give to Athena the Triton-born, to remain alone unstormed, and that shall profit thee and thy children. (*Greek Anthology* XIV:93; translated by Paton 1979:73)

The fifth-century Greek historian Herodotos (VII:142) describes the confused contemporary interpretations of this oracle. At the time some Athenians thought it referred to the thorn hedge of the Athenian Acropolis, others to the wooden hulls of Athens' ships. Misinterpretation of the oracle would prove fatal to the city, but, under the leadership of Themistokles, the Athenians took to their ships and won a major naval victory over the Persians.

This is just one example of what is sometimes referred to as the 'neck-riddle' (Norton 1942) in which the very life of an individual or group depends on the correct solution of an enigma. Other well-documented literary accounts of riddling include a collection of oracles in book 14 of the *Greek Anthology* (Paton 1979); the riddle in the Brahministic *Vajasaneyi Samhita* which describes a contest where the loser gives up everything; and the riddling between Odin and King Hendrik in the Icelandic *Hervarar Saga*. These cases may be compared with *Sunjata* where the exiled hero participates in a variation on a riddle contest in an encounter with a king who plans to slay Sunjata while competing in a board-game. During this game each participant asserts his intellectual power by making cryptic statements. In one version, Sunjata wins the contest with the following statement, which reads like a riddle:

> I don don, don don Kokodji.
> Formerly guests were sacred.
> I don don, don don Kokodji.
> But the gold came only yesterday.
> Whereas I came before yesterday.
>
> (S₄:30)

Sunjata thus informs his host that he knows about a bribe which had persuaded the king to challenge his guest.

It is important to remember, however, that the enigmatic statements offered in many of these examples are integral elements of the plot, rather than simple riddles offered for the audience to solve. As Abrahams (1972c:185) points out, they therefore serve as devices to heighten dramatic tension and lead to a satisfying dramatic resolution.

The presence of riddles as part of the plot of a story demonstrates that riddling is a practice which takes place in the culture which has generated that story. In actual performance, however, riddles have a range of very different functions. Perhaps the most obvious is their role as entertainment. Independent of setting, riddle sessions can be seen as an enjoyable and intriguing way of passing time with friends. But while riddles may be intellectually pleasing and entertaining, they also serve more serious functions. Since they require both a questioner and a respondent, they are essentially referential in nature and help to bind participants together as a group. Many riddles in a riddle contest will be known to all the participants and therefore serve as a demonstration of group knowledge and cohesiveness. Even when this is not the case, riddling is a highly participatory activity inasmuch as no one person dominates the performance. By the same token, the persons answering riddles are by no means passive partners in the process: they must examine the image to find the clue so that they can identify what is wrong and 'correct' the statement with their answer. If someone refuses to attempt an answer for the riddle, the questioner is frustrated and the riddle performance is broken. Many 'old chestnuts' have such an established position in the common cultural context that they serve an initiatory role, bringing successive generations of young children into the ranks of riddlers. Thus one of the first riddles learned by a young American is 'What is black and white and red all over?'–a newspaper, followed closely by the variant answer of 'a sunburned zebra'.

Another function of riddling is as an informal test of intelligence and personality. This function is particularly important, for instance, in the selection of a partner in arranged marriages in traditional Somalia. Andrzejewski (1973:93) gives the example of men who pose three questions when choosing a wife for their cousin from among three girls:

1. What is the best way of making boiled millet palatable?
2. What fence offers the best protection for camels?
3. What is the best sleeping mat for men?

The first two candidates give answers which go into a great deal of technical detail. The third, however, prefers to give simple answers which reveal both wit and wisdom:

1. To give it to a hungry man.
2. To be born in a powerful clan and to have a wife from a powerful clan.
3. Peace.

On the basis of these answers the cousins decided in favour of the third girl. Riddles are also posed as challenges to marriage in the story of Oidipous and in the exchange between the Norse god Thor and the crafty dwarf Alvis, who wanted to marry Thor's daughter Thrud in *The Elder Edda*.

On some occasions, riddles seem to question certain types of established order. They make a point of playing with conceptual borderlines. The crossing of such boundaries has the effect of showing that things are not quite as stable as they might seem. The riddle provides the poser with intellectual satisfaction and at the same time allows the group to explore and ponder their understanding of the order of things. This effect can be observed in many different settings. Isbell and Fernandez (1977), for instance, describe the way in which riddling begins near puberty in Quechua children and contributes to both sexual socialization and language development. Problems of sexuality and, indeed, many other recurrent social issues, can be seen as a focus for many West Indian riddles, too. The activities which surround death wakes provide a clear example of how this process works. The first night of the wake is given over to more serious observations such as speechmaking; but for up to eight nights afterwards, riddles, story-telling and other activities, often of a licentious nature, take the place of the more formal behaviour. Abrahams (1972c:12) cites the following example of a riddle, common at wakes, which seeks to atomize the problem of death:

A: Between the living and the dead;
     Seven tongues in one head
B: What is that?
A: Well there was a head.
B: What kind of head?
A: Like a cattle head.
B: Yeah
A: And seven black bird go inside the head.
B: Not so man. Speak your riddle good; your answer good.
A: Was an old cattle go in the mountain and dead. And then the head and a bird go and he lay six egg in the head. And after the six egg hatch, six young bird come out. And the mother, there is seven tongue in the head between the living and the dead. Right?

This riddle resolves the apparent opposition between life and death by suggesting that life can only go on because of death. The effect is to make the participants feel that they have some degree of control over an otherwise confusing and disorienting experience.

Riddles can mirror many other cultural aspects of oral societies; they play an important role in establishing a person's status and in furthering social development. Riddling often forms a part of highly competitive behaviour in which the aim is to assert power by causing confusion. On some occasions, this competition takes the form of a battle of the sexes; in the Solomon Islands, for instance, boys and girls sometimes sit opposite each other and take turns in posing riddles (Maranda 1971). Among the Vendas, a Bantu people of the Northern Transvaal in South Africa, young men who take part in riddling sessions are trying to establish their identity as individuals and as members of a junior social group. Riddles are widely used within Venda society as a means of assessing social status. They are used here, as in Somalia, as part of the courtship process, as a way of testing the marriageability of the suitor. Interestingly, however, the Venda male achieves greater recognition for his ability to pose riddles than for providing answers or even under-standing the content of a riddle posed by another. Two types of contest commonly take place (Blacking 1961). In the first:

> A asks B riddles, which B successfully answers. Eventually B is stumped
> but A does not give him the answer ... B must then ask A riddles until
> A too is stumped, A then reveals the answer to the original.

The second type of contest goes on longer and is easier to play. It also
has the advantage of saving face, because the second player can make
up for any lack of knowledge by striking a bargain:

> A asks B a riddle. B does not answer it; instead he 'buys' A's answer by
> posing another riddle. A answers his own first riddle and then 'buys'
> answer to B's riddle by posing another. B then answers his own first
> riddle and 'buys' ... and so on.

Tales of Us and Them

Rarely is verbal skill more important for an oral culture than in telling a
story. Sometimes narratives will take the form of story-telling sessions
where one tale triggers another. Afro-Americans, for instance, take part
in what they call 'lying sessions' or 'telling lies', story-telling rounds
where each narrator tries to top the one that went before Ferris (1972).
But the competitive element is by no means limited to Afro-American
communities. There is a story-telling session of sorts in *Odyssey* VIII–XII,
when the aoidos Phemios sings about the Trojan War and then Odysseus gives an account of his own adventures. In a similar vein, when
Abraham Lincoln, a story-teller of some considerable talent, came face
to face with another tale-teller, he is reputed to have responded immediately with a matching yarn (Dorson 1962:97). It is even recorded
that when an office seeker topped Lincoln's parable with a splendid folk
yarn of his own, the president promptly gave him the job. In such cases,
a close bond develops between the story-tellers.

Stories are, however, by no means restricted to special story-telling
sessions. Like proverbs they are often integrated into other activities
and create a bond between the narrator and the audience. Sermons, for
instance, are sometimes extended narratives which convey a theme,
although the way in which this is achieved will vary from one faith to
another. In Jewish sermons, a parable will be used to put across a
particular point. In Afro-American sermons, the preacher and members
of the congregation will tell the truth though 'story', or will testify to the
experience of being saved or to the power and goodness of God. But
'testifying' can also take place within a secular context focusing on
subjects such as racism at the hands of the White oppressor or testimo-

nials of the power of a gifted musician. In both cases, the story-teller is re-enacting the emotion through narrative in such a way that listeners can vicariously experience it. In the *Iliad* opposing warriors even tell each other stories on the battlefield. The encounter between the Lykian Glaukos and the Greek Diomedes in *Iliad* VI, for example, is marked by Glaukos' long tale explaining his ancestry to Diomedes. This tale reveals such a strong bond between the two opposing warriors that they decide to end their hand-to-hand conflict.

Most often, however, story-telling is such an integral part of the culture that tales are embedded into everyday conversation to make general observations about life, to explain a point or to make an argument. In this situation, the successful story-teller is someone with the ability to apply a story appropriately to an immediate situation. As Eastern European Jews often remark, 'A story is fine but one that is used at the right moment is even better' (Kirshenblatt-Gimblett 1977:287). This is by no means a talent valued only by Jewish speakers: Lincoln, among many others, has been praised for his ability to match the right tale to the right situation (Dorson 1962:97). When asked why he dismissed Cameron and not his entire cabinet, for instance, he replied with the anecdote of the farmer who trapped nine skunks and then let eight go because the one he killed made such a stench.

Even since folklore became a serious field of study in the nineteenth century, scholarly attention to oral narrative has focused on the distribution and collection of texts. The seminal collection of folktale motifs by Thompson (1955–8) has shown the regularity with which tales recur from one cultural context to another. In more recent years greater emphasis has been placed on the functions which folktales serve within a culture. In the following pages we look at three folktale types—tales of us and them, tales of now and then, and trickster tales, and consider some of the ways in which these tales, found time and again in many different cultures, all cement group solidarity.

Many elements of stories use dialects, regional customs and local history to emphasize the cultural bond within the oral community. We have already discussed in 'Thinking on Your Feet' the special linguistic forms often reserved for performances of epic in many cultures. Another example of such localized material is the cultural reservoir represented by a proverb which may function in one community but not in another. In this context the Japanese proverb 'The way your eyes look can say more than your mouth', which advocates silence after speech, can be compared with the counter-sentiment expressed in the Serbo-Croatian proverb '(Who) asks does not wander' (Saville-Troike 1982:172), which expresses a distruct for silence. Similarly the images and metaphors contained in riddles are culturally conditioned, and a riddle from one tradition may be impenetrable to a listener from another.

Sometimes regionalisms form whole narrative units. For example, the *Sunjata* epic unites diverse people from a wide geographic area in West Africa by means of localized tales. The final third of Bamba Suso's version of the epic (S_1) is devoted to local history of the region around the River Gambia where the performance takes place. The Homeric epics, on the other hand, appear to have undergone a process of delocalization. At one point regional versions of the epic probably existed, but sometime around the seventh century, while the texts of the epics were gradually becoming fixed, these regional elements reorganized into a panhellenic version of the epic, one which helped unite the diverse peoples of Greece into a cultural unit (Nagy 1979:6–11).

Wherever there is population movement, comic dialect tales also recur with remarkable regularity. They are particularly prevalent in the USA, wherever an ethnic community includes both first- and second-generation Americans. There are tales of the French, Finnish and Cornish in the Upper Peninsula of Michigan; Danish tales in Utah; Spanish-Mexican stories in the southwest; German in Pennsylvania; Jewish in the big cities. They occur with similar regularity in any setting where one linguistically or culturally distinct group comes into contact with another.

Dialect tales rely on the ability of the story-teller to mimic the fossilized pronunciation and grammar of the immigrants' first language as well as their facial expressions and hand gestures. They ridicule the culture shock and mishaps of the newcomer. The function of such dialect tales varies according to the story-teller. A story told by a member of the same ethnic group to other members of that community uses self-ridicule to reinforce the ties of the community within an alien culture; when the same story is told by an outsider to outsiders, however, it is the culture of the outsiders which is strengthened. Ridicule creates a barrier between the two groups and reinforces their cultural differences. There is an amazing degree of similarity, for instance, between the American Polack jokes, British stories about the Irish Paddy, the tales of the comic Afrikaaner Van de Moeve told by English-speaking Whites in South Africa, Sikh stories current throughout India or the jokes which the French target at Belgians (Davies 1987). In the fifth century BC the Greek comic playwright Aristophanes also made use of ethnic distinctions between Athenians and Spartans for humorous effect. In *Lysistrata* he brought before his Athenian audience Spartan officials who spoke and acted according to the Athenian stereotype of Spartans (Henderson 1987:xlv–1). Performed during a bitter war between the two cities, this play thus affirmed the cultural bond which tied Athenians together.

In a similar vein, the special language of the Afro-American toast, or epic poem, often impenetrable to White listeners, helps to define toasts as an exclusively Black speech event. Take, for instance the following toast, known as 'The Monkey and the Baboon' (Abrahams 1962:9):

He said, 'Mr. Monkey, if it ain't my friend.
We gonna play some "Georgia Skin".'
'Raise! That ain't my game.
Me and you can play some "Cooncan".'
'Why should we argue and fight, acting like a fool.
We'll just step in the hall and shoot a game of pool.'
So the baboon reached over to break the rack.
The monkey kicked him square in the—and he snatched him back.
He said, 'Unh, unh, not here.'
So they was fussing and fighting over who was going to make the break.
The giraffe was the houseman. You know naturally he had a stake.
So he said, 'We'll flip for it.'
So he flipped a coin about three feet in the air.
The baboon was itching to try to make a pin.
It was a two-headed coin, the monkey had to win.
The monkey grabbed a stick, and the baboon snatched the chalk,
And around the table them two mother—ers started to walk.
The monkey broke the rack. Got the one, two, three, four, and five.
Brought tears in the baboon's eyes.
Now the six, seven and eight
Was a natural take.
The nine and ten
Flew right in.
The 'leven ball crossed corner, the twelve just as well
The thirteen in the side pocket, combination, like a bat out of hell.
Baboon jumped up, said, 'It's a god-damn shame,
I can't beat this ugly mother—er in no kind of game.
We gonna play some "Cooncan".'
The monkey told the baboon, 'You know Brother Buzzard who live across the creek?'
He said, 'I cooncanned him for a solid week.'
He said, 'But you ain't gonna act right,
'Cause it took all me and my blade could do to keep out of a fight.
But you go find yourself a stump to fit your rump,
I'ma cooncan you tonight till you a—hole jump.'

It is no accident, for instance, that, until quite recently, toasts were completely unknown to Whites. Features of the toast such as sexual assertiveness, the use of taboo four-letter words and scorn for sentimental or abstract verbiage, were not likely to attract the favourable attention of conventional Whites. The language of the toast, which has even been interpreted as rebellion against White values (Dance 1978), thus reinforces a special bond within the Afro-American community.

Tales of Then and Now

There are also substantial numbers of oral performances which offer explanations for the way things are in the world today. In *Sunjata*, for instance, these aetiological elements explain, in particular, the intricate family structure upon which much of West African society is based. Thus the epic will offer etymologies for important Manding surnames such as Kante, which belongs to the descendants of Sumanguru. In one etymology (S_2:1319–44), hero and antagonist meet in a circumcision shed, where Sumanguru plans to slay Sunjata and where the hero converts the words of Sumanguru ('*N kang te*', 'It was not my voice', S_2:1323) into a new name for Sumanguru ('Call him Kante– –*n kang te*' S_2:1343).

Other aetiologies in *Sunjata* explain the special relationship between particular Manding families, such as that between the Keitas, the family of Sunjata, and the Kouyatés, the clan of his personal griot, Bala Fassigi. In an episode which occurs on the hero's return to his homeland in Bamba Suso's version, hero and griot journey through the bush and become terribly hungry. Discreetly removing some flesh from the calf of his leg, Sunjata treats the wound with some medicinal leaves, cooks the flesh and offers it to his unsuspecting *jalo*. As the journey continues the singer notices that Sunjata has developed a limp and inquires the cause. Sunjata then shows him the septic wound and tells him what he has done. The following comment by the singer reminds the audience that the special bond between the Keitas and the Kouyatés is based upon the relationship between Sunjata and his personal singer:

> There is a special relationship
> Between the members of the Keita family and the members of the Kuyaté family.
> Even today, if a member of the Kuyaté family deceives a member of the Keita family,
> Things will go badly for him.
> If a member of the Keita family deceives a member of the Kuyaté family,
> Things will go badly for him.
>
> (S_1:470–5)

The performance thus reaffirms the traditional social structure and unites 'then' with 'now', the heroic ancestors with their descendants who are members of the audience (Sienkewicz in press).

In the Afro-American tradition there are numerous tales explaining the origin of animals, as well as others explaining why people have dark skin, why their hair is kinked, and why they remain poor. Usually the explanations are based on alleged character defects such as tardiness, ignorance, laziness and greed, as can be seen in the tale which explains 'Why the Black Man's Hair is Nappy' (Dance 1978:8):

> All right now, we are going to our races; we going to find out where the Black people got their hair from, and how they got it. When it was time for the Lord to give hair, He called all three of these men, and this is what he said. Well, first he called the white man to come on and get his hair. All right, the white man he went right on up there and got his hair. So the Lord called the Jew man to get his hair. So the Jew man went up there and got his hair, and said, 'thank you, Lord'.
>
> So when it got down to the Black man, the Lord called him. And do you know what the Black man said? Black man said, 'Lord, ball it up and throw it to me'. And it's been balled up ever since.

While some observers, such as Weldon (1959:183), have interpreted these stories as evidence that contact with White people has resulted in self-hatred and a denial of blackness, such aetiologies can also be understood instead as a barely disguised satire of racism, as ridicule of illogical explanations for an oppressive situation imposed upon Blacks by White prejudices and White economic institutions. This story acknowledges the relationship between the Black man and White society just as the aetiologies in *Sunjata* explain family relationships. Black listeners to such tales are not laughing at the Black characters portrayed as much as they are recognizing the absurdity of their situation. In a similar way, members of the West African Kante family can enjoy the telling of the origin of their surname despite the fact that it occurs in a power struggle which their ancestor loses to Sunjata.

Aetiology is just one of several threads which intertwine the speech event with cultural considerations. Biebuyck and Mateene (1969:35), for example, describe the *Mwindo Epic* in the following terms:

> It contains a succinct survey of the many basic institutions and customs, some described in detail, others merely suggested or implied (e.g., kinship terminology, patterns of behaviour between kinsmen, marriage customs), aspects of political organization (e.g., local groups, political hierarchy), ritual, and religion. It provides a broad inventory of Nyanga material culture, and gives succinct references to basic techniques of agriculture and honey-harvesting. The epic also tries to account for the origin of certain institutions (cult of Lightning, fission of political entities, hunting taboos imposed on chiefs). It further provides a synopsis of basic

Nyanga values. And, finally, it permits us to enter the personal world of the narrator, who inserts many of his own reflections and meditations.

Looking After Yourself

The value of verbal skill is particularly strong in trickster or prankster tales. In these stories, common throughout the world, the underdog gets the better of an authority figure. Odysseus' use of wit and subterfuge to blind the Kyklops Polyphemos and escape from his cave in *Odyssey* IX has made him the archetypal trickster in Western culture. Real-life characters like Hershele Ostropoler, Shmerl Snitkever and Yosl Marshelik, renowned for their verbal wit, people the tales of Eastern European Jewish story-tellers (Kirshenblatt-Gimblett 1977). In *Sunjata*, it is especially the hero's sister who exhibits trickster qualities during her seduction of Sumanguru, the chief antagonist of the epic. Both West Africans and Afro-Caribbeans tell tales of Ananse the Spider Man who usually gets the better of much bigger and stronger adversaries through his guile. The Afro-American toast about the Monkey and the Baboon mentioned above also includes a trickster figure whose existence depends on his mental and physical agility. In fact, Afro-Americans have many different kinds of trickster tales (Dance 1978): Brer Rabbit, the rabbit who outfoxes the fox; Slave John, his human counterpart, who is constantly in conflict with Ole Massa; his contemporary parallel, the Bad Nigger, who rather than relying on wit, cunning and persuasion, resorts to physical force.

While Afro-American trickster tales have very frequently been interpreted primarily as opportunities for the acting out of hostility to White authority without the risk of physical danger, such an interpretation appears, in view of the variety of trickster tales told in non-slave contexts, to be too culturally specific. Another type of trickster tale found in the Afro-American repertoire suggests a broader explanation. In these tales, known as 'little boy' trickster tales, not only the conflict between Blacks and Whites but also the tension between Blacks inside and outside the Church is highlighted when the hypocrisy of the preacher is publicly revealed by a little boy (Dance 1978). Interestingly, little boy and preacher tales are by no means restricted to Afro-American communities. They are found widely in situations throughout Europe in which the Church aligns itself with upper-class society. The Aarne–Thompson (1928) index of folktales contains some 124 different examples.

The prankster tale, then, can be best understood outside a particular social setting, such as the American slave culture. Taken in broadest terms, the function of the prankster tale would appear to be both wish-fulfilment and catharsis, i.e. an expression of the subconscious urge by children (the little boy) to discover flaws in the authority of the adult world (the preacher); or, by extension, the prankster tale may be an attempt by any individual to overcome the everyday obstacles of power and authority. The same could also be said of tall tales in general, such as the story of Otto Walta which shows the individual pitted successfully against the powerful railroad company.

At the same time, all these tales also affirm the value of intelligence and verbal wit as a means to success. The key to Odysseus' victory over the Kyklops is the use of a pseudonym 'Nobody' in *Odyssey* IX:364– 412, and Brer Rabbit, caught in the embrace of the Tar Baby, employs a brilliant combination of psychology and verbal dexterity to persuade Brer Fox to hurl him into the briar patch instead of eating him (Harris 1925:16–19). It is not surprising that verbal skills are rewarded conspicuously in societies in which the art of speaking is so important.

The Many Fibred Cloth

Having looked at different genres, such as proverbs, riddles, genealogies and aetiologies, which carry social meaning in oral culture, we turn our attention now to ways in which these genres combine in actual performance. On some occasions, these smaller genres appear in isolation. The primary aim, for instance, of riddling competitions between men and women in the Solomon Islands, or Venda adolescents, is the exchange of riddles. Far more often, smaller generic forms are woven into the fabric of much longer performances. We are dealing, then, with multigeneity, with extended performances which are made up of many smaller genres. Mutigeneity, however, in no way implies disjointedness. While the individual threads or fibres may be very different, the overall effect of the finished cloth is of a unitary whole.

Any discussion of longer performances will focus sooner or later on the epic. Since this subject has generated a great deal of heated debate over the years, it receives special attention here. However, our aim is not necessarily to proclaim the epic as the pinnacle of performance in oral culture. Rather we want to unravel some of the confused motives surrounding the discussion of this genre and to argue that the multigeneity which is clearly a feature of the epic is also an integral part of longer performances of many different kinds.

To a great extent, the Homeric epics have determined the study of oral literature in the West. The *Webster's Dictionary* (McKechnie 1983) definition of the genre as 'a long narrative poem about the deeds of a traditional or historical hero or heroes of high station' suits the Homeric epics since it was designed to do so. Modern awareness of oral composition in performance, highlighted by Lord's study of the Yugoslav oral epic, initially arose because of the so-called Homeric question, the scholarly debate as to whether or not a single person composed the poems essentially in the form we know. Indeed, the admiration that these poems have received in the West for generations has resulted in an exalted position for the epic, whether oral or written, among the many forms of human composition. The epic is considered so important and such a quintessential art form that, if epic performances did not evolve in a particular society, that society was considered to be somehow deficient.

The intensity of passion connected with this subject is illustrated by the furore which Finnegan raised by suggesting in *Oral Literature in Africa* (1970:108–10) that the oral epic poem was not 'a typical African form'. The immediate and indignant scholarly reaction can be seen in Johnson's essay 'Yes, Virginia, there is an Epic in Africa' (1980) and other works asserting the existence of the epic form on that continent. In Finnegan's defence, it should be mentioned that reliable transcriptions of African epics were not readily available at the time her book was written. For example, she knew *Sunjata* only through prose reworkings, such as that of Niane (1965). With the recognition of indigenous African epics, African literature could finally find equal place with the literatures of other cultures, including the Greeks.

Or could it? Another difficulty has been with the poetic form which the genre inherited from the Greeks. Greenberg (1960) argued that, as a rule, prosodic poetry did not exist in sub-Saharan Africa, and Finnegan herself used the long prose narrative sections of performances from equatorial areas of Africa to question the existence of epic poetry on the continent. Scholars of African literature, like Bird (1972; 1976) and Johnson (1980; 1986), have spent a lot of ink since then to show that, to a certain extent, our Western expectations about rhyme, rhythm, and other 'poetic' forms are ethnocentric, that special poetic traits, very different from our own, can be found in African contexts. We have already talked about some of these characteristics of African poetry in 'Thinking on Your Feet'.

But perhaps we have asked the wrong questions. Maybe the issue is not whether or not oral African literature has poetic elements or whether or not there is an epic in Africa. The very same criticisms of inferiority have been levelled at the oral performances of other cultures, such as those of West Indians and Afro-Americans. Yet, our discussion of oral performance has shown that many features associated with poetry in a literate, Western context, features like rhythm, rhyme, special language, music, and, especially, metaphor, are regularly associated with traditional oral performance. Perhaps it is inappropriate to draw the literate distinction between prose and poetry into a discussion of oral performance. Afro-American sermons are, in many ways, as 'poetic' as the Homeric epics, even though the former appear written in prose and the latter in dactylic hexameter. In *spoken* form both sermons and epics sound much more alike, much more 'poetic'.

Johnson (1986:30–57) suggests that a special trait of African oral epic poetry is multigeneity, that the overlying narrative structure of the epic incorporates smaller elements which can also function as separate genres in the oral society. Johnson has identified some of these simpler generic forms as 'praise-names, folk etymologies, proverbs, incantations, curses, and oaths'. To these could be added forms like laments, genealogies, riddles, and so on. In this book we have again and again cited examples of these forms, not only in *Sunjata*, but also in other long oral performances, including the Homeric epics and Afro-American sermons and toasts. As a result of this survey, we suggest that the trait of multigeneity is not only a distinctive feature of oral epics but is also a common feature of long oral performances.

Multigeneity in oral performance can be seen, for instance, in Afro-American toasts. Typically, the dialogue between the protagonists in a toast is interspersed with description of the action as the story unfolds and the end is marked by a twist which can take the form of an ironic comment or even a boast such as this one:

> If anybody asks who pulled this toast,
> Just tell them old bullshitting Snell, from coast to coast.
> I live on Shotgun Avenue, Tommygun Drive,
> Pistol Apartment, and Romm 45.
>
> (Abrahams 1970b)

The wide range of forms in this type of performance is striking. Narrative, description, dialogue and boast all have their expected place, just as they do in the Homeric epics, in *Sunjata*, in the Afro-American sermon, or even in a South Asian marriage song.

The Finished Product

Oral communities are essentially small-scale, tightly-knit groups which share a common body of knowledge. Oral performance plays a vital role in cementing social cohesion of this kind. The use of proverbs, for instance, supports group solidarity by reinforcing commonly accepted values. 'Them and Us' tales perform a similar function by emphasizing common cultural bonds; so do 'Then and Now' stories, which offer a rationale for a particular form of behaviour and therefore support the status quo. Riddles, in contrast, give licence to explore ambiguous aspects of life which potentially threaten community ideals. Similarly, tales of craftiness identify flaws in the accepted order and operate as a kind of release valve which ensures a social equilibrium. In all these cases, good talkers draw on a joint stock of oral experience to reinforce community ideals.

In the oral community, where everything is ultimately related to everything else, multigeneity is the string which holds the web together. If any single feature sets oral performance apart from conventional literary genres, it is probably this tendency to include rather than exclude, to draw the audience and the community at large into the performance by means of referential elements, to incorporate a variety of traditional forms into the fibre of the performance. The epic clearly represents an excellent example of the many-fibred cloth of perform- ance, incorporating as it does a wide range of smaller genres. It is important to remember, however, that multigeneity of this kind is not only a feature of the epic but is also an integral element of longer performances of many different kinds.

Part IV

Stepping Back

Step after step the ladder is ascended.
G. Herbert, *Outlandish Proverbs* (1640)

In this section we step back and take stock of where we have been and where we are now. In the course of this book we have looked at the various perspectives which mould the oral experience. Often these perceptions differ radically from those associated with the literate tradition. As a result, strategies which are part of the aesthetic of oral performance have sometimes been seriously misunderstood. At best, orality is perceived to be quaint or exotic; at worst it is dismissed as unsophisticated or underdeveloped. In 'Repairing the Seams', we look at the question of cross-cultural communication, particularly as it affects the education of children from predominantly oral cultures who, for historical, political or economic reasons, now find themselves subject to the expectations of a literate society.

In 'Coming to a Close' we summarize the findings of our survey. We also make some projections. How has recent scholarship changed our perceptions of orality? What are the implications of these changed perceptions for future work on oral culture? To what extent can research within one discipline throw light on the methodologies and insights of another? How can attitudes towards the many vibrant oral cultures which are to be found side by side with literate traditions be changed in such a way that orality is treated as a valuable resource rather than a sign of backwardness, or a relic of the past?

10

Repairing the Seams

A pause in the wrong place, an intonation misunderstood and a whole conversation went awry.

E. M. Forster, *A Passage to India*

In this book we have presented oral culture as something which is alive and vibrant. It has its own aesthetic and deserves study in its own right, both as an art form and as a way of understanding in greater depth the social motives for communication within a given society. This approach can be characterized as the 'pure' study of oral culture. There is, however, an applied aspect to this subject and we feel it would be premature to end before looking at the range of ways in which an appreciation of the oral–literate continuum can help in everyday communication.

We live in a world which is becoming increasingly interdependent. Greater ease in communications and travel has made it possible for all but the most isolated of societies to come into contact with people from other countries. In many cases, the contact is ephemeral and at one remove – the package holiday of British tourists to Corfu; or the television documentary on Masai warriors in Kenya. In other situations, though, this contact can become an important part of everyday life. In the USA the so-called 'melting pot' has proven to be a myth and migrants from all over the world have adapted to American life while retaining many features of their linguistic and cultural heritage. In postwar Britain, nurses, bus drivers and factory workers have been recruited from the Caribbean and South Asia and the catering personnel in hospitals and hotels from Southern Europe, Morocco and the Philippines. In 1987 nearly 200 different languages were recorded among the children in the schools of London, one of the most cosmopolitan centres in the world (ILEA 1987).

Potential Minefields

In situations of this kind, different linguistic and cultural expectations come face to face on a daily basis and co-exist in varying degrees of tension. Our expectations about what is appropriate behaviour in conversation are, to a large extent, moulded by the culture into which we have been born. They are largely unconscious. It is only when we interact with people whose own cultural experience is different from our own that the seams begin to show. Often, it is only when someone breaks a rule that we even become aware of the existence of that rule.

Sometimes breakdowns in communication can be explained in terms of transfer from first to second language. Thus Gumperz (1982:173–4) describes the way in which South Asians ask questions with falling rather than a rising intonation and are perceived by British listeners as rude and uninterested. There is also a great deal of variation from one culture to the next in expectations as to when it is appropriate to talk. At one end of the spectrum, certain native American groups wait several minutes before responding or taking a turn in conversation (Saville-Troike 1982:23); at the other end of the spectrum, in Afro-Caribbean conversations it is considered perfectly acceptable for several people to speak at the same time (Reisman 1977:113–14). There are cross-cultural differences, too, in cohesion and coherence. For instance, Indian speakers often emphasize the sentence just before their main point but lower their voices when making the main point, even when talking in English. In many other societies, speakers expect the main point to be emphasized (Gumperz 1982:148–9).

Nor do cross-cultural difficulties result only from *how* the speaker chooses to say something. The actual content gives rise to similar misunderstandings. In some societies, it is considered better to get 'straight to the point'; in others, it is incumbent on the speaker to approach the subject more indirectly. Certain subjects are considered legitimate discussion points in some societies and are totally taboo in others. In a similar vein, Athabaskan Indians rarely ask questions and Australian Aboriginals never ask 'Why?'

In this chapter we argue that differences attributable to the oral–literate continuum also play an important role in cross-cultural misunderstanding. We do not wish, however, to oversimplify this process. As we have tried to show throughout this book, enormous differences exist within and between different cultures, both oral and literate. And yet there is a real sense in which the distinction between oral and literate traditions represents a psychological reality.

At first sight, the discourse styles of Athabaskan Indians have little in common with those of Afro-Americans: Athabaskans emphasize brevity rather than expansion, while Afro-Americans and Afro-Caribbeans set considerable store on verbosity. There is, none the less, a quality and a mind-set which bind together oral cultures as diverse as these:

members share a common set of expectations, emphasizing the import-ance of interaction between the speaker and the audience. Within this tradition, received wisdom, rooted in shared experience and common sense, is embodied in formulaic expressions such as proverbs and clichés. In marked contrast, literate societies place greater stress on decontextualized content and provide as much information as is necess-ary for someone in another time and place to follow what is happening. The importance of speaker–audience interaction is minimized. The literate view of knowledge is based upon facts and information which take the form of written records.

We are, of course, talking in relative and not absolute terms. Strategies that have been associated with oral and literate tradition can in fact be employed in any mode. The classroom or public lecturer relies on primarily literate strategies in an oral context, as does the television announcer reading from the autocue. Conversely, the writer of an informal letter to family and friends will draw heavily on oral strategies in a literate context. As we have already indicated, we are dealing essentially with an oral–literate continuum, not an artificial or idealized world in which some individuals can be labelled 'oral' and others 'literate'.

While acknowledging the dangers of oversimplification, we argue with Tannen (1984) that it is possible to highlight certain areas where strategies associated with the two ends of the oral–literate continuum are likely to give rise to serious misunderstanding when speakers associated with different traditions interact. The principles which underpin the organization of longer stretches of speech are fun-damentally different in oral and literate traditions. Various aspects of discourse style are affected, including coherence, or the underlying structure of what is said, and its cultural significance for those creating or comprehending it; the oral tendency to personalize conversation, drawing on the shared experience of speaker and audience, versus the literate preference for depersonalizing what is being said; the character-ization of formulaic language as 'quaint' or 'lazy' on the one hand, or 'wise' and socially desirable on the other; and conflicting expectations as to how listeners should indicate interest and attention.

Coherence

One of the most notable features of literate discourse is the tendency to develop thought in an essentially linear manner and to state explicitly the relationships between points. Significantly, there is no shortage of evidence that White, middle-class speakers of English also use an oral approximation of this style (Gumperz, Kaltman and O'Connor 1984; Michaels and Collins 1984). The examples from oral culture in the preceding pages, however, point to an underlying structure which departs in many important respects from the analytic linearity of literate discourse. If we take the example of the Afro-American blues lyrics, discussed in 'Spinning the Threads', we see that there are unvarying expectations about the structure of the verse, yet the order of the verses could be changed without substantially changing the integrity of the song as a whole. While observers from outside the Afro-American community often find blues lyrics confusing and difficult to understand, Afro-Americans consider a discourse structure of this kind unproblematic. Coherence is provided by shared knowledge of the traditions, the special language and expectations of what constitutes a blues song.

Similar observations have been made about oral narratives in a variety of traditions (Tannen 1981; Scollon and Scollon 1981). Very often stories are felt by literate observers to be episodic, disconnected and difficult to follow. It is not the case, however, that oral discourse lacks organizing principles. Erickson's (1984) analysis of coherence strategies in discussions of urban Afro-American adolescents, for instance, points to a very different discourse structure. The use of particular examples is by no means random but is underpinned by the semantic connection of similarity and contrast from one anecdote to the next. There are also internal constraints which are important for rhetorical effect. Within a set of anecdotes relating to a given topic, Erickson (1984:132) suggests that it is possible to identify a crescendo of dramatic emphasis in which the most dramatically ironic anecdote appears last. The inescapable conclusion is that Afro-American discourse style is a fully developed, internally consistent and effective rhetorical system.

The potential for misunderstanding, however, is considerable. Erickson (1984:98) describes a meeting between members of the faculty of a large university and representatives of inner-city communities. Afro-American speakers presented their arguments in close collaboration with their audience. They made extensive use of particular examples and anecdotes and thus drew on a typical oral discourse style. Many White faculty members experienced difficulty with this style. One woman retorted, 'I didn't come here to listen to a Baptist prayer meeting'. Ultimately, White participants came away from the meeting with the impression that 'those people' were incoherent, incomprehensible and unreasonable. Afro-American representatives, for their part, considered the White faculty to be equally unreasonable.

There is clearly a responsibility on the part of all parties in cross-cultural communication to appreciated the different ways in which discourse can be organized, and for the socially dominant group to avoid assuming either that there is only one way of handling discussion or that their own approach is inherently superior. Erickson (1984:84) sums up the situation in this way:

> [Afro-American rhetoric] is powerfully persuasive and engaging on the street corner of an urban black ghetto, but . . . fails to persuade or even attract serious attention in mainstream school classrooms, employment interviews, or in negotiation sessions between grass roots neighborhood residents and mainstream representatives of business, government, and social service organizations with whom neighborhood residents must occasionally deal. Miscommunication in these types of institutional gatekeeping situations contributes to the perpetuation of disadvantage and lack of influence of the individuals and groups who employ these nonstandard ways of speaking.

Oral tradition places more emphasis on personal topics, binding together speaker and audience in a single referential web. Strategies are geared towards personalization and bringing the conversation to life with actual instances and examples. Speech is immediate and interactive. Listeners can indicate approval or disapproval and speakers are therefore able to mould their performance accordingly. In contrast, writers are removed from their audience. It is important for writing to decontextualize content so that readers in different times and places can understand what is taking place. Those people who tend towards the oral tradition in their speech will make extensive use of personalization; those who veer towards the literate tradition will tend to use strategies which decontextualize the subject of conversation.

In the oral tradition, speakers include detail, characterization, plot and related digressions as a normal part of their discourse style. From the Mende of West Africa to Eastern European Jews and from Afro-Americans to the Xhosa of Southern Africa, these strategies are the building blocks of story-telling and part of the shared expectations of what constitutes successful performance. They are also an integral part of normal conversational interaction. Tannen (1980b), for instance, reports an experiment in which Greek Americans and non-Greek Americans viewed a film without a soundtrack and afterwards were required to recount what they had seen. The two groups responded quite differently: Greek Americans tended to make up a story about the film, 'interpreting' what they had seen. When they made judgements about the film, these tended to be about the characters' behaviour or the message of the film. In contrast, non-Greek Americans recalled details more accurately and listed them as though they were performing a memory task. When they offered judgments, these tended to focus on the film-maker's technique and to draw heavily on cinematic jargon. As Tannen (1980a:2) points out:

> The Greeks . . . seemed concerned with presenting themselves as acute judges of human behaviour and good storytellers, exercising strategies associated with the in-group setting or oral tradition. By performing a memory task and presenting themselves as acute critics of cinematic technique, the Americans in the study were exercising strategies associated with schooling or literate tradition.

There is evidence that differences in strategy of this kind lead to negative stereotyping in both directions. Vassiliou et al. (1972), for instance, have shown that Greeks characterize Americans as cold but organized while Americans tend to stereotype Greeks as enthusiastic and spontaneous but disorganized. On the basis of the responses to the Tannen experiment, it is not difficult to understand the triggers for such stereotypes.

This fundamental difference in attitude towards personalization, on the one hand, and towards decontextualization, on the other hand, has far-reaching implications in cross-cultural communication. Those who identify more closely with the literate tradition are likely to dismiss an oral style as unnecessarily verbose, because of the literate expectation that the speaker 'get to the point'. Smitherman (1977:161–3) provides another example of this phenomenon in an American context. She cites the case of a 20-year-old Black male who was charged as an accessory to an armed robbery. His attorney had already entered a plea of not guilty for him at the pre-trial hearing and the White judge had a copy of the young man's statement in front of him. At this point the judge made the cultural 'mistake' of asking the defendant if he had anything to add. The young man responded by launching on a long and elaborate account of what had taken place. He was still in full flow when the judge, no doubt fearful that this tale would take up an enormous amount of court time without adding anything to the evidence in front of him, asked the attorney and his client to approach the bench. He ordered the young man bound over for trial and went on to the next case. The perceptions of judge and defendant as to what constituted appropriate language behaviour were clearly miles apart.

A similar phenomenon in interaction between Greek and non-Greek Americans has been labelled 'the brevity effect' by Tannen (1981:2). Americans argued that the response 'OK' was casual and sincere because it was brief; when a husband said 'OK' to his wife it was therefore interpreted as meaning 'yes'. In contrast, Greeks felt that it was unenthusiastic and considered it to mean 'no'. For them to have placed another, more positive interpretation on this response, they would have expected more elaboration on the part of the spouse.

We have dealt at length in chapters 2 and 8 with the role which formulaic language plays, not simply as an aid to composition in performance but as a symbol of the shared knowledge and experience of both performer and audience. Speakers who make use of formulaic language thus have the assurance both of the wisdom of what they are saying and of social approval of their contribution. Attitudes such as these stand in marked contrast to those which are prevalent in literate societies, where an important part of the training is in the avoidance of the formula and the search for the fresh and original. In the oral tradition, a cliché is something to be valued and respected. In the literate tradition, the cliché is a joke, something to be avoided at all costs.

This difference in emphasis between oral and literate is neatly captured in Havelock's (1963:66–7) retelling of a poignant incident which reputedly took place during the Gallipoli campaign of World War I. The terrible slaughter which had resulted from massed charges by Turkish soldiers on Allied positions made it necessary to negotiate a truce so that both sides could bury their dead in no man's land. The understandable tension gradually dissipated as the working parties carried out their unpleasant task and, by the time the operation came to a close, the common soldiers on both sides exchanged greetings and farewells. Interestingly, in reply to the Australian 'Goodbye, old chap; good luck', the Turks offered a proverb: 'Smiling may you go and smiling may you come back'. As Havelock (1963:67) comments:

> Here briefly, in an hour of crisis, a semi-literate and a literate culture confronted each other. Each as it speaks under stress resorts to its fundamental idiom of communication. For the one this is laconic and casual prose; for the other it is the rhythm and parallelism of the shaped and preserved formula.

So what happens when speakers from an oral tradition come into contact with speakers from the literate tradition? Tannen (1980c) suggests a number of possible outcomes. One strategy is to retain formulae from the other language or translate them from the mother tongue. Thus, Jewish Americans often utter Yiddish formulaic expressions such as 'God bless them' in English conversation, either in Yiddish or translated into English. This strategy, of course, is likely to be successful only in conversation with other Yiddish–English bilinguals who share the same values and expectations. In conversation with people from other backgrounds, the solution is not so clear-cut. One possibility is to drop the formulae altogether, though this is a course of action which is likely to lead to a great deal of frustration. Since formulaic language is such an integral part of discourse strategies, the attempt to remove it from conversation is likely to leave the speaker with the same feeling of incompletion experienced by an English speaker when an interlocutor leaves out a 'please' or 'thank you'. Another possibility is to carry on using the formulae regardless, though the speaker who chooses to do this runs the risk of sounding odd, quaint or insincere, depending on the listener's attitude to formulaic language.

Whereas there is no shortage of evidence that literate people tend to stereotype formulaic language negatively, Tannen (1980c:332) also points to a reverse phenomenon:

> I can recall a time before I knew Modern Greek, when I heard Greeks use expressions in English that I now know to be formulaic in Modern Greek. At the time they struck me as highly imaginative, poetic and charming. I have a suspicion that this phenomenon contributes to the fact that young American women travelling in Greece often find young Greek men inexpressibly charming and poetic. It is an instance of the broader phenomenon ... that in communicating with speakers from a different culture, one cannot distinguish between individual and culturally shared style.

Similar misunderstandings centre on the use of rhetorical language in the oral tradition. The trend in writing is to distance oneself and present a 'logical' and 'dispassionate' argument. Yet in a society where importance is attached to the notion of presenting oneself through words, in savouring the power of words, the emphasis is quite different. We have already seen the divergence in opinion on questions of boasting in literate and oral societies. In oral communities boasts are sometimes self-proclamatory; on other occasions, they are self-deprecating. Whichever the case, they are part of the presentation of self for the enjoyment of an audience. They remain none the less part of a performance and will not necessarily be taken at face value within the social context in which they are offered. Problems therefore arise when a member of an oral culture makes a boast in a situation where not all members of the audience share the same value set. Smitherman (1977:83), for instance, discusses the essentially defensive rhetoric of militants such as the Black Panthers in the 1960s with their battle cries of: 'Death to the racist exploiters!' 'Off the Pigs!' and 'Defend our communities by any means necessary'. Many White observers, however, interpreted these responses literally and retaliated physically against what they perceived to be a real threat to their personal security.

Tannen (1980a:3) distinguishes two main styles in naturally occurring conversation, which she calls 'high involvement' and 'high considerateness'. Interestingly, she notes that these styles correlate closely with the oral–literate distinction. High involvement speakers feel the need for interpersonal involvement; high considerateness speakers, in contrast, particularly concerned with not imposing upon others, place emphasis on content and verbalization. One area where this difference in orientation is particularly noticeable is in the overlap between speaker and interlocutor in cross-cultural communication. In the literate tradition, it is considered polite for listeners to show deference to speakers by allowing them to hold the floor and by making their own contributions only after the speaker is finished. Any interruption before this point is therefore seen as both rude and insensitive. In the oral tradition, the expectations are quite different. By making comments while the speaker is in full flow, the listener is indicating support and interest; the lack of such overlap would indicate disinterest or hostility.

Problems therefore arise when speakers from two different traditions, both totally convinced of the inherent rightness of their own approach, come together in ignorance of the effect which their individual discourse style is likely to have on the other party. In an American setting, for instance, the lack of support or countercomment from many White speakers is likely to be interpreted by Black speakers as evidence of inattention. In order to put this situation to rights, Black speakers may well intersperse their contributions with questions such as 'Do you hear me?' or 'Are you listening?' White interlocutors, for their part, may take these questions literally and, since they are indeed paying attention, may find them irritating. In so doing, they demonstrate that they have failed to understand that the Black speaker is simply inviting them to respond. Similar problems occur when the White speaker is holding the floor. Responses from the Black interlocutor of 'Tell it' or 'I hear you' which are intended to register support are more likely to be perceived as unwelcome interruptions.

The meeting between White faculty members and Afro-American community representatives described above provides a clear example of the way in which call and response strategies can be misunderstood. When the White faculty member commented that she had not come to listen to a Baptist prayer meeting, a Black speaker responded with 'You just insulted my religion!' This remark was intended simply as a humorous riposte and was greeted with laughter and applause from an appreciative Afro-American audience. Many White faculty members, however, interpreted it at face value and were further confirmed in their view of Afro-Americans as unreasonable.

Oral and Literate Traditions and the School

There is thus enormous potential for misunderstanding when speakers from one tradition attribute to speakers from the other qualities and characteristics which bear little relationship to reality. Negative stereotyping of this kind tends to work in both directions, but, in the Western world at least, it seems reasonable to assume that the consequences are more serious for those who prefer oral strategies. In most cases, and for a variety of historical reasons, members of oral cultures belong to less powerful strata of society.

As we have emphasized on various occasions throughout this book, we are dealing with a continuum of strategies and not a simple oral–literate dichotomy. It would be quite misleading, of course, to expect every Afro-American or Afro-Caribbean to have equal access to the skills associated with oral culture. By the same token, it would be wrong to emphasize the essentially oral tradition of South Asians at the expense of their long, rich and varied written tradition. These provisos apart, some important generalizations can be made about the implications of the oral–literate continuum for equality of opportunity in cross-cultural contact.

Differing expectations as to what constitutes an appropriate discourse style can have adverse effects for those who prefer oral strategies in many different settings, including the workplace and .the courtroom. School is another setting in which speakers from different traditions inevitably come into contact. In many areas of the Western world today, classrooms are populated with children from a wide variety of cultural backgrounds. Not only do the children differ from one another but, in many cases, the experience and expectations of students and teachers are highly divergent. Because negative stereotyping by teachers has wide-reaching implications not only for the current well-being of children, but also for their entire future, we would like to focus our attention for the rest of this chapter on cross-cultural communication in an educational setting.

We all have a basic familiarity with oral strategies. In our early years, of course, language learning necessarily takes place within an essentially oral framework, and, if strategies associated with the literate tradition are acquired at all, these are learned later in life. In some societies, however, verbal strategies and language attitudes associated with the literate tradition have come to be expected in a wide range of settings and are superimposed on strategies associated with the oral tradition. This is certainly the case in middle-class English-speaking families. Speakers from many other cutural and ethnic backgrounds, in contrast, prefer discourse strategies associated with the oral tradition in these same settings. Children using a predominantly oral discourse style clearly find themselves at a disadvantage in school systems which fail to recognize the legitimacy of oral strategies.

A brief overview of the research literature on language and education can leave little doubt as to the close links between the standard language and literacy, on the one hand, and non-standard varieties and orality, on the other. The exclusive emphasis on the standard language in educational settings has a number of unfortunate consequences. Of particular concern is the fact that dialect speakers have tended to be stereotyped as less able than standard English speakers (Giles and Powesland 1975). It is also regrettable that the traditional oral culture of the vast majority of the population, preserved today in such activities as oral narrative and the oratory of trades unionists, has received little attention from either teachers or researchers. The emphasis has been rather on the inherent limitations of non-standard speech.

Negative attitudes towards non-standard speech can be traced back several hundred years (Milroy and Milroy 1985) but seemed to surface with renewed vigour in the 1960s and 1970s. The main catalyst for this resurgence in the debate on the adequacy of Black and other non-standard varieties of English was the work of Bernstein (1973). Postulating two polar language codes, the 'elaborated' and the 'restricted' codes, Bernstein argued that the different distributions of these codes within society accounted for the differential rates of educational achievement. Although he denies that this was ever his intention, Bernstein's work was widely interpreted on both sides of the Atlantic as suggesting that the elaborated code could be equated with standard English and the restricted code with non-standard speech.

Bernstein's ideas have attracted bitter criticism from a wide range of writers (Stubbs 1976; J. Edwards 1979; Gordon 1981). It has been argued, for instance, that his theory of language codes is both untestable and unrelated to linguistic evidence. When discussed within the framwork of the oral–literate continuum, however, it is possible to see the Bernstein debate in a new and interesting light. The 'elaborated' code corresponds to the literate tradition, which tends to decontextualize content by fully explaining the background information. The 'restricted' code, on the other hand, draws on the shared knowledge of speaker and hearer and is thus necessarily context-bound. In other words, the restricted code corresponds to the oral tradition.

The terms 'elaborated' and 'restricted', however, are extremely value-laden: they assume that the responsibility is on the restricted code users to conform to the norms and expectations of the elaborated code users. The dichotomy in terminology also implies a simple division rather than a continuum in which all speakers use both sets of strategies, although in varying degrees. But perhaps most damaging in its ethno-centrism is the assumption that the 'elaborated' code or literate strategies demanded by the educational system represent the only route to learning.

The inherent limitations of the deficit position, which holds that certain varieties of language are inferior to others, can be illustrated quite clearly by comparing some of the observations made by certain academic writers on the language of British coal miners with actual examples of discourse from this same group of speakers. Gahagan and Gahagan (1970:11–12), for instance, make the following comments in *Talk Reform: Exploration in Language for Infant School Children:*

> A miner may have restricted language with respect to all areas of experi-ence except coal, where he probably makes such discriminations that it would take the rest of us months to learn and for which he has a rich technical vocabulary. The coalminer might have a number of terms for coal found in the language generally, that is, his vocabulary in this area is an extended one. Nevertheless, his use of these terms in the structure of his speech generally would coincide with what we believe to be the features of restricted code. The restricted code user operates with a smaller range of fine linguistic distinctions than the elaborate code user, except perhaps with respect to particular circumscribed areas . . .

Compare these observations with the following extract from an ex-tended conversation with Jimmy Miller, a Scottish miner and an active trade unionist. Miller is not only an effecive orator but has a keen appreciation of the rhetoric which he uses in his speeches.

> I won't change my style. My style of speaking. All that happens to me when I go on a public platform is that I slow down my tempo of speech so that it reaches the back of the hall. And I speak the same way on the platform as I speak every day in the pit. Because I think, I don't know what happens to us. I found it happening to me earlier on and I decides to stop it. You begin to talk as you've read and the books are all written by bloody middle-class people and you don't communicate to working-class people by using middle-class language. And I begin to make it a hobby . . . I began to take a phrase and strip it and strip it and strip it until I could get the bare bones; and then I'd maybe turn it upside down because sometimes a worker sees a thing better upside down. You know? Because his humour comes to the thing. You know, he sees it and you make the illustration like that. And I do that to, oh, scores and scores of times.
>
> I was illustrating the millions that the Coal Board has thrown away and the Governement had robbed the mining industry of and I tell my audience, 'Have you ever thought what one million means? If Adam and

Eve'd been born in the year dot—and this is 1967—and they'd saved three quid a week between them, working five shifts each, they wouldn't have a million yet . . .' (Miller et al. 1974:9)

Miller deliberately cultivates an oral style—note the repetition ('strip it and strip it and strip it'), the involvement of the audience ('you know') and the vivid imagery of the didactic fable. The effect is both reflective and immediate. Only from a literate perspective does a speaker of this kind appear to 'operate with a smaller range of fine linguistic distinctions' (Gahagan and Gahagan 1970:12) than other, more literate speakers. Miller's speech is certainly different from the middle-class literate norm, but this in no way implies that it is deficient. In some ways and in some contexts, in fact, his speech is more effective than that of a speaker using literate middle-class techniques.

It would seem that the characterization of working-class discourse as limited and illogical is based more on social stereotyping than on objective observation and analysis. Much recent research by writers such as Tizard and Hughes (1984) and Wells (1987) has shown that the main differences in language use occur not between middle- and working-class children but between home and school. At home conversations are frequently longer and more equally balanced between child and adult. Children ask more questions and spend more time in conversation with adults. Parents play much more with their children, talk to them much more and answer many more questions than do teachers. The widespread notion that professionals should offer parents advice and suggestions on how to talk to their children (Bullock 1975) is seriously challenged by research findings such as these.

H. 'Rap' Brown, the Afro-American activist well known for his involvement in the civil rights struggle, is another eloquent critic of middle-class assumptions. In his autobiography (Brown 1969) he describes how he grew up in the streets of Baton Rouge, Louisiana:

> The street is where the young bloods get their education. I learned how to talk in the street, not from reading about Dick and Jane going to the zoo and all that simple shit. The teacher whould test our vocabulary every week, but we knew the vocabulary we needed. They'd give us arithmetic to exercise our minds. Hell we exercised our minds by playing the dozens . . . And the teacher expected me to sit up in class and study poetry after I could run down shit like that. If anybody needed to study poetry, she need to study mine. We played the dozens for recreation, like white folks play Scrabble.

A similarly blinkered approach to learning determines that there is only one right answer, which, in the context of the school, is likely to be the one influenced by the literate tradition. Aronowitz (1984), for instance, describes the way in which many Black children approach school tasks as real-world problems, rather than as decontextualized tasks: in answering questions on reading tests, they go beyond the information given in the paragraph to choose an answer which takes into consideration their broader experience.

All too often teachers are guilty of forming impressions of children and their potential on the basis of their language behaviour in the classroom and with no awareness of the ways in which the formal school environment moulds that behaviour. Non-standard English-speaking children are often judged in these terms with little understanding of how their language behaviour can be shaped by situational constraints. Perhaps the most important critique of these shortcomings is contained in Labov's (1973b) polemical article entitled 'The logic of non-standard English'. He describes two interviews with Leon, an eight-year-old Afro-American boy. In the first interview little progress is made and Leon gives short non-committal responses to the questions put to him. In the second meeting, however, his best friend is invited to come along, everybody (including the interviewer) sits down on the floor, food is passed around and taboo subjects are introduced into the conversation. The social distance between interviewer and child has been reduced and Leon shows himself to be a perfectly normal eight-year-old who speaks fluently and intelligently.

The same insensitivity to situation which is lampooned by Labov is also to be seen in a British context. Pollak's (1972) study of young children in London draws attention to the astonishingly small number of West Indian children who knew their own names and sex. The reader is left to speculate on whether the children felt it was more polite to remain silent than to reply when faced with an unknown adult, or whether a little girl wearing her best dress and with her hair in plaits was simply incredulous at being asked if she was a girl or a boy. The literate tendency to decontextualize is surely totally inappropriate in situations such as this.

A thread which runs through much of the work on verbal deprivation is the verbal skills which are supposedly lacking in Black and other non-standard English-speaking children. Often the writers seem totally unaware that the children they are discussing are privy to a lively and varied oral culture which places a premium on words. Pollak (1972:92), for example, interprets the failure of West Indian children to complete a nursery rhyme when offered the first line as evidence that there is no tradition of nursery rhymes in the Caribbean. Yet there is no shortage of documentation that, in addition to the traditions of story-telling, riddling, proverbs, ritual invective and oratory which we have discussed at various points in this book, there is a well-developed corpus of nursery rhymes which includes both English and more specifically West Indian examples (Elder 1973).

The foundations for the development of verbal skills in Black communities are laid at a very early stage. We have already discussed contraverting routines such as sounding and playing the dozens in adolescents and pre-adolescents. Erickson (1984:68–9) describes the precursor of such activities, 'stylin'' or 'show time', in which Afro-American children between the ages of three and seven or eight take part in exchanges which escalate in intensity. An adult starts with something like 'Don't touch that refrigerator', and the child replies with 'I gonna'. From this point the threats become more and more drastic. At the end of the routine, an adult says admiringly, 'Oh, he so bad' while other members of the audience show their approval with laughter and other comments.

Not surprisingly, this kind of behaviour is sometimes transferred from home to school, where it risks creating serious misunderstanding on the part of teachers. Lein (1975) describes the way in which Black migrant-worker families travelling north and south along the eastern seaboard of the USA in the growing seasons interpret teacher imperatives as an invitation to take part in the kind of contraverting routine described above. Children who are apparently refusing to cooperate are often judged by teachers as recalcitrant or emotionally disturbed. Nor is this pattern of response restricted to Afro-American children; Gomes (1979) refers to a similar sequence of escalating threats between a Cape Verdean child and a White teacher.

A clue to what may be taking place on a regular basis in multiethnic classrooms is contained in the work of Michaels and Collins (1984). In a discussion of 'sharing time', a daily classroom activity where children were invited to describe an object or give a narrative account of some past event, they identify two distinct discourse styles – one characteristically White, the other typically Black. White children tend to use a topic-centred style in which a single clearly identified topic is chosen and usually developed in a linear manner. Black children, in contrast, prefer a 'topic-associating' style made up of a series of implicitly linked topics.

The children's teacher related easily to the topic-centred style which she expanded through comments and questions. The children who adopted a topic-associated style, however, posed difficulties for the teacher who often could neither discern the underlying theme nor predict where the talk was going. Inappropriate questions and comments sometimes threw the children off course while those children who continued talking were characterized as 'filibusters' and were often cut short. Deena, a first-grade girl, complained, for instance, that her teacher 'was always stoppin' me, sayin' "that's not important enough", and I hadn't hardly started talkin'!' Michaels and Collins (1984:242) sum up this situation in the following terms: 'Differential treatment and negative evaluation in activities such as sharing time in part result from and also reinforce systematic differences in discourse style. In effect, some students are given instruction in how to talk in a lexically and grammatically explicit fashion, while other students are systematically excluded from that practice and instruction.'

Differences between oral and literate discourse strategies give rise to misunderstanding in other spheres, too. In an analysis of classroom debating techniques used by White and Afro-American students, Kochman (1981:34–5) observes that Afro-Americans tend to apply to the classroom the same rules used for personal interaction in the Afro-American community at large, where it is expected that individuals with better speaking abilities dominate the conversation. For Afro-Americans a debate, inside or outside the classroom, becomes a contest of wits and abilities. As Kochman notes, '. . . blacks do not simply debate an idea; they debate the person debating the idea. Consequently, individuals in the group assess their own debating skills relative to others in the group, and if they feel they cannot generate the kind of dynamic balance necessary to establish parity for their view, they do not contend'; while Whites, on the other hand, 'debate the idea rather than the person debating the idea. This allows those who disagree to enter into the discussion without having to match the forcefulness the opposition, since they are not in direct contention. This mode would seem to allow the greatest possible involvement, since participation is not dependent upon strong debating skills.'

In such a situation an outspoken Afro-American student runs the risk of being labelled overly aggressive by an evaluator using White standards or a White student debating an 'idea' may suddenly feel uncomfortable and may cease to pursue the discussion when an Afro-American opponent makes a more personal challenge.

Watson (1988), in an examination of language and mathematics education for Aboriginal Australian children, offers yet another perspective on the processes which regularly undermine children more comfortable with oral than literate discourse styles. In considering the main reasons why Aboriginal children seriously underachieve in this area of the curriculum, she looks, for instance, at the different semantic organizations of Aboriginal and Indo-European languages: in mathematics children are developing a schema of meaning which grows from the semantic structure of Indo-European languages. In order to use number names efficiently, for instance, children need to be at ease with what teachers call 'number skills'—the base ten recursive series, which is by no means a universal feature of semantic organization in the languages of the world.

Differences in semantic systems, however, are not the only problem. The easiest way for teachers to interact with large groups of children is through the use of pencils and paper. Symbols like 1 and 100 constitute a specific form of literacy—'numeracy'—and take precedence over the the oral mode of making meaning in the mathematics of ordinary 'street life'. Mathematics lessons are thus dominated by written communication. Closely related to this emphasis on writing is a sense of progression in learning, offered in discrete episodes. Watson (1988: 268–9) sums up the very real dilemmas posed by this style of learning for many Australian Aboriginal children in the following terms:

> People in oral cultures ... learn by apprenticeship—fixing a car with an experienced person for example; by discipleship (a kind of apprenticeship) through repeating what they hear, by mastering proverbs, by assimilating other formulated materials, by participating in a kind of corporate retrospection in evening talk or in ceremony, but not by study.
>
> In oral culture, pictorial memory is well developed; there is a highly developed capacity to identify and remember pictorial pattern. Problem solving, and understanding of the meanings of theoretical words is associated with metaphor, which often invoke physical, landscape images. Knowing is necessarily holistic. Literate cultures tend to view learning as progressive. Holism in approach to knowing and problem solving can be discarded, for the whole problem can be captured in writing, and laid out in a tabulated form which enables a sequential and progressive approach to learning about the problem.

The characteristics of conventional mathematics lessons and, indeed, many other areas of the curriculum, are often not well-suited to the purposes of Aboriginal learners. Careful thought is needed to explore ways in which schools can be transformed to allow children from different cultural backgrounds to operate most effectively.

Our main focus up to the present has been on speakers of non-standard dialects of English, both Black and White. The underlying theme has been the class bias and ethnocentrism of the socially-dominant group which has interpreted differences in language structure and language strategies as evidence of inferior cognitive processes. One of the consequences of this assumption of inferiority is that many of the 'experts' in the dominant group—teachers, educational psychologists, speech therapists, health visitors and paediatricians—have concentrated on what children lack, rather than on the linguistic resources which they bring with them to the classroom (cf. Edwards 1983).

A similar observation can be made about reactions to both indigenous people in many different countries and to the second- and third-generation immigrants populating the schools of London, Sydney, Toronto or New York. These multilingual communities are by no means homogeneous. They include, for instance, families who are from all corners of the world and who are steeped in literacy and the world of books. For the most part, however, they are made up of people from rural or peasant backgrounds in Europe, South and East Asia, Africa and the Caribbean for whom oral culture plays an important part in everyday life.

Writers like Tannen (1980b) have demonstrated how the impact of the oral tradition can be felt not only in the attitudes and expectations of first-generation Greek Americans but also in those of their children and grandchildren. Although English may be the dominant language of the second and third generations, many of the discourse patterns of the original settlers remain intact. This is by no means a uniquely Greek phenomenon. It is reasonable to assume that settlers from the parish of Saint Thomas in Jamaica, or the Sylhet region of Bangladesh or the New Territories of Hong Kong can also be distinguished from the literate middle classes in their adopted countries not only because they speak a different language but also because their approach to communication is different, It is impossible, of course, to completely disentangle language and discourse strategies in cross-cultural communication; but, in any discussion of the attitudes of mainstream English society to speakers of other languages, the oral–literate dimension deserves to be taken into consideration.

The present discussion has focused mainly on the United Kingdom and the USA, the countries of which we have first-hand experience. This is not to suggest, however, that these are the only countries which demonstrate a low level of awareness of the educational implications of oral culture. Other examples could have been drawn from all over the English-speaking world including Canada (Cummins 1988) and Australasia (Baldauf and Luke 1989). There is also evidence for similar patterns of behaviour on the European continent, especially in the Netherlands (Appel 1988) and Sweden (Tingbjörn 1988).

A Possible Way Forward?

Discussions of linguistic diversity in the various settings we have considered have usually been framed in terms of what some bilingual or Black children lack, namely the ability to speak standard English, rather than in terms of the rich and varied linguistic resources which they bring with them to the school. Such an approach is likely to have a number of unfortunate consequences. The exculsive emphasis on the values and strategies of the dominant culture may well lead to negative stereotyping. The relation between low teacher expectation and educational underachievement has long been suspected and may have particularly serious consequences for entire cultural groups. Equally important, the definition of instructional goals by mainstream educators is likely to leave whole areas of experience either undervalued or overlooked completely.

We have presented in this book an outline of the skills, qualities and expectations of oral cultures that has no point of contact with the picture of verbal and cultural deprivation in Black and working-class populations which pervades the educational literature of the 1960s and 1970s and which can still be detected in many schools today. We have described oral culture as a source of creativity with an aesthetic of its own; a force which binds together a community through shared experience and expectations and ensures social stability. The educational literature, for the most part, emphasizes the linguistic and cultural deprivation of populations which have often, in a superb stroke of irony, been considered non-verbal.

In general, teachers can respond in two ways to the oral tradition which forms a central part of many children's lives. One possibility is to look on oral culture, and the language used in its transmission, as a deviation from the norm, an obstacle to be overcome; from this point of view, the task of the school is to teach children the strategies and standard language associated with literacy. The second response looks upon oral culture not as a problem, but as a resource to be nurtured. Considered from this perspective, oral skills in no way compete with the teaching of literate strategies. Instead, children are more likely to make more progress in the book-based culture of the school when their language and culture are valued and accepted than when they are criticized and rejected. This latter response is clearly exemplified in the work of Michael Rosen (1982:389), a children's writer who spent a year as writer-in-residence at Vauxhall Manor School in London.

> Judith had told something like eight or nine Anansi stories on tape – some of which we made into booklets – before it occurred to me that we could lend her a tape-recorder and ask her to record her mother. This she did. Her mother, an 'ordinary' working class woman, is as fine a storyteller as anyone anywhere. You don't have to go to the Brothers Grimm, or to this or that Book of Beautiful Tales. Great storytellers are amongst us. If you happen to have some of these stories on tape and play them in school, what happens? The parent's culture becomes part of the school curriculum – even if it's only for five minutes at a time. And there was Farrah

too, who speaks Punjabi at home and told me she didn't like stories, who told me she only really liked books on magnetism, but who finally let on that her grandmother tells her stories. The result of that is a tape of an old lady telling an epic in Punjabi which Farrah translated for us.

Rosen's description of his work at Vauxhall Manor illustrates how story-telling can involve children whose experiences in oral culture are often overlooked or undervalued. There is also a growing recognition of the value of story as a vehicle for learning in many different teaching situations. Discussing recent developments in story-telling workshops for English teachers worldwide, Garvie (1988) points out that interaction between teller and audience provides an ideal language-learning environment. The power of telling–as opposed to reading–a story has implications for children of all backgrounds and all ages. Bingham (personal communication) vividly captures the excitement at the discovery of the traditional art of story-telling in the following terms:

> Although I embarked on the first session with trepidation, and a copy of Joseph Jacobs' *English Fairy Tales* firmly on my lap, the sight of seven pairs of eyes fixed unwaveringly on my every gesture soon dispelled any inhibitions. Neither had I anticipated the freedom which would result from dispensing with the written word. I soon found that my eyes were free to lock with my listeners' who would become riveted under my gaze. My arms were free to gesticulate and I discovered the added emphasis that could impart: the fear that could be conveyed by use of hands, the extra flourish with which a sword could be drawn. It was possible to gauge from the children's faces and bodies when they were really enrapt and this encouraged me to embellish that part of the story which had them in its grip. It was a chastening experience to realise the power over the audience which the role of the storyteller gives. I was able to pause for dramatic effect and it was a positive delight as I watched their eyes dilate with mine, and heard them gasp just as I did. I was amazed at how often my facial expressions were mirrored back in the children's. Or how they would imitate a particular gesture which obviously appealed.

Teachers are, in many cases, awakening to the potential of story-telling as part of their own repertoire. They are also showing a growing interest in involving both parents and professionals in story-telling performances for children in school.

Familiarity with oral culture has implications for other areas of curriculum development, too. Au and Jordan (1981), for instance, discuss the ways in which the reading performance of Hawaiian children has been improved by adopting teaching strategies which are closer to the cultural experience of the community. Initially children

Plate 10   *Grace Hallworth, British Black story-teller with an audience of school children.*
Photograph: Laurie Sparham, Network.

had been taught using a phonics approach which emphasized sound–
symbol relationships: the results, as indicated by standardized testing,
were disappointing. There was a marked improvement, however,
when teachers began to devise special reading lessons which resembled
talk-story and story-telling, two important speech events in Hawaiian
culture.

The identification of areas of possible breakdown in communication
of this kind has been greatly facilitated by the development of ethnog-
phic research techniques. Much recent analysis points to potential
conflict between mainstream and minority cultures in the school. In
formal education, it is the teacher who determines the precise nature of
most classroom interaction: who speaks on which subject at any given
time. From the pupil perspective, there is great emphasis on the need to
perform on demand. In many cultures, expectations such as these
present real difficulties. Boggs (1972), for instance, discusses the way in
which Hawaiian children become silent when called upon by name but
take part enthusiastically in choral responses and are happy to volunteer

information to receptive teachers. Philips (1972) reports that Native American children in the Warm Springs Reservation, Oregon, work happily when occupied in independent study and approach their teachers whenever they need information. They also take an active part in small group projects run by the children and supervised by the teacher at a distance. However, they participate only reluctantly in large groups or in small goup settings such as reading groups which are closely controlled by the teacher and which require individual perform- ances. There is clearly a need for teacher sensitivity towards differences such as these.

It is vitally important to acknowledge, respect, learn from and build upon the predominantly oral cultures shared by large numbers of children in our schools. By looking on diversity as a resource rather than a problem, we may avoid the worst excesses of negative stereo- typing behaviour and help teachers to think in terms of verbal skills rather than linguistic deprivation. The integration of oral culture into the mainstream curriculum also has important implications for the pupils. Those children most comfortable in the literate tradition will hopefully broaden their own horizons and learn the important lesson that there is never a single solution for a problem, while the children versed in oral culture are likely to grow in confidence and self-worth. As both types of children begin to appreciate the value of each other's way of speaking, they will also come to recognize the points of intersec- tion, where the literate and the oral worlds meet, where Homer and the rapper are the same. Only then will the seams really be repaired.

11

Coming to a Close

Here is my journey's end, here is my butt,
And my sea-mark of my utmost sail.
Shakespeare, *Othello* (Act V, Scene ii, lines 267–8)

What conclusions can we draw at the end of this journey into the oral world? In this last chapter we direct our attention to three areas: the insights which can be drawn from interdisciplinary study of oral performance; a few practical suggestions for researchers of oral culture; and some broader applications of this approach to oral culture.

Interdisciplinary Perspectives

Although oral cultures have been studied in many different disciplines, including folklore, anthropology, sociolinguistics, classics and literary criticism, for many years there was little pooling of ideas. Only in relatively recent times has there been any significant interdisciplinary convergence. The research of Parry (1930; 1932) and Lord (1960), addressed originally to classicists interested in the Homeric question, has gradually affected other areas, including linguistics and anthropology, so that scholars, such as Ong (1982), Rosenberg (1987) and Smith (1977; 1989), working more or less independently, are now reaching a consensus on a number of important points. For instance, there is widespread agreement that orality and literacy are best seen as the poles of a single continuum rather than as a dichotomy. It is also widely accepted that the notion of performance is essential for an appreciation of orality, and that performance necessarily involves both good talkers and their audience. Equally significant is the emergent understanding of the ways in which the social organization of an oral culture moulds this performance.

Social organization also moulds the way in which literates think about performance. For example, whenever we have noted in this book how oral performance tends to include rather than exclude, to synthesize rather than analyse, we have inevitably fallen into a binary way of thinking common to the Western literate tradition, at least since the time of Plato and the development of his concept of the Form. Yet the tendency to think in pairs like 'nature and nurture' or 'concrete and abstract' is antithetical to the synthetic approach of oral culture, which rests more comfortably with 'both/and' rather than 'either/or' (Goody 1977).

Exponents of the deficit hypothesis in the so-called 'different–deficit' debate which raged in educational circles in the 1960s and the 1970s saw non-standard language as an inadequate vehicle for learning. It is objectively true that the literate tradition associated with Bernstein's elaborated code tends to decontextualize information, while the 'restricted code' of oral tradition makes heavy use of contextualization. Many writers, however, went on to make unfounded generalizations on the basis of this observation. Because writing is often associated with the discussion of abstract thought, it was assumed that the oral language of non-standard speakers was suitable only as a vehicle of concrete thought. Yet there is ample evidence that this is not the case. Afro-American preachers regularly use non-standard speech to deal with concepts as abstract as transubstantiation, while commentators such as Labov (1973b) have cited examples of highly philosophical discussions by Afro-American youths about life after death.

The same binary thinking can be felt in the very opposition of 'oral' and 'literate'. Although we have repeated on a number of occasions that we use expressions such as 'the oral community' or 'the literate community' as a convenient form of shorthand, there is a strong temptation to think in terms of a dichotomy between the two traditions, between orality and literacy. The evidence, however, points overwhelmingly towards a continuum between orality and literacy which blurs the edges of many traditional assumptions.

There is a tendency, for instance, for literate observers in the Western industrial world to think of orality as something exotic, a phenomenon associated with other parts of the world rather than an everyday feature of life around us. Yet the nineteenth and twentieth centuries have witnessed uprecedented population movements from country to town. In the process, the small, tight-knit rural–and predominantly oral–communities in North America and Europe have made the transition to more centrally organized societies, mediated by the written word. Yet rural communities tend to retain many elements of an essentially oral culture. There has also been considerable movement from one country to another as a result of both immigration and international trade. Native American, African, Mediterranean and Eastern European oral traditions are thus part of the fabric of the North American experience, in the same way as South Asian and Caribbean oral cultures have made their mark on British life.

This juxtaposition of oral and literate traditions is not, of course, a recent phenomenon. We have attempted to show the way in which literacy developed in ancient Greece alongside an oral tradition which continued to exert an important influence. In West Africa, the oral epic has continued cheek by jowl with the literate tradition of Islam. In the USA, the delivery of the Afro-American sermon has retained its oral roots for over two hundred years in spite of the fact that preachers are among the most highly educated members of the community. Children's lore continues to be transmitted as a primarily oral tradition, even in those settings where the importance of the written word is paramount.

It is significant, however, that the importance attached to orality and literacy within the different traditions is very different. While oral cultures continue to value the spoken word, the literate tradition tends to hold orality in very low esteem: this can be illustrated, on the one hand, by its dismissal of the special language of West Indian oratory as flowery or obsequious and, on the other hand, by its widespread ignorance of Afro-American speech events such as toasting and playing the dozens, and of South Asian wedding songs.

The low status of many contemporary oral cultures stands in marked contrast to the high prestige accorded by Western societies to the ancient Greeks. Not only are the Homeric epics celebrated for their literary form; the very language and the myths on which they draw have sometimes been proclaimed as transcending the limits of the Greek experience, as reaching out to all cultures and all times. Yet the themes, the structures, the formulae and special language associated with the Homeric epics can be shown to be essentially oral: the same features which emerge from an analysis of the ancient Greek tradition recur time and again in oral cultures widely separated by time and space. The inescapable conclusion is that the same status which is enjoyed by the Homeric poems—or indeed by other oral epics such as *Beowulf* or the *Chanson de Roland*—should be accorded to contemporary forms of oral culture.

Another point of contact between the study of oral culture past and present is the insight which contemporary studies offer in the reconstruction of the past. The written text poses no problems for the scholar who wishes to analyse such oral characteristics as archaisms or the frequency of formulaic phrases. Students of the *Iliad* or *Beowulf*, however, can only speculate on features of performance. By observing contemporary good talkers in interaction with an audience, for instance, it is possible to construct a much clearer picture of the dynamics of performance and of how these might ultimately have moulded the written text.

This rapidly developing awareness of the centrality of performance for an understanding of orality is undoubtedly the major achievement of researchers in many different disciplines in recent years. While Lord first drew attention to the importance of the performer, the emphasis has since expanded to include the audience: the oral tradition depends on the interaction of good talkers and their audiences. Performance is thus dynamic, never static, and changes from one occasion to the next. The very act of transcription inevitably transforms performance into an artifact of the literate observer, rather than a link in the chain of a vibrant and resilient tradition. Central to this tradition is the delicate balance between stability and creativity: on the one hand, stability is rooted in the themes, the formulae, the tunes and structures passed down from one generation to the next; on the other hand, creativity finds expression in the way in which individual performers combine these traditional elements and apply them in appropriate situations.

There has also been a growing awareness of the way in which an appreciation of the social structure of oral cultures is essential to an understanding of performance. Small-scale, tight-knit communities are able to exert considerable control over their members. A feature of this control is oral referring in performance which binds all members of the community, living and dead, into a single referential web. In addition to their role as entertainers, 'sweet talkers' act as historians and teachers, helping to preserve both the memory of individuals who might be forgotten in the absence of written records, and the values of the group. 'Broad talkers', while apparently contravening accepted norms, function as a steam valve for anti-community impulse and ultimately serve a similar function to sweet talkers. Without an understanding of the social factors which frame performance, however, a literate observer risks seriously misunderstanding the forms and functions of oral perform- ance.

The progress which has been made in recent decades in the study of orality points to a number of important lessons which future researchers in this field will ignore at their peril. The most important of these is the need to tap the insights of the insider, to avoid the temptations of interpreting one society through the cultural matrix of another. It is only by listening carefully that we can guard against imposing our own, possibly misguided, view of what is significant. There are many diffe- rent ways in which this might be achieved. The most desirable route is, of course, to ensure that, wherever possible, a given society is studied by an insider. The main obstacle to this course of action is, however, the reluctance of the outside 'experts' to relinquish their 'authority' (Alladina 1986). Another possibility is collaboration between outside expert and insider, though the potential for cultural imperialism is just as great. There can be little doubt, however, that the most effective collaboration is a product of participant observation in the anthropological tradition.

Anthropologists are not, however, immune from criticism. As Finnegan (1969:59) notes, very often they have been guilty of giving greater prominence to material artifacts than to oral culture. They have also tended to give insufficient information on the context of performance, presenting lists of proverbs, for instance, rather than explaining the situations in which they are used. Many anthropologists have emphasized the narrative content of oral performance, while dismissing elaboration and descriptive passages as digressions rather than as integral parts of the oral aesthetic. None the less, in our opinion, many of the most insightful studies of oral culture are the product of researchers trained in the anthropological tradition. The most effective access to another culture is achieved only by spending an extended period of time as part of the group being studied.

Another important lesson from the study of orality is the need for an awareness of the implicit limitations of the written text. No single transcription can successfully convey the dynamic nature of performance, though the availability of multiple transcriptions can go at least some way towards alerting the literate observer to this feature of orality. The seven published versions of *Sunjata*, for instance, show evidence of considerable variability, and are suggestive of the many ways in which performers respond to their audience. Most often, however, the reader is presented with a single, static text, which may seriously distort the reality of performance: the oral poetry of Afro-American preachers with its underlying rhythms and tonal semantics is reduced to the bland prose of the transcription.

Recent work on oral culture has called not only for different approaches to study and transcription of performance, but also for a redefinition of what constitutes orality. As we have already indicated, oral and literate traditions have long existed side by side, a long-standing phenomenon which the population movements of the nineteenth and twentieth centuries have only served to reinforce. In such a situation, literacy functions as a resource for good talkers rather than as a threat to their existence. Oral culture is an important part of contemporary society and the student of orality in the Western world need never stray far from home.

An Oral Perspective on the World?

So what are the applications of this new understanding of orality? We have already looked at the ways in which members of oral and literate cultures frequently misunderstand the strategies and intentions of the other group. In large-scale societies which draw on people from many different backgrounds, an understanding of these different perspectives is of importance for a wide range of situations—from the courtroom to the workplace, from the school to the supermarket. While many features come into play in such cross-cultural miscommunication—including differences in language, intonation patterns and non-verbal behaviour—strategies associated with oral and literate traditions would also seem to be important: the use of formulaic language and the tendency to contextualize information, for instance, which are more often characterized as oral rather than literate.

It is important to remember, however, that when we discuss differences between orality and literacy, we do not do so in a social vacuum. The literate assumption that the oral tradition is in some way inferior to the literate has important implications for the status of those most comfortable using oral strategies. The heavy emphasis on the written word in formal education, for instance, clearly places children from oral cultures at a disadvantage. It also has the effect of marginalizing and devaluing the very real skills which they bring with them to the school: an appreciation and enjoyment of the spoken word which in many cases is manipulated with considerable verbal and mental agility. In any discussion of equality of educational opportunity in the schools of London, New York, Toronto or Melbourne, and awareness of the different strategies and aesthetics of oral performance would represent an important challenge to the all-pervading ethnocentricism which is the hallmark of mainstream society.

References

Aarne, A. and Thompson, S. (1928) *The Types of Falk-tale: A Classification and Bibliography* (2nd revision). Helsinki: Suomalainen Tiedeakatemia, Academia Scientiarum Fennica.

Abrahams, R. (1962) 'The Toast: a neglected form of folk narrative.' In H. P. Beck (ed.), *Folklore in Action: Essays for discussion in honor of MacEdward Leach*. Philadelphia: The American Folklore Society Inc., pp. 1–11.

Abrahams, R. (1967) 'The shaping of folklore tradition in the British West Indies.' *Journal of Inter-American Studies* IX: 456–80.

Abrahams, R. (1968a) 'Introductory remarks to a rhetorical theory of folklore.' *Journal of American Folklore* 81:143–58.

Abrahams, R. (1968b) '"Speech Mas" on Tobago.' In W. M. Hudson (ed.), *Tire Shrinker to Dragster*. Austin: The Encino Press, pp. 125–44.

Abrahams, R. (1970a) 'Traditions of eloquence in Afro-American communities.' *Journal of Inter-American Studies and World Affairs* 12:505–27.

Abrahams, R. (1970b) *Deep Down in the Jungle: Negro Narrative Folklore from the Streets of Philadelphia* (revised edn). Chicago: Aldine.

Abrahams, R. (1970c) 'Patterns of performance in the British West Indies.' In. N. Whitten and J. Szwed (eds), *Afro-American Anthropology: Contemporary Perspectives*. New York: The Free Press, pp. 163–78.

Abrahams, R. (1972a) 'The training of the man of words in talking sweet.' *Language in Society* 1(1): 15–30.

Abrahams, R. (1972b) 'Joking: the training of the man-of-words in talking broad.' In T. Kochman (ed.), *Rappin' and Stylin' Out: Communication in Urban Black America*. Chicago: University of Illinois Press, pp. 215–40.

Abrahams, R. (1972c) 'The literary study of the riddle.' *Texas Studies in Literature and Language* 14: 177–97.

Abrahams, R. (1976) *Talking Black*. Rowley, MA: Newbury House.

Achebe, C. (1980) *Things Fall Apart*. New York: Astor-Honor.

Adkins, A. W. H. (1969) 'Threatening, Abusing and Feeling Angry in the Homeric Poems.' *Journal of Hellenic Studies* 89:7–21.

Ali, Muhammad (1975) *The Greatest: My Own Story*. New York: Random House.

Alladina, S. (1986) 'Black People's Languages in Britain–A Historical and Contemporary Perspective.' *Journal of Multilingual and Multicultural Development* 7(5): 349–59.

Andrzejewski, B. W. (1973) 'Modern and traditional aspects of Somali drama.'

In R. Dorson (ed.), *Folklore in the Modern World.* The Hague: Mouton, pp. 87–102.

Appel, R. (1988) 'The Language education of immigrant workers' children in The Netherlands.' In T. Skutnabb-Kangas and J. Cummins (eds), *Minority Education: From Shame to Struggle.* Clevedon, Avon: Multilingual Matters, pp. 57–78.

Arewa, E. O. and Dundes, A. (1964) 'Proverbs and the Ethnography of Speaking.' *American Anthropologist* 66(6): 70–85.

Aronowitz, R. (1984) 'Reading Tests as Texts.' In D. Tannen (ed.), *Coherence in Spoken and Written Discourse.* Norwood, NJ: Ablex, pp. 245–64.

Au, K. and Jordan, C. (1981) 'Teaching reading to Hawaiian children: finding a culturally appropriate solution.' In H. Trueba, G. Guthrie and K. Au (eds), *Culture and the Bilingual Classroom.* Rowley, MA: Newbury House, pp. 139–52.

Baldauf, R. and Luke, A. (eds) (1989) *Language Planning and Education in Australasia and the South Pacific.* Clevedon, Avon: Multilingual Matters.

Barnstone, W. (translator) (1972) *Greek Lyric Poetry.* New York: Schocken.

Basgöz, I. (1975) 'The Tale Singer and His Audience.' In D. Ben-Amos and K. S. Goldstein (eds), *Folklore, Performance and Communication.* The Hague: Mouton, pp. 142–203.

Bauman, R. (1975) 'Verbal art as performance.' *American Anthropologist* 77: 290–311.

Bernstein, B. (1973) *Class, Codes and Control,* Vol. 1. London: Routledge & Kegan Paul.

Beuchat, P. (1965) 'Riddles in Bantu.' In A. Dundes (ed.), *The Study of Folklore.* Englewood Cliffs, NJ: Prentice Hall, pp. 182–205.

Biebuyck, D. (1978) *Hero and Chief.* Berkeley and Los Angeles: University of California Press.

Biebuyck, D. and Mateene, K.C. (eds and translators)(1969) *The Mwindo Epic from the Banyanga.* Berkeley and Los Angeles: University of California Press.

Biedelman, T. O. (1989) 'Agonistic Exchange: Homeric Reciprocity and the Heritage of Simmel and Mauss.' *Cultural Anthropology* 4: 227–59

Bird, C. (1972) 'Aspects of Prosody in West African Poetry.' In B. Kachru and H.F.W. Stahlke (eds) *Current Trends in Stylistics.* Edmonton, Alberta: Linguistic Research, Inc., pp. 207–15.

Bird, C. (1976) 'Poetry in the Mande: its Form and Meaning.' *Poetics* 5: 89–100.

Blacking, J. (1961) 'The social value of Venda riddles.' *African Studies* XX.

Blake, C. F. (1978) 'Death and Abuse in Marriage Laments: The Curse of Chinese Brides.' *Asian Folklore Studies* 37: 13–33.

Blake, C. F. (1979) 'The feelings of Chinese daughters towards their mothers.' *Folklore* 90: 91–7.

Boggs, S. (1972) 'The Meaning of Questions and Narratives to Hawaiian Children.' In C. Cazden, V. John and D. Hymes (eds), *Functions of Language in the Classroom.* New York: Teachers College Press.

Brown, H. R. (1969) *Die Nigger Die!* New York: The Dial Press.

Brown, H. R. (1972) 'Street Talk.' In T. Kochman (ed.), *Rappin 'and Stylin'
Out: Communication in Urban Black America.* Champaign-Urbana: University
of Illinois Press, pp. 205–7.

Bryant, M. (1983) *Riddles Ancient and Modern.* New York: Peter Bedrick.

Bullock, Sir A. (1975) *A Language for Life.* London: HMSO.

Burnett, A. P. (1983) *Three Archaic Poets.* Cambridge, MA: Harvard University
Press.

Burton, R. F. (1969) *Wit and Wisdom from West Africa.* New York: Biblo and
Tannen.

Butler, S. (1922) *The Authoress of the Odyssey* (2nd edn). London: Jonathan
Cape.

Callois, R. (1968) 'Riddles and Images.' *Yale French Studies* 41.

Campbell, D. A. (1967) *Greek Lyric Poetry.* New York and London: Macmillan.

Cole, M. and Scribner, S. (1974) *Culture and Thought: A psychological introduction.* New York: Wiley.

Cosentino, D. (1982) *Defiant Maids and Stubborn Farmers: Tradition and invention in Mende story performances.* Cambridge: Cambridge University Press.

Cross, T. P. and Slover, C. H. (1969) *Ancient Irish Tales* (2nd edn). New York:
Barnes and Noble.

Crowley, D. (1956) 'Midnight robbers.' *Caribbean Quarterly* IV: 263–74.

Crowley, D. (1966) *I Could Tell Old Story Good: Creativity in Bahamian Folklore.*
Berkeley and Los Angeles: University of California Press.

Cummins, J. (1988) 'From multicultural to anti-racist education: an analysis of
programs and policies in Ontario.' In T. Skutnabb-Kangas and J. Cummins
(eds), *Minority Education: From Shame to Struggle.* Clevedon, Avon: Multilingual Matters, pp. 127–57.

Dalphinis, M. (1985) *Caribbean and African Languages: Social History, Language,
Literature and Education.* London: Karia Press.

Dance, D. C. (1978) *Shuckin' and Jivin': Folklore from Contemporary Black
Americans.* Bloomington and London: Indiana University Press.

Davies, C. (1987) 'Language, identity and ethnic jokes about stupidity.' *International Journal of the Sociology of Language* 65: 39–52.

Détienne, M. (1979) *Dionysus Slain* (translated by M. and L. Muellner).
Baltimore: Johns Hopkins University Press.

Dillard, J. (1962) 'Some variants in concluding tags in Antillean folk tales.'
Caribbean Studies 2(3): 16–25.

Dillard, J. (1963) 'Beginning formulas for Antillean folk tales, etc.' *Caribbean
Studies* 3(3): 51–5.

Dollard, J. (1939) 'The Dozens: Dialect of Insult.' *The American Imago* 1:
3–25.

Dorson, R. (1962) 'Oral styles of American folk narrators.' In H. P. Beck (ed.),
Falklore in Action: Essays for discussion in honor of MacEdward Leach. Philadelphia: The American Folklore Society Inc., pp. 77–99.

Dorson, R. (1973) *America in Legend: Folklore from the Colonial Period to the
Present.* New York: Pantheon Books.

Dover, K. J. (1964) 'The Poetry of Archilochos.' In *Archiloque* (Fondation
Hardt Entretiens 10), Geneva, pp. 183–222.

Dundes, A., Leach, J. and Özkök, B. (1972) 'The strategy of Turkish boys verbal dueling.' In J. J. Gumperz and D. Hymes (eds), *Directions in Sociolinguistics: The Ethnography of Communication.* New York: Holt, Rinehart & Winston, pp. 130–60.

Edwards, B. (1793) *The History, Civil and Commercial, of the British Colonies in the West Indies.* Dublin.

Edwards, J. (1979) *Language and Disadvantage.* London: Edward Arnold.

Edwards, V. (1979) *The West Indian Language Issue in British Schools.* London: Routledge & Kegan Paul.

Edwards, V. (1982a) *Langauge Variation in the Multicultural Classroom.* Reading: University of Reading Centre for the Teaching of Reading.

Edwards, V. (1982b) 'Oral literature in the British Gujarati communities: Wedding Songs.' Report to the British Academy.

Edwards, V. (1983) *Language in Multicultural Classrooms.* London: Batsford.

Edwards. V. and Katbamna, S. (1989) 'The Wedding Songs of British Gujarati Women.' In J. Coates and D. Cameron (eds), *Women in their Speech Communities.* London: Longman, pp. 158–74.

Edwards, W. (1978) 'Tantalisin and Busin in Guyana.' *Anthropological Linguistics* 20(5): 194–213.

Egudu, R. N. (1975) 'Negative expression for positive attribute in Igbo language: an aspect of Igbo idiom.' In F. C. Ogbalu and E. N. Emanjo (eds) *Igbo Language and Culture.* Oxford: Oxford University Press, pp. 174–85.

Elder, J. D. (1973) *Song Games from Trinidad and Tobago.* (2nd edn). Port of Spain, Trinidad: National Cultural Council Publications.

Erickson, F. (1984) 'Rhetoric, Anecdote and Rhapsody: Coherence Strategies in a Conversation among Black American Adolescents.' In D. Tannen (ed.), *Coherence in Spoken and Written Discourse.* Norwood, NJ: Ablex, pp. 81–154.

Evans, J. J. (1988) *Diarhebion Cymraeg. Welsh Proverbs* (5th edn). Llandysul: Gomer Press.

Fanon, F. (1970) *Black Skins, White Masks.* New York: Grove Press.

Ferris, W. R. (1972) 'Black prose narrative in the Mississippi Delta: an overview.' *Journal of American Folklore* 85: 140–51.

Finnegan, R. (1969) 'Attitudes to the study of oral literature in British Social Anthropology.' *Man (N. S.)* 4 (1): 59–69.

Finnegan, R. (1970) *Oral Literature in Africa.* Oxford: Clarendon Press.

Finnegan, R. (1977) *Oral poetry: its nature, significance and social cantext.* Cambridge: Cambridge University Press.

Finnegan, R. (1988) *Orality and Literacy.* Oxford: Basil Blackwell.

Fluck, H. (1931) *Skurrile Riten in griechischen Kulten.* Endingen: Druck von Emil Wild.

Foley, J. M. (1977) 'The Traditional Oral Audience.' *Balkan Studies* 18: 145–53.

Fowler, B. F. (1968) 'Hell-fire and folk humour on the frontier.' In W. M. Hudson (ed.), *Tire Shrinker to Dragster.* Austin: The Encino Press, pp. 51–62.

Fox, C. (1977) 'Our ancestors spoke in pairs: Rotinese views of language, dialect and code.' In R. Bauman and J. Sherzer (eds), *Explorations in the*

Ethnography of Speaking. Cambridge: Cambridge University Press, p. 65–85.

Fyfe, W. H. (1982) 'The Poetics'; 'Longinus on the Sublime'; 'Demetrius on Style.' In W. H. Fyfe and W. R. Roberts (translators), *Aristotle. Works*, Vol. 23. Cambridge, MA: Harvard University Press.

Gahagan, D. and Gahagan, G. (1970) *Talk Reform: Exploration in Language for Infant School Children.* London: Routledge & Kegan Paul.

Gardner, R. (translator)(1958) *Cicero. The Speeches. Pro Caelio. De Provinciis Consularibus, Pro Balbo.* Cambridge, MA: Harvard University Press.

Garvic, E. (1989) *Story as Vehicle.* Clevedon, Avon: Multilingual Matters.

Gentili, B. (1988) *Poetry and its Public in Ancient Greece* (translated by A. T. Cole). Blatimore and London: The Johns Hopkins Press.

Giles, H and Powesland, P. (1975) *Speech Style and Social Evaluation.* London: Academic Press.

Goldstein, K. S. (1964) *A Guide for Field Workers in Folklore.* Hatboro, PA: Gale.

Gomes, L. A. (1979) 'Social interaction and social identity: A study of two kindergarten children.' Cambridge, MA: Harvard Graduate School of Education dissertation.

Goody, J. (1977) *Domestication of the Savage Mind.* Cambridge: Cambridge University Press.

Goody, J. (1987) *The Interface Between the Written and the Oral.* Cambridge: Cambridge University Press.

Goody, J. and Watt, I. (1968) 'The Consequences of Literacy.' In J. Goody (ed), *Literacy in Traditional Societies.* Cambridge: Cambridge University Press, pp. 27–68.

Gordon, J. (1981) *Verbal Deficit: A Critique.* London: Croom Helm.

Greenberg, J. (1960) 'A Survey of African Prosodic Systems.' In S. Diamond (ed.), *Culture in History.* New York: Columbia University Press, pp. 925–50.

Gregory, D. (1965) *Nigger: An Autobiography.* New York: Pocket Cardinal.

Grimble, A. (1957) *Return to the Islands.* London: Murray.

Gumperz, J. (1982) *Discourse Strategies.* Cambridge: Cambridge University Press.

Gumperz, J., Kaltman, H. and O'Connor, M. (1984) 'Cohesion in Spoken and Written Discourse: Ethnic Style and Transition to Literacy.' In D. Tannen (ed.), *Coherence in Spoken and Written Discourse,* Norwood, NJ: Ablex, pp. 3–20.

Haley, G. (1972) *A Story, A Story.* London: Methuen.

Halpert, H. (1951) 'A pattern of proverbial exaggeration from West Kentucky.' *Midwest Folklore* 1: 41–7.

Hannerz, U. (1969) *Soulside.* New York: Columbia University Press.

Harris, J. C. (1925) *Uncle Remus: His Songs and Sayings.* New York and London: D. Appleton and Co.

Hatto, A. T. (1980) 'Kirghiz.' In A. T. Hatto (ed.), *Traditions of Heroic and Epic Poetry,* Vol. 1. London: Modern Humanities Research Association, pp. 300–27.

Havelock, E. (1963) *Preface to Plato.* Cambridge, MA: Belknap Press of Harvard University Press.

Havelock, E. (1982) *The Literate Revolution in Greece and its Cultural Consequences.* Princeton: Princeton University Press.

Havelock, E. (1986) *The Muse Learns to Write: Reflections on orality and literacy from antiquity to the present.* New Haven: Yale University Press.

Henderson, J. (ed) (1987) *Aristophanes: Lysistrata.* Oxford: Clarendon.

Henry, E. (1975) 'North Indian wedding songs.' *Journal of South Asion Literature* 11(I–II): 61–93.

Herington, J. (1985) *Poetry into Drama: Early Tragedies and the Greek poetic Tradition.* Berkeley: University of California Press.

Hollingworth, B. (1989) 'Education and the Vernacular.' In J. Cheshire, V. Edwards, H. Münstermann and B. Weltens (eds) *Dialect and Education: Some European Perspectives.* Clevedon, Avon: Multilingual Matters, pp. 293–302.

Holmes, L. D. (1969) 'Samoan oratory.' *Journal of American Folklore* 82: 342–52.

Holt, G. S. (1972) 'Stylin' outta the black pulpit.' In T. Kochman (ed.), *Rappin' and Stylin' Out: Communication in Urban Black America.* Champaign-Urbana: University of Illinois Press, pp. 189–204.

Hrdičková, V. (1969) 'Japanese professional storytellers.' *Genre* 2: 179–210.

Huizinga, J. (1949) *Homo Ludens: a study of the play element in culture.* London: Routledge & Kegan Paul.

Ingham, J. M. (1968) 'Culture and personality in a Mexican Village.' Unpublished Ph. D. dissertation, University of California, Berkeley.

Inner London Education Authority (ILEA) (1987) *Language Census.* London: ILEA Research and Statistics.

Innes, G. (1974) *Sunjata. Three Mandinka Versions.* London: School of Oriental and African Studies.

Isbell, B. J. and Fernandez, F. A. R. (1977) 'The ontogenesis of metaphor: riddle games among Quechua speakers seen as cognitive discovery procedures.' *Journal of Latin American Lore* 3(1): 19–49.

Jackson, B. (1974) '*Get your Ass in the Water and Swim Like Me.*' *Narrative Poetry from Black Oral Tradition.* Cambridge, MA: Harard University Press.

Jackson, L. A. (1986) 'Proverbs of Jamaica.' In D. Sutcliffe and A. Wong (eds), *The Language of the British Black Experience.* Oxford: Basil Blackwell, pp. 32–6.

Jarrett, D. (1984) 'Pragmatic Coherence in an Oral Formulaic Tradition: I Can Read Your Letters/Sure Can't Read Your Mind.' In D. Tannen (ed.), *Coherence in Spoken and Written Discourse.* Norwood, NJ: Ablex, pp. 155–72.

Johnson, J. W. (1979) *The Epic of Sun-Jata according to Magan Sisòkò.* Bloomington, IN: Bloomington Folklore Group, Indiana University.

Johnson, J. W. (1980) 'Yes, Virginia, there is an Epic in Africa.' *Research in African Literature* 11: 308–26.

Johnson, J. W. (1986) *The Epic of Son-Jara.* Bloomington, IN: Indiana University Press.

Jones, A. M. (1964) 'African Metrical Lyrics.' *African Language Studies* 5: 52–63.

Keenan, E. (1977) 'Norm-makers, norm-breakers: uses of speech by men and women in a Malagasy community.' In R. Bauman and J. Sherzer (eds),

Explorations in the Ethnography of Speaking. Cambridge: Cambridge University Press, pp. 125–43.

Kirshenblatt-Gimblett, B. (1977) 'The concept of varieties of narrative performance in East European Jewish culture.' In R. Bauman and J. Sherzer (eds), *Explorations in the Ethnography of Speaking.* Cambridge: Cambridge University Press, pp. 283–308.

Kochman, T. (1972) 'Towards an Ethnography of Black American Speech Behavior.' In T. Kochman (ed.), *Rappin' and Stylin' Out: Communication in Urban Black America.* Urbana, IL: University of Illinois Press, pp. 241–64.

Kochman, T. (1981) *Black and White Styles in Conflict.* Chicago and London: University of Illinois Press.

Labouret, H. (1951) 'A propos du mot "griot".' *Notes Africaines* 50: 56–7.

Labov, W. (1972) 'Rules for ritual insults.' In T. Kochman (ed.), *Rappin' and Stylin' Out: Communication in Urban Black America.* Chicago: University of Illinois Press, pp. 265–314.

Labov, W. (1973a) 'The Linguistic Consequences of being a lame.' *Language in Society* 2: 81–115.

Labov, W. (1973b) 'The logic of non-standard English.' In N. Keddie (ed.), *Tinker, Tailor . . . the myth of cultural deprivation.* Harmondsworth: Penguin, pp. 21–66.

Labov, W., Cohen, P., Robins, C. and Lewis, J. (1981) 'Toasts.' In A. Dundes (ed.), *Mother Wit from the Laughing Barrel: Readings in the Interpretation of Afro-American Folklore.* London and New York: Garland Publishing Inc., pp. 329–47.

Ladner, J. (1972) *Tomorrow's Tomorrow. The Black Woman.* New York: Anchor Doubleday.

Lattimore, R. (translator) (1959) *The Odes of Pindar.* Chicago and London: University of Chicago Press.

Lattimore, R (translator) (1960) *Greek Lyrics* (2nd edn). Chicago and London: University of Chicago Press.

Lattimore, R. (translator) (1961) *The Iliad of Homer.* Chicago and London: University of Chicago Press.

Lattimore, R. (translator) (1975) *The Odyssey of Homer.* New York: Harper and Row.

Laye, C. (1984) *The Guardian of the Word. Kouma Lafôlô Kouma.* New York: Random House.

Lein, L. (1975) '"You were talkin' though, oh yes you was." Black migrant children: Their speech at home and at school.' *Anthropology and Education Quarterly* 6 (4): 1–11.

Lesky, A. (1966) *A History of Greek Literature* (2nd edn, translated by J. Wills and C. de Heer). New York: Thomas Y. Crowell Co.

Levine, L. W. (1977) *Black Culture and Black Consciousness.* New York: Oxford University Press.

Lord, A. B. (1960) *The Singer of Tales.* Cambridge, MA: Harvard University Press.

Lord, A. B. (1963) 'Homer and Other Epic Poetry.' In A. J. B. Wace and F. H. Stubbings (eds), *A Companion to Homer.* New York: Macmillan, pp. 179–214.

McKechnie, J. L. (1983) *Webster's New Universal Unabridged Dictionary* (2nd edn). New York: Simon & Schuster.

McWhirter, N. (ed.) (1980) *Guinness Book of Records.* New York: Sterling Publishing Co.

Maranda, E. K. (1971) 'Theory and practice of riddle analysis.' *Journal of American Folklore* 84: 51–61.

Martin, R. (1989) *The Language of Heroes: Speech and Performance in the 'Iliad'.* Ithaca, NY: Cornell University Press.

Massignon, G. (1968) *Folktales of France.* Chicago: University of Chicago Press.

Mayer, P. (1951) 'The joking of pals in Gusii age-sets.' *African Studies* 10: 24–41.

Merkelback, R. and West, M. L. (1970) 'Fragmenta Selecta.' In F. Solmsen (ed.), *Hesiodi Theogonia, Opera et Dies, Scutum.* Oxford: Clarendon Press.

Messenger, J. (1959) 'The role of proverbs in a Nigerian judical system.' *Southwestern Journal of Anthropology* XV: 64–73.

Meyer, G. (ed.) (1985) *Proverbes Malinké.* Paris: Conseil International de la Langue Française.

Michaels, S. and Collins, J. (1984) 'Oral Discourse Style: Classroom Interaction and the Acquisition of Literacy.' In D. Tannen (ed.), *Coherence in Spoken and Written Discourse.* Norwood, NJ: Ablex, pp. 219–44.

Miller, D. Miller, J and Paker, C. (1974) 'Every force Evolves a Form.' *Language and Class Workshop* 2: 8–10.

Milroy, J. and Milroy, L. (1985) *Authority in Language.* London: Routledge & Kegan Paul.

Mitchell, H. (1970) *Black Preaching.* Philadelphia and New York: Lippincott & Co.

Murray, G. (1924) *The Rise of the Greek Epic,* (3rd edn). Oxford: Clarendon Press.

Nagy, G. (1979) *The Best of the Achaeans.* Baltimore and London: The Johns Hopkins Press.

Niane, D. T. (1965) *Sundiata: An Epic of Old Mali.* London: Longman.

Nilsson, M. P. (1968) *Homer and Mycenae.* New York: Cooper Square Publishers.

Norton, F. J. (1942) 'The prisoner who saved his neck with a riddle.' *Folklore.* 52: 27–57.

Okpewho, I. (1979) *Epic in Africa.* New York: Columbia University Press.

Olrik, A. (1919) *Folkelige Afhandlinger.* Copenhagen.

Ong, W. (1967) *The Presence of the Word.* New Haven, CT: Yale University Press.

Ong, W. (1978) 'Literacy and Orality in Our Times.' *Association of Departments of English (ADE) Bulletin* 58 (September): 1–7.

Ong, W. (1982) *Orality and Literacy: The technologizing of the word.* London and New York: Methuen.

Opie, I. and Opie, P. (1977) *The Lore and Language of Schoolchildren.* London: Paladin.

Page, D. (1959) *History and the Homeric Iliad.* Berkeley and Los Angeles:

University of California Press.

Papadaki d'Onofrio, E. and Roussou, M. (1990) 'The Greek Speech Community.' In S. Alladina and V. Edwards (eds) *Babel and Beyond: Multilingualism in the British Isles*. London: Longman.

Parkin, D. (1980) 'The Creativity of Abuse.' *Man (N. S.)* 15: 45–64.

Parry, M. (1930) 'Studies in the Epic Technique of Oral Verse-Making. 1: Homer and Homeric Style.' *Harvard Studies in Classical Philology* 41: 73–147. Reprinted in A. Parry (ed.) (1971) *The Making of Homeric Verse: The Collected Papers of Milman Parry*. Oxford: Clarendon Press, pp. 266–324.

Parry, M. (1932) 'Studies in the Epic Technique of Oral Verse-Making. II: The Homeric Language as the Language of an Oral Poetry.' *Harvard Studies in Classical Philology* 43: 1–50. Reprinted in A. Parry (ed.) (1971) *The Making of Homeric Verse: The Collected Papers of Milman Parry*. Oxford: Clarendon Press, pp. 325–64.

Paton, W. R. (translator) (1979) *The Greek Anthology* (5 vols). Cambridge, MA: University of Harvard Press.

Peabody, B. (1975) *The Winged Word. A Study in the Technique of Ancient Greek Oral Composition as Seen Principally Through Hesiod's Works and Days*. Albany: State University of New York Press.

Perrin, B. (translator) (1914) 'The Life of Themistocles.' In T. E. Page and W. H. D. Rouse (eds), *The Life of Themistocles*. London: William Heinemann, and New York: Macmillan.

Philips, S. (1972) 'Participant Structures and Communicative Competence: Warm Springs Children in Community and Classroom.' In C. Cazden, V. John and D. Hymes (eds), *Functions of Language in the Classroom*. New York: Teachers College Press, pp. 370–94.

Pollak, M. (1972) *Today's Three Year Olds in London*. London: Heinemann.

Pomeroy, S. B. (1975) *Goddesses, Whores, Wives and Slaves*. New York: Schocken.

Radcliffe-Brown, A. R. (1940) 'On Joking Relationships.' *Africa* 13: 193–210.

Radcliffe-Brown, A. R. (1952) *Structure and Function in Primitive Society*. Chicago: The Free Press.

Radloff, W. (1885) *Proben der Volkslitteratur der nördichen türkischen Stämme. Part V. Der Dialect Kara-Kirgisen*. St Petersburg: Comisseionäre der Kaiserlichen Akademie der Wissenschaften.

Rees, A. and Rees, B. (1961) *Celtic Heritage*. London: Thames and Hudson.

Reisman, K. (1977) 'Contrapuntal conversations in an Antiguan village.' In R. Bauman and J. Sherzer (eds), *Explorations in the Ethnography of Speaking*. Cambridge: Cambridge University Press, pp. 110–24.

Rosen, M. (1982) 'Three Papers: Writers in inner city residence; In their own voice; Our culture–a definition of its parts.' In Talk Workshop Group (ed.), *Becoming Our Own Experts: The Vauxhall Papers*. London: ILEA English Centre, pp. 378–91.

Rosenberg, B. A. (1970a) *The Art of the American Folk Preacher*. New York: Oxford University Press.

Rosenberg, B. A. (1970b) 'The Formulaic Quality of Spontaneous Sermons.'

Journal of American Folklore 83: 3–20.

Rosenberg, B. A. (1975) 'Oral sermons and oral narrative.' In D. Ben-Amos and K. S. Goldstein (eds) *Folklore, Performance and Communication.* The Hague: Mouton, pp. 75–105.

Rosenberg, B. A. (1987) *Can These Bones Live? The Art of the American Folk Preacher.* Chicago: University of Illinois Press.

Rouse, W. H. D. (translator) (1956) *Great Dialogues of Plato.* New York and Scarborough, Ontario: New Ameircan Library.

Salmond, A. (1977) 'Rituals of Encounter among the Maori: sociolinguistic study of a scene.' In R, Bauman and J. Sherzer (eds), *Explorations in the Ethnography of Speaking.* Cambridge: Cambridge University Press, pp. 192–212.

Saville-Troike, M. (1982) *The Ethnography of Communication.* Oxford: Basil Blackwell.

Scheub, H. (1977) 'Xhosa narratives.' In W. R. Bascom (ed.), *Frontiers of Folklore.* Boulder, Colorado: Westview Press for the AAAS, pp. 54–78.

Scollon, R. and Scollon, S. (1979) *Linguistic Convergence: an ethnography of speaking at Fort Chipewyan. Alberta.* New York and London: Academic Press.

Scollon, R. and Scollon, S. (1981) *Narrative, Literacy and Face in Interethnic Communication.* Norwood, NJ: Ablex.

Shtern, Y. (1950) *Khetder un bas-medresh.* New York.

Sienkewicz, T. J. (in press) 'The Greeks Are Too Like the Others.' In D. C. Pozzi and J. M. Wickersham (eds), *Myth and Polis.* New York: Cornell University Press.

Sithole, E. T. (1972) 'Black folk music.' In T. Kochman (ed.), *Rappin' and Stylin' Out: Communication in Urban Black America.* Chicago: University of Illinois Press, pp. 65–82.

Slater, P. E. (1968) *The Glory of Hera.* Boston: Beacon Press.

Smith, J. D. (1977) 'The Singer or the Song? A Reassessment of Lord's "Oral Theory".' *Man (N. S.)* 12: 141–53.

Smith, J. D. (1989) 'How to Sing a Tale: Epic Performance in the Pābūjī Tradition.' In J. B. Hainsworth (ed.), *Traditions of Homeric and Epic Poetry,* Vol. II, London: Modern Humanities Research Association.

Smitherman, G. (1977) *Talkin and Testifyin: The Language of Black America.* Boston: Houghton Mifflin Company.

Steiner, G. (1975) *After Babel: Aspects of Language and Translation.* London: Oxford University Press.

Steiner, G. (1984) *Antigones.* New York and Oxford: Oxford University Press.

Stubbs, M. (1976) *Language, Schools and Classrooms.* London: Methuen.

Sutton-Smith, B. (1959) *The Games of New Zealand Children.* Folklore Studies 12. Berkeley, California: University of California Press.

Tannen, D. (1980a) 'Oral and literate strategies in discourse.' *The Linguistic Reporter* 22(9): 1–3.

Tannen, D. (1980b) 'A comparative analysis of oral strategies: Athenian Greek and American English.' In W. Chafe (ed.), *The Pear Stories: Cognitive, cultural and linguistic aspects of narrative production.* Newark, Delaware: University of Delaware Press, pp. 51–87.

Tannen, D. (1980c) 'Implications of the oral/literate continuum for cross-cultural communication.' In J. Alatis (ed.), *Current Issues in Bilingualism.* Georgetown University Round Table on Languages and Linguistics, Washington D. C.: Georgetown University Press, pp. 326–47.

Tannen, D. (1981) 'Talking New York: It's not what you say, it's the way that you say it.' *New York*, March 30th: 30–33.

Tannen, D. (1984) 'The pragmatics of cross-cultural communication.' *Applied Linguistics* 5(3): 189–95.

Thompson, R. F. (1974) *African Art in Motion.* Los Angeles: University of California Press.

Thompson, S. (1955–1958) *Matif-Index of Folk-literature.* Bloomington: University of Indiana Press.

Tingbjörn, G. (1988) 'Active bilingualism–the Swedish goal for immigrant children's language instruction.' In T. Skutnabb-Kangas and J. Cummins (eds), *Minority Education: From Shame to Struggle.* Clevedon, Avon: Multilingual Matters, pp. 103–26.

Tizard, B. and Hughes, M. (1984) *Young Children Learning.* London: Fontana.

Tolosana, C. L. (1973) 'Verbal art in modern rural Galicia.' In R. Dorson (ed.), *Folklore in the Modern World.* The Hague: Mouton, pp. 281–300.

Torres, J. (1971) *. . . Sting Like a Bee.* London and New York: Abelard-Schuman.

Van Sickle, J. (1975) 'Archilochus: A New Fragment of an Epode.' *Classical Journal* 71: 1–15.

Vassiliou, V., Triandis, H., Vassiliou, G. and McGuire, H. (1972) 'Interpersonal contact and stereotyping.' In H. Triandis (ed.), *The Analysis of Subjective Culture.* New York: John Wiley.

Watson, H. (1988) 'Language and Mathematics Education for Aboriginal Australian Children. *Language and Education* 2(4): 255–73.

Webster, T. B. L. (1964) *From Mycenae to Homer* (2nd edn). New York: W. W. Norton.

Weldon, F. O. Jr (1959) 'Negro Folktale Heroes.' In M. C. Boatright, W. H. Hudson and A. Maxwell (eds) *And Horns on the Toads.* Dallas: Southern Methodist University Press.

Wells, G. (1987) *The Meaning Makers: Children Learning Language and Using Language to Learn.* London: Hodder & Stoughton.

West, M. L. (ed.) (1966) *Hesiod. Theogony.* Oxford: Clarendon Press.

Williams, A. P. (1972) 'Dynamics of a black audience.' In T. Kochman (ed.), *Rappin' and Stylin' Out.* Urbana, IL: University of Illinois Press, pp. 101–6.

Wright, R. (1963) *Lawd Today.* New York: Walker.

Yankah, K. (1983) 'To Praise or Not to Praise the King: The Akan *Apae* in the Context of Referential Poetry.' *Research in African Literature* 14: 381–400.

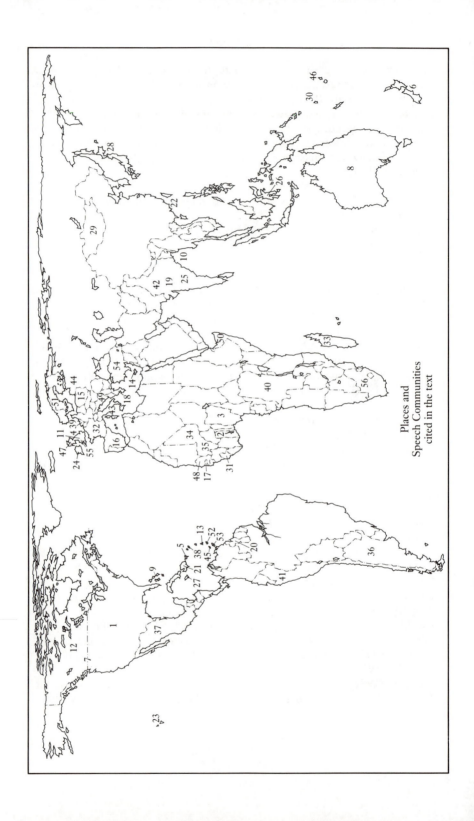

Places and
Speech Communities
cited in the text

Index of Places and Speech Communities

The number in brackets following each entry refers to the code on the accompanying map

Index